The

MEANING

of the

CROSS

PETER NEWMAN

For God's Elect
The Bride of Christ

Now to Him who is able to keep you from stumbling,
and to make you stand in the presence of His glory
blameless with great joy, to the only God our Savior,
through Jesus Christ our Lord, be glory,
majesty, dominion and authority,
before all time and now and forever.
Amen. Jude 24 & 25

CONTENTS

PREFACE

This book is a series of forty teachings with a common theme: the purpose and power of Christ's death on the cross. The teachings are progressive, beginning with the meaning of the new birth and baptism and ending with God's eternal purpose for His church and the marriage supper of the Lamb. Each chapter contains Scripture references so the teachings can be used for individual or group Bible studies. Since the forty chapters were originally written as individual teaching tracts and not intended to be put into book form, there is some intentional repetition and overlap in the chapters to emphasize and explain the meaning of Christ's death on the cross. We believe this repetition is worthwhile because the central Biblical truth of the cross of Christ has been grossly neglected for too long with devastating consequences for the church. For this reason, an exceptional emphasis on the cross is now essential in order to awaken and enable the church to fulfill God's divine plan. We believe this is the same emphasis on the cross that Jesus Christ said was necessary in the lives of all His disciples. Jesus said, "If anyone wishes to come after Me, he must deny himself, and *take up his cross daily* and follow Me." Luke 9:23

While reading this book, you may have additional questions on the meaning and application of the cross in your life. Please turn to the *Appendix C: Questions and Answers* at the end of the book where you may find answers to these specific questions. When you are finished reading this book, you may still want to learn more. We invite you to visit our website at www. ChristCrucified.info where you will find gospel tracts, teaching articles, podcasts and other resources that may help you. All proceeds from this book go to support Christian evangelism and provide aid to members of the body of Christ in need.

INTRODUCTION

I n this book, you hold in your hands the key to understanding the most momentous act in human history – the crucifixion of Jesus Christ. This epoch event was predetermined by God from before the beginning of time to accomplish His eternal purpose. Christ's death on the cross is the basis of the New Covenant, the cornerstone of the church and the power of the gospel. Although there is no truth of greater importance to God's people than the meaning of Christ's death on the cross, it is astonishing that there is no truth of which there is greater ignorance among professing Christians. For by Christ's death on the cross, God not only provided His people the way of salvation, He also provided them the way to overcome sin and live wholly devoted to Him. Yet most Christians simply do not know how to act on this full provision of the cross of Christ.

This is the dilemma that all Christians have faced through the centuries: After being saved, how is it possible to live in this sin-filled world without becoming compromised by sin? Although they know they are saved by faith, very few Christians know how to live by faith. Consequently, they trust Jesus as Savior and hope one day to go to

God's people can be ignorant about a lot of things, but if they are ignorant about the meaning of the cross, they are in real trouble.

heaven but, in between, they struggle vainly to live in this sin-sick world by the best of their ability and often mistake their self-effort for faith. This is not only tragic, it is alarming because God's people can be ignorant about a lot of things, but if they are ignorant about the meaning and power of the cross, they are in real trouble. As God said in Hosea 4:6: "My people are destroyed for lack of knowledge."

This book unveils the glorious mystery of the cross, which the Bible also calls the mystery of the gospel. The mystery of the cross is like the centerpiece of a divine jigsaw puzzle that is the key to understanding the whole gospel. When the full meaning of Christ's death on the cross is clearly grasped, the whole Bible and all its truths fit together to form the eternal purpose of God in Christ Jesus. Salvation is only the beginning and not the end of God's intention for His people, for the cross of Christ is the door that leads to eter-

> *The mystery of the cross is like the centerpiece of a divine jigsaw puzzle that is the key to understanding the whole gospel.*

nal union and intimate relationship with God. When God's people know how to act by faith on the power of Christ's death on the cross, they will come into a true knowledge of God, and Christ will be able to fully express His resurrection life in them and through them.

May God use this book to awaken His people to His eternal purpose, which has been made possible by the cross of Christ. And, once awakened, may His people, the bride of Christ, triumphantly take their rightful place in this age and the age to come.

"I determined to know nothing among you except Jesus Christ and Him crucified."

1 CORINTHIANS 2:2

CHAPTER ONE

The Mystery
of the Gospel

"We speak God's wisdom in a mystery,
the hidden wisdom which God predestined before the ages to our glory;
the wisdom which none of the rulers of this age has understood;
for if they had understood it they would not have crucified the Lord of glory."

1 CORINTHIANS 2:7-8

"God has chosen to make known... the glorious riches of this mystery, which is
Christ in you, the hope of glory."

COLOSSIANS 1:27

Jesus Christ lives in us, His people! This is God's glorious mystery, hidden for ages and now revealed to His church through the New Covenant. Imagine what God's people of the Old Covenant would have thought if they had known the Messiah would live in them. This is why the Bible calls the New Covenant a better covenant. To understand this divine mystery, which the apostle Paul called the mystery of the gospel (Ephesians 6:19) requires divine revelation. Unless we receive divine revelation that Jesus is the Christ, we cannot be born again. In the same way, without divine revelation we cannot understand the mystery of how Jesus Christ can live in us. "For beyond question, great is the mystery of godliness (1 Timothy 3:16)."

The cross is at the heart of this mystery. The crucifixion of Jesus Christ is the triumph of the ages. God's eternal purpose was for His Son to live in fullness in His church, which is His body (Ephesians 1:22-23). Jesus fulfilled His Father's desire by willingly coming to earth to die on the cross for us. Jesus Christ not only gave His life to forgive us from the penalty of sin (Romans 5:8-9); He also gave His life to free us from the power of sin (Romans 6:6-8). Since we were born into sin, God freed us from Satan's dominion and sin's captivity by including us in His Son's death. To do this, God spiritually immersed everyone who is born of the Spirit into Christ's death (Romans 6:3). Thus the mystery of the cross is also the mystery of the gospel.

The mystery of the cross is also the mystery of the gospel.

Like two sides of a precious coin, there are two divine facts that compose the mystery of the whole gospel. The first divine fact is "we died in Christ" and the second is "Christ lives in us." These are the undivided facts of Christ's completed work on the cross. Without the first divine fact, there would be no second. Before God's Holy Son could inhabit us, God had to first remove our unholy nature. Thus God used the death of His only Son to perform a divine heart transplant. When Christ died on the cross, God replaced our sinful heart with His Son's divine heart (Romans 6:1-11; Colossians 2:11-3:4). God then raised Jesus Christ from the dead and exalted Him as the eternal King of glory. God incorporated us into His Son's death so that His resurrected Son might live in us (Romans 6:5;

Colossians 1:27). Therefore, the whole gospel can be stated as "Christ died for us and included us in His death so He might live in us." Paul personally expressed it this way, "I have been crucified with Christ and I no longer live, but Christ lives in me; and the life I now live in the body, I live by faith in the Son of God (Galatians 2:20)."

In another sense, these two divine facts of the gospel form the two sides to the door of salvation. Jesus said, "I am the door; if anyone enters through Me, he will be saved (John 10:9)." The front of this divine door is "we died in Christ." The other side of the door is "Christ lives in us." Of course, these two spiritual transactions occurred simultaneously at our new birth when by faith we entered into Jesus Christ, who is our door of salvation. The Bible says when we were born again of the Spirit we were spiritually united with Christ in both His death and resurrection (Romans 6:5). Although we may not comprehend this mystery of the gospel when we are initially saved, we must embrace both these divine facts by faith to walk in the gospel of Christ after we are saved. In order to overcome the world and inherit the kingdom of God, we must abide by faith in

We cannot count ourselves to be alive in Christ unless we believe and act on the truth that we have died in Christ.

Christ's death and resurrection. First, we must believe when Christ died we died with Him. Next, we must believe Christ now lives in us. Our glorious redemption in Christ is only limited by our unbelief. For example, what if we believe we died in Christ but we do not believe Christ lives in us? Then Christ's ability to sovereignly overcome in us is limited by our unbelief. Or, what if we believe Christ lives in us but we do not believe our sinful nature has died with Christ? Then Christ's ability to live His overcoming life in us is still limited by our unbelief. For as long as we continue to believe that sin still has power over us, God will not overrule our free will and unbelief.

We cannot just mentally consent to the facts of the gospel that Christ died and rose again and then expect to be saved. The eyes of our heart must first be enlightened by divine revelation and then we must receive the Son of God as our Lord (Romans 10:9). This is the true faith that saves us. In the same way, we cannot just mentally agree with the facts of the gospel that we have died in Christ and then expect the Son of God to live His overcoming life in us. Unless we know in our hearts by divine revelation that our sinful nature has died, we will be stuck in Romans 7:24 crying, "What a wretched man I am! Who will set me free from this body of death *(this sinful nature)?*" If we don't believe in our spirit that we have died in Christ, we will try to live the Christian life by our natural ability. We will mistake our positive attitude, passionate energy, and personal attributes for Christ's life. This is tragic and grievous since only the Holy Spirit gives divine life; our natural soul-life has no divine life or power (John 6:63).

Therefore, walking in the power of Christ's resurrection life requires two stepping-stones of faith. We cannot just lightly skip over the first (we died in Christ) and hope to stand firm on the second (Christ lives in us). We cannot count ourselves to be alive in Christ (Romans 6:11) unless we believe and act on the truth that we have died in Christ (Romans 6:6). This is the mystery and power of the gospel of Christ.

"For you have died and your life is now hidden with Christ in God. When Christ, who is your life, is revealed, then you also will be revealed with Him in glory."

COLOSSIANS 3:3-4

CHAPTER TWO

Water Baptism-
Our Betrothal

"Do you not know that all of us who were baptized into
Christ Jesus were baptized into His death?"

ROMANS 6:3

When Jesus Christ gave His Great Commission, He commanded all new disciples to be water baptized. "Go therefore and make disciples of all the nations, baptizing them in the name of the Father and the Son and the Holy Spirit (Matthew 28:19)." Water baptism outwardly expresses the divine transformation that occurred in a believer when they were born again of the Spirit. Through baptism, new believers declare their union with Jesus Christ and His death and resurrection. Thus water baptism is the betrothal or commitment ceremony of new members of the bride of Christ to Jesus, their bridegroom. Our actual marriage ceremony to the Lamb of God will take place at the end of this age. Whenever anyone was saved in the early church, they were normally water baptized the same day. This was God's way for new disciples to be taught that their old sinful nature had died and they were now a new creation in Christ. Knowing you have died with Christ is crucial if you want to become Christ's disciple and overcoming bride. This is the spiritual lesson that God wants every Christian to learn from water baptism.

The Greek word for baptize is *baptizo*, which means to immerse. When you receive Jesus Christ as your Lord and Savior, the Bible says you are spiritually immersed into Christ's death so that you might have His new resurrection life (Romans 6:3-5). Therefore, in water baptism, there are two stages that express this truth of the gospel. First there is a burial and then there is a resurrection. Whenever anyone was baptized in the early church, they were immersed under water, which represented the burial of their old man *(their sinful nature)*. "We have been buried with Him through baptism into death (Romans 6:4; see also Colossians 2:12)." This burial in water baptism confirms that when we were born again, our sinful nature died. Burial

Water baptism is the betrothal or commitment ceremony of new members of the bride of Christ to Jesus, their bridegroom.

also signifies that God has removed that sinful nature from us. Therefore, our sinful nature not only died; it can never come back to haunt us since God has taken it away. "For we know that our old self was crucified with Him in order that our body of sin *(our sinful nature)* might be done away with, so that we would no longer be slaves to sin (Romans 6:6)."

In this way, water baptism reveals the heart of the New Covenant. God knew we needed forgiveness for our sins, but He also knew we needed deliverance from our sin nature. Otherwise, we would remain captives to sin. Therefore, when Jesus Christ died, He bore not only our sins on the cross; He also bore our sin nature on the cross with Him. "God made Christ who had no sin to be sin on our behalf, so that we might become the righteousness of God in Him (2 Corinthians 5:21)." Since our bondage to sin came when we were born sinners; our deliverance from sin came when God included us in Christ's death. "We are convinced that one died for all, therefore all died (2 Corinthians 5:14)." Since we no longer have a sinful nature, sin is no longer is master over us. "Because anyone who has died has been freed from sin (Romans 6:7)."

In the next phase of water baptism, we are raised in His new resurrection life out of the watery grave. This demonstrates that Jesus Christ now lives in us (2 Corinthians 13:5; Romans 6:4-5). But we must always remember our old man *(our sinful nature)* had to be buried before we could be raised up a new man in Christ. Before God could make us a new creation, He had to first deal with the old creation. God had to take care of not only its fruit *(our sinful actions)*; He had to remove its very root (our sinful nature). "Therefore, if anyone is in Christ, he is a new creation; the old has gone, the new has come (2 Corinthians 5:17)!" Thus water baptism demonstrates how God replaced our sinful nature with His holy nature by including us in the

Each time God adds new believers to the church, they act out through baptism their inclusion in the death, burial and resurrection of Christ.

death, burial and resurrection of His Son, Jesus Christ. We might consider this new birth a divine heart transplant by which God replaced our terminally sin-sick heart with His Son's divine heart to save us from the power of sin and certain doom.

This divine exchange is not a future promise reserved for us when we go to heaven; it is God's present reality that He wants us to experience now if we will receive it by faith. The intent of Christ's crucifixion was to produce this total transformation within our inner being so we would no longer be defeated by sin but live daily in Christ's resurrection power. Since water baptism is for new disciples, we can mistakenly think teaching on water baptism is elementary and not for older Christians. However, we cannot grow into Christian maturity unless we abide by faith in the truth of God's Word that we have died with Christ and Christ is now our life (Colossians 3:3-4). In fact, God knows it is impossible for us to live the Christian life and follow Christ in truly devoted discipleship if we do not know our old sinful nature is dead and gone.

Therefore, we cannot realize we are dead to sin (Romans 6:11), if we do not truly know we were crucified with Christ (Romans 6:6). This is the way faith works. The Bible says Jesus Christ died for the whole world but if you do not know He died for you, you cannot be saved. In the same way, the Bible says Christians have been freed from sin but if you do not know you have died with Christ, you cannot overcome sin. This is why instruction on the spiritual meaning of water baptism is so essential. Each time God adds new believers to the church, they act out through baptism their inclusion in the death, burial and resurrection of Christ. In this way, water baptism always reminds the church of this great provision of Jesus Christ's death on the cross.

"Therefore we have been buried with Him through baptism into death,
so that as Christ was raised from the dead through the glory of the Father,
so we too might walk in newness of life."

ROMANS 6:4

CHAPTER THREE

The Foundation
of the Cross

"According to the grace of God which was given to me, like a wise master
builder I laid a foundation, and another is building upon it. But each man
must be careful how he builds on it. For no man can lay a foundation other
than the one which is laid, which is Jesus Christ."

1 CORINTHIANS 3:10-11

Whenever the church in Corinth met, the spiritual gifts seemed to abound (1 Corinthians 1:7). However, the spiritual gifts, which are spiritual tools and can be exercised spontaneously by faith, do not reflect the character of spiritual fruit, which is produced over time by a persevering faith (Luke 8:15). The Corinthians mistakenly thought they were spiritually mature because they did not lack in the gifts. However, the apostle Paul, who had spiritually fathered them in the Lord, rebuked the Corinthians for being worldly-minded and remaining immature infants in Christ (1 Corinthians 3:1-3). Paul then had to instruct them once again on the foundation for their Christian life and growth. Paul's need to go "back-to-basics" with the

Corinthians now works to our benefit since it enables us to also receive the apostle's foundational teaching.

Paul reminded the Corinthians that the power of God and the foundation of their faith was in the message of the cross (1 Corinthians 1:18). He emphasized that the gospel he preached to them was Christ crucified (1 Corinthians 1:23). According to the New Testament record, what did Paul teach about the power of Christ's crucifixion? Paul taught that Christ's death on the cross had provided believers with a "divine exchange." In other words, Jesus Christ, through His crucifixion, exchanged our sinful life with His holy life. Christ became cursed so that we might be blessed (Galatians 3:13-14). Christ paid for our sins so that we might be forgiven (Ephesians 1:7). Christ became sin so that we might become righteous in Him (2 Corinthians 5:21). Christ died so that we might live through Him (2 Corinthians 5:14-15). Paul's apostolic mission was to establish the church on this revelation of Jesus Christ and the power of His crucifixion. That is why he declared, "I am determined to know nothing among you except Jesus Christ and Him crucified (1 Corinthians 2:2)."

Many Christians have bypassed the cross and are trying to be moral by their willpower and self-effort rather than trusting in the indwelling power of Christ to transform them.

Paul taught that everything we need *in order to live the Christian life* has been provided for us *in Christ* (Ephesians 1:3). As Christians, we know Christ died on the cross to provide us forgiveness for our sins. However, this is not the only divine provision given to us by Christ's death. For Christ's crucifixion also provided the way for us to become members of His body (Ephesians 2:23). This is the central purpose of the New Covenant, which was made possible by God including us in His Son's death and resurrection (Romans 6:5). Christ not only died for us (Romans 5:8), our sinful nature also died with Him (Romans 6:8). Our sinful nature has been crucified and removed from us so that we would be freed from the power of sin and Christ could live in us (Romans 6:6-7; Colossians 1:27). In this sense, God performed a divine heart transplant by replacing our terminally sin-sick heart with His Son's divine holy heart. Paul sums up this all-important consequence of Jesus Christ's crucifixion by his testimony, "I have been crucified with Christ and I no longer live but Christ lives in me (Galatians 2:20)."

The Corinthians were not the only ones who had to be reminded that Christ crucified is the precious foundation of our faith - both our justification and our sanctification. Paul had to constantly appeal to the early church that true spiritual growth could only be based on Jesus' completed work on the cross. Tragically, it is a common problem for Christians to not know (because of ignorance or unbelief) what Christ fully accomplished for us by His crucifixion. That is why Paul had to regularly ask believers in the first century church, "Did I not clearly explain Jesus Christ's crucifixion to you?

Until we see that God has dealt a deathblow to our sinful nature, we may think we possess some inherent ability or usefulness to Christ within ourselves.

Do you not know you have been immersed into Christ's death? Do you not know your body is a temple of God and the Holy Spirit lives in you? Do you not know Jesus Christ lives in you?" (See Galatians 3:1; Romans 6:3; 1 Corinthians 3:16; 2 Corinthians 13:5).

Some might say this is the ABCs of the gospel. Yes, it is the ABCs but it is also the XYZs. Our faith must begin and end at the cross. The trouble is that many Christians have bypassed the cross and are trying to be moral by their willpower and self-effort rather than trusting in the indwelling power of Christ to transform them (Galatians 3:3). But if we attempt to build our spiritual life by any other foundation than Christ crucified, we are doing so by our natural strength. Paul compared this to building with wood, hay and straw. If we rely on our natural resources, we only produce dead works, which will not stand the test of fire at the judgment seat of Christ (1 Corinthians 3:12-15). If we are trying to be good Christians by the best of our ability, we are living as mere men, perhaps even moral men, yet still inherently incapable of living the overcoming Christian life (1 Corinthians 3:1-3).

Why did Paul focus his foundational teaching on Christ crucified rather than Christ risen? It is not a question of relative importance but of divine order. Death always comes before resurrection (Romans 6:5). The basis for experiencing the power of Christ's resurrection is to abide (stay rooted by faith) in the power of Christ's death on the cross. Until we see by divine revelation that God has dealt a deathblow to our sinful nature and removed it, we may think we possess some inherent ability or usefulness to Christ within ourselves. However, when God reveals to us that the divine purpose and verdict of the cross was to also make sure our sinful nature was crucified with Christ, *so that it would be taken out of the way,* we will cease to have confidence in our natural ability to do His work and bear His fruit. Indeed, if we do not get out of the way, we become a hindrance to God and He cannot and will not work through us. The foundation of the New Covenant is Christ crucified. Our faith will only rest in the power of God (and not the power of our personality) when we know our sinful nature has died with Christ and been removed from us, and we then trust Christ to sovereignly live through us (Romans 6:1-14; Galatians 2:20).

"May I never boast except in the cross of our Lord Jesus Christ, through which the world has been crucified to me, and I to the world."

GALATIANS 6:14

CHAPTER FOUR

The Divine Exchange

"Those who wait on the Lord will renew their strength; they will mount up
with wings like eagles, they will run and not get tired,
they will walk and not become weary."

ISAIAH 40:31

The heart of the New Covenant is the divine exchange God provided for us by the crucifixion of His only Son, Jesus Christ. The Book of Isaiah is sometimes called the gospel of the Old Covenant because it prophetically heralds Christ's coming and sacrificial death on our behalf. This is probably why Isaiah is the most quoted Old Testament prophet in the New Testament. In the verse above, Isaiah prophetically and poetically portrays Christ's divine exchange. The Hebrew word for wait is *qavah* whose root meaning is "braided together" and the Hebrew word for renew is *chalaph* whose root meaning is "exchange." In other words, those who are spiritually braided together with the Lord will have their natural strength exchanged for God's strength. The prophet Ezekiel also foretold of this divine exchange of the New Covenant when he declared God would replace our old sin-hardened heart with His new spiritual heart (Ezekiel 36:26-27).

After His crucifixion and resurrection, Jesus Christ personally revealed this divine exchange to the apostle Paul (Galatians 1:11-16; 2:20). As a result, this was the gospel Paul proclaimed: "God made Christ who had no sin to be sin for us, so that we might become the righteousness of God in Him (2 Corinthians 5:21). What exactly is this divine exchange? By His death on the cross, Christ exchanged our unholy nature with His holy nature and reconciled us to God (Romans 5:10; 1 Corinthians 1:30; Colossians 1:21-22; 1 Peter 2:24; 1 John 5:11-12). Thus by the sacrifice of His Son, God translated us from our Adamic sinful nature into Christ's divine nature (2 Peter 1:4). Therefore, when we receive Jesus as our Lord and are born again by God's Spirit (John 3:3-8), our sinful nature is crucified and removed (Romans 6:6; Colossians 2:11), and we become a new creation in Christ (2 Corinthians 5:17; Galatians 6:15). The Son of God now lives in us (Romans 8:10; 2 Corinthians 12:9; 13:5; Galatians 1:16; 2:20; Colossians 1:27).

> *The Christian life is not a changed life; it is an exchanged life.*

The Christian life is not a changed life; it is an exchanged life. There is a great difference. If my old car is in need of repair, I could change its carburetor. If it breaks down again, I could try changing its transmission. If it fails again, I could keep changing more parts and hope it will work. Or, I could decide my old car is beyond repair and exchange it for a brand new car. This is similar to the divine exchange God accomplished in us. He knew our old man *(with its sinful nature)* was beyond repair and could not be changed, fixed or improved. Therefore, God completely disposed of our old sin nature and exchanged it for Christ's divine nature. "If anyone is in Christ, he is a new creation; the old has gone, the new has come (2 Corinthians 5:17)."

The divine exchange is like a spiritual grafting. We were once unholy branches but now we have been grafted into Christ - God's holy root (Romans 11:16-21). Jesus said, "I am the vine, you are the branches; he who abides in Me and I in him, he bears much fruit, for apart from Me you can do nothing (John 15:5)." When we know we have been united with Christ in His death and resurrection (Romans 6:5), we can cease from our works and enter into His spiritual rest (Hebrews 4:10). If we abide in the power of Christ's crucifixion, then the power of His resurrection life will certainly abide in us. Since we no longer live but Christ now lives in us (Galatians 2:20), we can trust Christ to bear His fruit in us (Romans 7:4).

God used the crucifixion of Christ to exchange our terminally sin-sick heart with His Son's divine heart and save us from the power of sin and death.

Hudson Taylor, pioneer missionary to China, wrote of this divine exchange, "The Lord Jesus tells me I am a branch. I am part of Him and I have just to believe and act upon it. I have seen it long enough in the Bible but I believe it now as a living reality. In a word, 'whereas once I was blind, now I see.' I am dead and buried with Christ - aye, and risen too and ascended; and now Christ lives in me. I now believe I am dead to sin. God reckons me so and tells me to reckon myself so. Oh, the joy of seeing this truth: I pray that the eyes of your understanding may be enlightened, that you may know and enjoy the riches freely given us in Christ."

The divine exchange is like a spiritual heart transplant. God used the crucifixion of Christ to exchange our terminally sin-sick heart with His Son's divine heart and save us from the power of sin and death. Of course, Jesus had to willingly die for us so we could receive this transplant. Thus

God included us in His Son's death so that His resurrected Son might live in us. The Bible also describes this divine surgery in terms of spiritual circumcision. "In Him you were also circumcised with a circumcision made without hands, in the removal of the sinful nature by the circumcision of Christ… when you were dead in your sins and in the uncircumcision of your sinful nature, God made you alive with Christ (Colossians 2:11-13)."

This divine exchange is not a future promise reserved for us when we go to heaven; it is God's present reality that He wants us to experience now if we will receive it by faith. The intent of Christ's crucifixion was to produce this total transformation within our inner being so we would no longer be defeated by sin but live daily in Christ's resurrection power.

"I have been crucified with Christ and I no longer live, but Christ lives in me.
The life I live in the body I now live by faith in the Son of God,
who loved me and gave Himself up for me."

GALATIANS 2:20

CHAPTER FIVE

The Cross in the Wilderness

"As Moses lifted up the serpent in the wilderness, even so must the Son of Man be lifted up; so that whoever believes in Him will have eternal life... And I, if I am lifted up from the earth, will draw all men to Myself." But He was saying this to indicate the kind of death by which He was to die."

JOHN 3:14-15; 12:32-33

In this passage of Scripture, Jesus compared His impending death on the cross to Moses lifting up the serpent in the wilderness. This Old Testament story can be found in the Book of Numbers (see Chapter 21:4-9). When the people of Israel journeyed in the wilderness, they complained in unbelief against God. As a result, poisonous serpents bit them and many of them died. After the people confessed their sins and repented, God told Moses to make a bronze serpent and fasten it to a standard or stake. God said if anyone was dying from the poisonous venom and they gazed at the serpent on the stake, they would live.

Why did Jesus compare His death on the cross to this story of the serpent on the stake? The Bible says Satan is the serpent of old (Revelation 12:9) who rules this world (John 14:30; 2 Corinthians 4:4). Sin and spiritual death entered the human race when Adam disobeyed God and yielded to Satan (Romans 5:12-21). Since then, everyone (except for Jesus Christ the Son of God) who is born into this world is born with a sinful nature (Psalm 51:5; Ephesians 2:1-3).

Therefore, the story of the serpent in the wilderness is initially a picture of how Satan poisoned man's nature with sin leading to spiritual death. But thanks to God's plan of redemption for mankind, this is not the end of the story. For ultimately, the serpent nailed to the stake in the wilderness helps us understand how Christ's death on the cross has freed us from Satan's power of sin. The Bible calls this the "mystery of the gospel" (Ephesians 6:19).

God is now telling us to fix our eyes by faith on Jesus and the power of His cross to spiritually live.

The mystery is this: How can a man born with a sinful nature be reborn with God's divine nature? This is essentially the same question Nicodemus asked Jesus: How can someone be born again and enter the kingdom of God (John 3:3-7)?

Since we were born sinners and our bondage to sin came by our birth, God in His wisdom and power delivered us from our sin nature by including us in His Son's death (Romans 6:3-5). God's plan of salvation was not to *improve* our serpent-controlled, sin nature but to *kill* it and remove it (Romans 6:6). Therefore, when Jesus Christ died on the cross, He took our sin nature upon Himself (2 Corinthians 5:21; Galatians 3:13). When Christ died, we died with Him (Romans 6:3-8). Thank God that old serpent nature of our sinful man has been crucified with Christ!

John the Baptist declared, "Behold, the Lamb of God who takes away the sin of the world (John 1:29)!" Thus, by His death, Jesus Christ completely redeemed us from sin. He redeemed us from the penalty and condemnation of sin (Romans 8:1; Ephesians 1:7). He also completely delivered us from the power of sin (Romans 6:7). He delivered us from the power of this fallen world (Galatians 1:4; 6:14). And finally, Christ redeemed us from the power of the devil (Colossians 1:13; 2:15; Hebrews 2:14; 1 John 3:8). What a complete redemption we have obtained through Christ's death on the cross!

Our redemption was accomplished through a "divine exchange" that took place on the cross. By dying on the cross on our behalf, Jesus Christ willingly paid the price for our sins and exchanged His own divine life for our sinful life (2 Corinthians 5:21; Colossians 1:21-22; 1 Peter 2:24). By this holy and mighty sacrifice of His only Son, God translated us from our sinful Adam nature into Christ's divine nature (2 Peter 1:4). Therefore, when we receive Jesus as our Lord and are born again by God's Spirit (John 3:3-8), our sinful, self-centered nature is removed (Colossians 2:11) and we become a new spiritual creation in Christ (2 Corinthians 5:17).

If we are trying to serve Christ through our natural ability, we are practicing a moral code apart from the cross, which nullifies the power of Christ from working in us.

In a sense, God performed a divine heart transplant and replaced our terminally sin-sick heart with His Son's divine heart to save us from the power of sin and certain doom. Thus God included us in His Son's death so that His resurrected Son might now sovereignly live in us (2 Corinthians 13:5; Colossians 1:27).

When the people of the Old Covenant faced death in the wilderness, God told them to fix their eyes by faith on the serpent fastened to the stake in order to physically live (Numbers 21:8). God is now telling us, His people of the New Covenant, to fix our eyes by faith on Jesus and the power of His cross in order to spiritually live (Hebrews 12:2). When we abide (stay rooted by faith) in the Biblical truth that our old sinful nature was put to death with Christ on the cross, we will experience deliverance and healing from the power of sin (Romans 6:6-7). Therefore, the power of the gospel (Romans 1:16) is the message of the cross (1 Corinthians 1:18) that Jesus Christ died for our sins (Romans 5:8) and we also died with Him (Romans 6:8). Thus the serpent in the wilderness was a prophetic picture of how our sinful nature would be put to death on the cross with Christ.

Jesus' last words on the cross were, "It is finished (John 19:30)." When the Galatians lost sight of Christ's finished work on the cross and tried to live the Christian life based on their human efforts, the apostle Paul warned they were severed from Christ and had fallen from grace (Galatians 3:1-4; 5:4). If we are trying to serve Christ through our natural ability, we are practicing a moral code apart from the cross, which nullifies the power of Christ from working in us. The basis for our living Christ's resurrection life (the Spirit-filled life) is to know by faith that our sinful nature has been crucified with Christ. When we know that our sinful nature is dead and gone, then our life will not be based on trying to imitate Christ through our willpower and self-effort. Instead, we will trust Jesus Christ to live His life through us.

"And the testimony is this, that God has given us eternal life, and this life is in His Son. He who has the Son has the life; he who does not have the Son of God does not have the life."

1 JOHN 5:11-12

CHAPTER SIX

Abide in Christ

*"I am the true vine, and My Father is the vinedresser. Every branch in Me
that does not bear fruit, He takes away, and every branch that bears fruit, He
prunes it so that it may bear more fruit. You are already clean because of the
word which I have spoken to you. Abide in Me and I in you. As the branch
cannot bear fruit of itself unless it abides in the vine, so neither can you unless
you abide in Me. I am the vine, you are the branches; he who abides in Me and
I in him, he bears much fruit, for apart from Me you can do nothing."*

JOHN 15:1-5

The moment we were born of the Spirit, God grafted us into Jesus
Christ (Romans 11:16-24). When God grafted us into His Holy Son,
He also severed our spiritual connection to Satan by removing our unholy
sinful nature (Romans 6:6; Colossians 2:11). Now that God has planted
us in Christ, our responsibility is to abide in Christ by faith. Jesus Christ
said, "Abide in Me and I in you." This is both a command and a promise.
If you abide in Christ, He will abide in you. The Greek word for abide is
meno, which means "to actively dwell in." This can also be expressed as
"stay rooted in" or "remain united to."

As with all of God's promises, this one is also conditional upon the obedience of our faith. If you stay united to Christ by faith, He will remain united to you and you will bear spiritual fruit. However, if you do not stay rooted in Christ, you will not bear spiritual fruit. Therefore, whether your spiritual grafting into Christ takes hold and bears fruit depends on whether you "hold fast" by faith to Jesus Christ (Luke 8:15; 1 Corinthians 15:2; Hebrews 3:14). It is vital that we stay rooted by faith to Christ because we have no spiritual life in ourselves apart from Christ. Without Christ's life, we cannot bear His fruit. This is why Jesus told His disciples, "Truly, truly, I say to you, unless you eat the flesh of the Son of Man and drink His blood, *you have no life in yourselves* (John 6:53).

Most Christians do not understand what it means to "abide in Christ." Many think that they automatically abide in Christ as long as they have been saved. However if a Christian practices sin, the Bible says this is not true. "No one who abides in Him continues to sin; no one who continues to sin has seen Him or known Him (1 John 3:6)." We cannot abide in Christ unless we abide in the truth of His word. Jesus said, "If you abide in My word, then you are truly My disciples and you will know the truth and the truth will set you free (John 8:31-32)." Therefore, we can abide in Christ's life and bear His fruit only if we believe and

When we try to bear spiritual fruit by our self-effort, we cut ourselves off from the life of the vine, which is Christ.

act on the truth. What is the foundational truth of Christian living? We can only abide *(live)* in Christ *if* we know that we have *died* in Christ. We must believe and act on the truth that our sinful nature has died in Christ and been removed in Christ (Romans 6:3-11). Otherwise, we will try to bear spiritual fruit by the best of our natural ability and mistake our self-effort for faith.

When we try to bear spiritual fruit by our self-effort, we cut ourselves off from the spiritual life of the vine, which is Christ (Galatians 3:3; 5:4). Just as we could not crucify ourselves, we cannot sanctify ourselves apart from Christ's completed work on the cross. We will only experience Christ's resurrection life *if* we abide (stay rooted by faith) in Christ's death. "Now if we have died with Christ, we believe that we shall also live with Him (Romans 6:8)." This is the way abiding in Christ works. When we stay rooted by faith in the truth of Christ's death (when Christ died, we died with Him), Christ's life will be formed in us. "For you have died and your life is hidden with Christ in God. When Christ, who is our life, is revealed, then you also will be revealed with Him in glory (Colossians 3:3-4)."

As we abide in Christ, the Bible says that God will periodically prune us so we can bear more fruit and grow into Christ's fullness. How does God prune us? Once again, He uses His Word. To paraphrase and adapt Hebrews 4:12, "The Word of God is living and active and sharper than any pruning shears and able to cut away everything which is carnal and soulish from our lives." Sometimes we will turn away from worldly attitudes and activities when God's Word convicts us. Other times, God uses difficult situations to discipline and prune us. "But God disciplines us for our good, so we may share His holiness (Hebrews 12:10)." When we are being pruned, we may not under-stand what God is doing since His *God has grafted us into His Son; this is our glorious salvation and just the beginning of God's pruning and sanctifying work in our life.* pruning can be painful. At times, we may feel as if God has pruned us so far back that we are left with only a stump. However, when God causes the new growth of Christ's life to emerge within us, we will reap the fruit of abiding in Christ and His completed work on the cross. "All discipline for the moment seems not to be joyful, but sorrowful; yet to those who have been trained by it, afterwards it yields the peaceful fruit of righteousness (Hebrews 12:11)."

Being pruned by our heavenly Father can be painful, but it is far better to undergo His training in righteousness than to bear no fruit at all. "If you are not disciplined… then you are illegitimate children and not true sons (Hebrews 12:8)." These are people who were once grafted into Christ (John 15:2), but they proved themselves unworthy of being God's children because they resisted His divine pruning and never bore any spiritual fruit. Jesus said, "If anyone does not abide in Me, he is thrown away as a branch and dries up, and they gather them, and cast them into the fire and they are burned (John 15:6; see also Romans 11:20-22)."

God has grafted us into His Son. This is our glorious salvation and just the beginning of God's pruning and sanctifying work in our life. Let us then be diligent to stay rooted by faith in Jesus Christ and in the power of His death so that the power of His life might bear much fruit in us.

"My Father is glorified by this, that you bear much fruit, and so prove to be My disciples… you did not choose Me but I choose you, and appointed you that you would go and bear fruit, and that your fruit would remain."

JOHN 15:8 & 16

CHAPTER SEVEN

The Fruit of the Cross

"Every tree that does not bear good fruit is cut down and thrown into the fire.
So then, you will know them by their fruits."

MATTHEW 7:19-20

A few years ago, the Lord gave me a vision. I found myself high above the earth looking down on a vast forest. As I descended, I could see all the trees were lush with green leaves. As I drew closer, I could see beneath the canopy of leaves. I suddenly asked the Lord, "Where's the fruit?" Out of thousands of trees, only a few trees in the entire forest had any fruit. Most of the trees had no fruit. The Lord then gave me the interpretation of the vision. The forest was the church. The leaves were its gifts and ministries and the fruit was the expression of Christ's life. Although the church was flush with gifts and ministries, it had precious little of Christ's life.

We often mistake the spiritual gifts described in 1 Corinthians, Chapter 12 as the evidence of Christ's abundant life in the church. However, Jesus said not everyone who ministers spiritual gifts in His Name will enter the kingdom of heaven (Matthew 7:21-23). Although we should seek to use the spiritual gifts as tools to build up the body of Christ (1 Corinthians 14:1), we should also remember the gifts, in themselves, are not an accurate reflection of the spiritual health of the church. If the gifts are not clear evidence of Christ's life, then what about the fruit of the Spirit? Galatians 5:22-23 describes this fruit as love, joy, peace, patience, kindness, goodness, faithfulness, gentleness and self-control. These are attributes of God's divine character. Therefore, we cannot develop spiritual fruit by our human efforts. We cannot grow in God's love by trying harder to be kinder and gentler. We cannot get more of God's patience by determining to be more patient. We cannot overcome pride by trying to be more humble. We cannot overcome lust by resolving to have more self-control.

We may think if only we were stronger we could become more holy and overcome sin. But God's way of salvation wasn't to make our old man *(our sin nature)* stronger. Instead, His righteous verdict for our old man *(our sin nature)* was execution not reformation. Therefore, our old man of sin was crucified with Christ. He completely destroyed and removed that inward sin factory, which continuously caused us to sin (Romans 6:6). This was God's wisdom and power in the cross of Christ (1 Corinthians 1:18, 23, 24). By His crucifixion, Jesus Christ exchanged our sinful nature with His divine life (2 Corinthians 5:21). When Christ died, we died with Him (2 Corinthians 5:14).

Although God may use our natural talent, He does not want us to have any confidence in our natural ability to produce spiritual fruit.

Our old sinful nature was spiritually removed (Colossians 2:11) and Christ now lives in us (2 Corinthians 13:5). Now that Christ's new nature has replaced our old sinful nature, we are freed from sin and no longer have to sin (Romans 6:7). After we are saved, God's way of spiritual growth is not to make us stronger in our natural self. Instead, God's divine power is revealed in our weakness as we learn to rely by faith in His Son who lives in us (2 Corinthians 12:9).

Have you ever seen imitation fruit in a store display? Although it looks real, it lacks the fragrance of true fruit. That's the same way it is with imitation spiritual fruit. Many of us have, by means of our natural personality and strength of will, changed our behavior to create imitation fruit. This can be called "behavioral Christianity" since we have modified our behavior to conform to Christian virtues. However, this is false Christianity. Satan can, through man's soul-power, imitate almost everything in the church, including the gifts and fruit of the Spirit. However, the one thing the devil cannot counterfeit is the fragrance of Christ's life (2 Corinthians 2:14-16). The appearance of imitation fruit is no substitute for Christ's life. We may appear to be gentle, peaceful and disciplined but if these "virtues" spring from our natural personality instead of our living by faith in Christ, they are not true fruit and they do not have the fragrance of Christ's life (John 6:63).

If we abide in Christ and He abides in us, we will bear fruit that has His fragrance. If we still think we can bear spiritual fruit by our own doing, then we do not need the power of the cross.

If we still think we can bear spiritual fruit by our own doing, then we do not need the power of the cross of Christ (Galatians 2:20-3:3). When Jesus said, "Apart from Me you can do nothing (John 15:5)," He did not mean we could not do anything. By our own initiative and talent, there are many things we could do. Jesus meant we could not produce anything of true spiritual value without His initiative and His power. Although God may use our natural talent, He does not want us to have any confidence in our natural ability to produce spiritual fruit (Philippians 3:3). Our faith must rest in His Son alone to accomplish His work through us. If we rely on our natural talent to do Christian work and produce Christian fruit, we may look healthy and productive to others but Jesus Christ won't recognize our fruit.

However, if we abide (stay rooted by faith) in spiritual union with Jesus Christ, His fruit will flow naturally from us (Romans 7:4). This is the same way the life of the vine flows through its branches to bear fruit. If we abide in Christ and He abides in us, we will bear fruit that has Christ's fragrance (John 15:5). God has already put us in Christ (1 Corinthians 1:30). Our response should be to fix our eyes on Jesus and His completed work on the cross (Hebrews 12:2). Jesus is not only the author of our faith; He is also the finisher of our faith. If we know in our spirit that we have been crucified in Christ so that Christ might live in us (Galatians 2:20), we will see the futility of our natural efforts to produce fruit. We will then look by faith for Christ to produce His fruit in us that we cannot possibly produce ourselves (2 Corinthians 3:5-6). May God open our eyes to see what His Son has accomplished on the cross so that we might bear His lasting fruit with the sweet and true fragrance of Christ.

"Abide in Me, and I in you. As the branch cannot bear fruit of itself unless it abides in the vine, so neither can you unless you abide in Me. I am the vine, you are the branches; he who abides in Me and I in him, he bears much fruit, for apart from Me you can do nothing."

JOHN 15:4-5

CHAPTER EIGHT

The Hiding Place

"You are my hiding place; You will protect me from trouble. You will surround me with songs of deliverance."

PSALM 32:7

God the Father has given us His Son to be our hiding place in time of trouble. This is a great promise but if we do not know Christ as our hiding place, we will not be able to experience God's provision when we need it.

Understanding the secret of how Christ is our hiding place starts at the cross. Everyone who professes to be a Christian knows Christ died for our sins (Romans 5:8). However, many Christians do not know that we died with Christ (Romans 6:8). Yet this was the central purpose of Christ's Atonement. When Christ was crucified, He not only bore our sins on the cross; He bore our sin nature on the cross with Him (2 Corinthians 5:21). Therefore, when Christ died, our sinful nature died with Him (Romans 6:6). Not only have we died with Christ, we have been raised with Christ (Colossians 2:12). By the grace of God the Father (the cost was the crucifixion of His only Son), our sinful nature has been removed and replaced with

His Son's divine nature (2 Corinthians 13:5). This is the divine exchange that God has provided for us in His New Covenant through the blood of Christ.

We might call this a divine heart transplant. Of course, Jesus had to willingly die for this heart transplant to take place. When Jesus died on the cross, God exchanged our terminally sin-sick heart with His Son's divine holy heart to save us from the power of sin and certain doom (Romans 6:1-11). Thus God included us in His Son's death so that His resurrected Son might now live in us (Colossians 1:27). The Bible also describes this divine surgery in terms of spiritual circumcision: "In Him you were also circumcised with a circumcision made without hands, in the removal of the sinful nature by the circumcision of Christ... when you were dead in your sins and in the uncircumcision of your sinful nature, God made you alive with Christ (Colossians 2:11-13)."

God included us in His Son's death so that His resurrected Son might now live in us.

There is another Scripture that sums up this divine transformation that has taken place within us: "For you have died and your life is now hidden with Christ in God (Colossians 3:3)." Why is our new life hidden with Christ? One reason is that the divine operation accomplished by Christ's death on the cross was spiritual. In other words, Christ's divine exchange occurred within our spirit. Since it is spiritual in nature, it is not visible to the carnal man since he is not governed by the Spirit and cannot see the things of the Spirit (John 3:3; 1 Corinthians 2:14). However, that does not make what God did any less true. "For we walk by faith not by appearances (2 Corinthians 5:7)." Although a miraculous, inward transformation has taken place in our spirit, who we are in Christ will not be completely visible to the world until Christ returns. "When Christ, who is our life, is revealed, then you will be revealed with Him in glory (Colossians 3:4)."

However, all those who are governed by the Spirit no longer merely recognize anyone who is in Christ by their outward natural personality, since they are able to see them by faith as a new spiritual person in Christ (2 Corinthians 5:16-17).

Jesus Christ personally revealed this mystery of the cross (*we died in Christ so Christ might live in us*) to the apostle Paul (Galatians 1:11-16; Colossians 1:25-27). This is the gospel Paul lived and preached: "I have been crucified with Christ and I no longer live but Christ lives in me and the life I now live in the body, I live by faith in the Son of God (Galatians 2:20)." Since Paul knew the mystery of Christ's "exchanged life," he knew Christ was his hiding place. This is what Paul meant when he said he had learned the secret of being content in Christ in every situation, whether he was in prosperity or in adversity (Philippians 4:11-13). When we know we have died in Christ to the world (Galatians 6:14) and Christ

If we practice living out the truth of the cross by faith, Jesus Christ will be our hiding place in time of trouble.

is now our life (Colossians 3:3), we can live in the midst of this hostile world without being spiritually harmed by our enemy, the devil (1 John 5:18). We can function very effectively here on earth in body and soul while our spirit is firmly fixed in the heavenly realm where we are seated with Jesus Christ (Ephesians 2:6). "Therefore, if you have been raised with Christ, keep seeking the things above, where Christ is seated at the right hand of God. Set your mind on the things above, not on the things that are on earth (Colossians 3:1-2)."

Just because Christ is our hiding place does not mean we will not suffer physical or emotional pain and loss. However, if Christ is our hiding place, His divine life within us will always be sufficient. When Paul proclaimed nothing could separate us from Jesus Christ - neither trouble, persecution or peril (Romans 8:35), he spoke from his personal experience. He had suffered hunger and homelessness, shipwrecks, beatings, lashings, imprisonments and stoning for Christ's sake. Yet he overcame all these difficulties in the strength of Jesus Christ, His hiding place (Philippians 4:11-13).

Jesus said great trouble would come upon the earth in the last days and warned us to be ready (Matthew 24:21-44). The only secure way to prepare for the trouble ahead is to know we have been crucified with Christ and make Christ our life each day. If we practice living out the truth of the cross by faith, Jesus Christ will be our hiding place in time of trouble. This is similar to getting ready for a great storm. We must prepare beforehand by securing our house. Jesus said, "Everyone who hears these words of Mine and *acts on them,* may be compared to a wise man who built his house on the rock... and the rain fell, the floods came and the winds blew and slammed against that house; and yet it did not fall, for it had been founded on the rock (Matthew 7:24-25)." If we wait to secure our house during the storm, it is too late. In the same way, if we think we can get spiritually ready and find the hiding place when the trouble is already on us, it may be too late.

"For in the day of trouble He will hide me in His shelter; in the secret place of His tabernacle He will hide me; He will lift me up on a rock."

PSALM 27:5

CHAPTER NINE

The Rest of the Cross

"Therefore, just as the Holy Spirit says, 'Today if you hear His voice, do not harden your hearts as when they provoked Me, as in the day of trial in the wilderness.'... And to whom did He swear that they would not enter His rest, but to those who were disobedient? So we see that they were not able to enter because of unbelief."

HEBREWS 3:7-8; 18-19

Jesus Christ commands His disciples "to be perfect, as your heavenly Father is perfect (Matthew 5:48)." Yet Jesus also promised, "Come to Me, all who are weary and heavy-laden, and I will give you rest. Take My yoke upon you and learn from Me... and you will find rest for your souls. For My yoke is easy and My burden is light (Matthew 11:28)." Many Christians would admit their experience has fallen far short of Christ's command and promise. His yoke of discipleship has not seemed easy or light and His commandments have seemed difficult to keep. Why is this? A look at God's ways in the wilderness with Israel may help us to understand why and help us find His promised rest today.

The Lord saved His people Israel by the blood of the Passover lamb (Exodus 12:1-13) and delivered them from a kingdom of slavery (Exodus 13:3). He then baptized them in the sea and in the cloud of His Presence (symbolic of baptism in water and the Spirit/Exodus 13-14; 1 Corinthians 10:2). Then what does God do after His people are saved and baptized? Does He immediately bring them into the bounty of the Promised Land? No. Instead He led them into the wilderness (Deuteronomy 8:15) - a "great and terrible" desert lacking in food and water and inhabited by deadly serpents and scorpions (symbolic of demonic spirits/Luke 10:19-20). In this wilderness, God miraculously protected and provided for them with food and water (a picture of Christ/John 6:31-58; 2 Corinthians 10:3-4).

God's promised rest is fulfilled by Christ's completed work on the cross.

The Lord's intent in the wilderness was to test His people and reveal whether they would trust and obey Him (Deuteronomy 8:2). The Bible says God used the wilderness to discipline His people as a father trains his son (Deuteronomy 8:5). God's goal was to humble His people so they would learn to depend on Him alone for their sufficiency (Deuteronomy 8:3). God wanted His people to realize that they had no ability or righteousness of their own to possess the Promised Land (Deuteronomy 8:17; 9:4-5). However, Israel failed to understand the Lord and His ways during their wilderness testing. Despite the fact that they had witnessed His miraculous works (Hebrews 3:9) and zealously built His tabernacle (Exodus 39:42), they did not trust God and did not recognize His purpose in the wilderness (Hebrews 3:10-12). Therefore, the Bible calls them "a stubborn and rebellious generation, a generation that did not prepare its heart and whose spirit was not faithful to God (Psalm 78:8)." As a result of their unbelief, most of God's people died in the wilderness without entering His promised rest (Hebrews 3:17-19).

Today, God still disciplines every son and daughter who belongs to Him (Hebrews 12:6-7). After we are baptized in water and the Spirit, the Lord will often lead us into a "wilderness" experience where we suffer hardship and affliction. The apostle Paul said, "We do not want you to be unaware, brethren, of our affliction... that we were burdened excessively, beyond our strength... so that we would not trust in ourselves but in God (2 Corinthians 1:8-9)." The Greek word for affliction is *thlipsis.* It is also translated as tribulation and simply means pressure. God has designed our experience in the wilderness to press us beyond our natural ability so that by faith we will enter into Christ's rest. The wilderness is God's school of the Spirit. The wilderness is where God reveals to us the hidden attitudes and motives of our hearts (Hebrews 4:12). The wilderness is the crucible God uses to purify our faith in His Son, Jesus

By resting in His victory on the cross, we can trust Christ to live in us and His yoke becomes easy.

Christ (1 Peter 1:6-7). The wilderness is intended to show us that we are incapable of living the overcoming Christian life in our natural strength (2 Corinthians 1:8-9; 3:5) and to enlighten the eyes of our heart to see what His Son has accomplished for us on the cross. When we finally come to the end of ourselves, God will reveal the mystery of Christ's crucifixion to us. This is the divine revelation that God has included us in His Son's death so His risen Son might live in us (Romans 6:3-11; Colossians 1:27).

When you know *(believe and act on)* the Biblical truth that when Christ died, your sinful nature died with Him, you are then free to serve God without the fear of being defeated by sin (Romans 6:1-14). When you are convinced of this historic and divine fact of your inclusion in Christ's death, you can then live by faith in the Son of God who lives in you (Galatians 2:20; Colossians 1:27). When you know *(believe and act)* that you no longer have sinful nature, you will learn to no longer rely on your natural ability to serve God (Philippians 3:3) and Christ will become your true food and drink (John 6:55-56). So then, you enter into the rest of the cross when you know that "you have died and your life is hidden with Christ in God (Colossians 3:3)."

Israel failed to enter God's rest because of their unbelief. Although they professed faith in God, they trusted in their own righteousness and strength instead of God (Psalm 78:36; Isaiah 29:13). Today, God's promised rest is fulfilled by Christ's completed work on the cross. The secret to entering God's rest is to know that we have died with Christ and we no longer live. We will then cease from our depending on our own works and enter into His spiritual rest and His works (Hebrews 4:10). By resting in His victory on the cross, we can trust Christ to sovereignly live in us and His yoke becomes easy (Galatians 2:20).

"Therefore, let us fear if, while a promise remains of entering His rest, any one of you may seem to have come short of it. . . so there remains a Sabbath rest for the people of God. For the one who has entered His rest has himself also rested from his works, as God did from His.

HEBREWS 4:1, 9-10

CHAPTER TEN

The Church of the Living God

"And God placed all things under Christ's feet and appointed Him to be head over everything for the church, which is His body, the fullness of Him who fills all in all."

EPHESIANS 1:22-23

". . . stay connected to the head, from whom the entire body, being supplied and held together by the joints and ligaments, grows with a growth which is from God."

COLOSSIANS 2:19

In God's divine order, everything reproduces after its own kind. Plants reproduce plants, animals reproduce animals and humans reproduce humans. In the same manner, just as earthly seed reproduces the image of the earthly, only heavenly seed can reproduce the image of the heavenly. According to God's plan of redemption, Christ is the heavenly seed that reproduces His church. Jesus said, "Unless a grain of wheat falls into the earth and dies, it remains alone; but if it dies, it bears much fruit (John 12:24)." Jesus spoke here of His death on the cross by which He would birth His church.

We see two kinds of church today – the false church, which bears the image of the earthly *(man)* and the true church, which bears the image of the heavenly *(Christ)*. "You have come to… the city of the living God, the heavenly Jerusalem… the church of the firstborn who are enrolled in heaven (Hebrews 12:22-23)." The primary evidence that separates the true church from the false church is *life*. In Biblical terms, there are three different kinds of life. First, there is physical life. In the New Testament Greek, this is called *bios,* from which we get the English word *biology,* the study of physical life. This

> *Now that we have been born of the Spirit, we have God's DNA (Divine Nature from Above) and Christ's zoe life.*

is the life Jesus portrayed when He said the Word of God, after it has been received by someone, can be "choked with the worries and riches and pleasures of this *life* (Luke 8:14)." Next, there is soul-life or *psyche,* from which we get the English word *psychology,* the study of self- or soul-life. This is the life Jesus described when He said, "He who has found his *life* will lose it, and he who has lost his *life* for My sake will find it (Matthew 10:39)."

And finally, there is spiritual life or *zoe.* Of the three kinds of life, only *zoe* life is eternal. This is the divine life Jesus described when He said, "I have come that they may have *life,* and have it more abundantly (John 10:10)." This is the life John referred to when he wrote, "He who has the Son has the *life*; he who does not have the Son of God does not have the *life* (1 John 5:12)." Before we were saved, we had no *zoe* life. Jesus said, "You have no *life* within yourselves (John 6:53)… That which is born of the flesh is flesh and that which is born of the Spirit is spirit (John 3:6)." Our life before we received Christ consisted of our physical life and soul life, both of which we inherited from our natural parents, and our inward sinful nature, which we spiritually inherited from Adam, the first man. But when Jesus Christ died on the cross, God performed a divine heart transplant and replaced our terminally sinful heart with His Son's divine heart. Now that we have been born of the Spirit, we have God's *DNA (Divine Nature from Above)* and Christ's *zoe* life.

Therefore, the true church is a divine organism. She is the church of the living God - the body of Christ. "Now you are Christ's body and individually members of it (1 Corinthians 12:27)." In the natural, when any of the body's major organic systems such as the nervous system or cardiovascular system is obstructed, the body quickly loses its vitality. Its immune system is compromised; its members stop functioning; and the body itself can die. Likewise, if the church relies on her natural ability instead of abiding in Christ, she blocks Christ's life from nourishing her. The church must stay connected to Christ's headship in order to be sustained by His life. Jesus emphasized this vital aspect

> *The church must stay connected to Christ's headship in order to be sustained by His life.*

of knowing Him when He said to the churches in the Book of Revelation, "He who has an ear, let him hear what the Spirit says to the church." When the church fails to hear and obey Christ's voice, her fellowship and connection to Him is lost. The result is spiritual degeneration, death and a form of religion without real *zoe* power. The only way the church can stay united to Christ is to know she has died in Christ and she now lives in Christ. This is God's divine order. Death always comes before resurrection *life.* When God's people do not know they have died with Christ, they try to do in the natural power of their soul what they can only do in the power of Christ's death. Unless the church abides *(believes and acts on)* on the power of Christ's crucifixion, she cannot express the power of His resurrection *life.*

Jesus said we would know the true church by its fruit. What is the true fruit of the church with Jesus Christ enthroned as her head? The primary fruit is a love for Jesus Christ and His body. The Bible says, "Though you have not seen Him *(Jesus)*, you love Him (1 Peter 1:8)." And Jesus said, "By this everyone will know that you are My disciples, if you love one another (John 13:35)." The Greek word used here for love is *agape,* the only love that is from God. "We know love by this, that He laid down His life for us; and we ought to lay down our lives for the brethren (1 John 3:16)." When the church is disconnected from Christ her head because she does not abide in the truth and tries to live by her own power, she is incapable of producing Christ's life and love.

The other prime fruit of a church under the headship of Christ is holiness or sanctification. Jesus Christ will produce a holy church because He is the holy seed. Therefore, the Lord has called us to come out and separate from the world (2 Corinthians 6:17). If you belong to Christ's body, there is no exception to this call. "Like the Holy One who called you, be holy yourselves also in all your behavior; because it is written, 'You shall be holy for I am Holy (1 Peter 1:15-16).'" Thus the witness of the true church submitted to Christ is God's life, love and holiness. And the church can only produce this fruit if she abides in Christ – by knowing and living in the power of His death and resurrection.

"We will in all things grow up into Him who is the head; that is, Christ. From Him the whole body, joined and held together by every supporting ligament, grows and builds itself up in love, as each part does its work."

EPHESIANS 4:15-16

CHAPTER ELEVEN

The Freedom
of the Cross

*"Everyone who sins is a slave to sin... so if the
Son sets you free, you will be free indeed."*

JOHN 8:34-36

*"Now having been freed from sin and enslaved to God, you derive your
benefit, resulting in sanctification, and the outcome, eternal life."*

ROMANS 6:22

At the beginning of His ministry, Jesus Christ declared, "The Spirit of
the Lord is on Me, because He has anointed me to preach the gospel
to the poor. He has sent Me to proclaim freedom for the prisoners (Luke
4:18)." Jesus fulfilled this mission by dying on the cross. God used His
Son's death to set us free from the kingdom of darkness and bring us into
His kingdom of light (Colossians 1:13). "God set you free when He sent
His own Son... to be a sacrifice for our sin (Romans 8:3)."

Before we were saved, we were slaves to the fear of the destructive power of sin in our life (Romans 8:15). But through the cross, Christ has set us free from the guilt and condemnation of sin. "For by the death of Christ we are set free... our sins are forgiven (Ephesians 1:7)." When we were still lawless and rebels to God, we were enslaved to sin. But through His death, Christ freed us from this power of sin. "We know that our old self was crucified with Him so that our sinful nature might be done away with, so that we would no longer be slaves to sin (Romans 6:6)." When we were still unbelievers, many of us were afraid of physically dying. But, even as believers, many of us are still afraid of sin's power; wrongly believing we are still captive to sin. However, by His death, Jesus has freed us from this fear of death and sin's stranglehold. "So that by His death He might destroy him who holds the power of death - that is, the devil – and free those who all their lives were held in slavery by their fear of death (Hebrews 2:14-15)"

Therefore, by Christ's death on the cross, we have been forever freed from the fear of sin's dominion and the fear of death. It is crucial for us to know that sin is no longer master over us and death no longer has dominion over us. "For the law of the Spirit of life in Christ Jesus has set you free from the law of sin and death (Roman 8:1)." Why? Because the Bible says that through Christ's death we have been "brought into the glorious freedom of the children of God... for you

Since we were born into sin, God freed us from sin's captivity by including us in His Son's death so that we could be born again into His resurrection life.

have not received a spirit of slavery leading to fear again, but you have received a spirit of adoption as sons by which we cry out, 'Abba! Father!' (Romans 8:15; 21)." Before we were born of the Spirit, we were enemies of God. But by His Son's death on the cross, God has set us free to be His bondslaves.

How did God deliver us from the power of sin and produce this miraculous change of heart in us - from godless, rebellious sinners to devoted bondslaves of God?   The way God accomplished this glorious liberation for us was simply profound and powerful: Since we were born into sin, God freed us from sin's captivity by including us in His Son's death (Romans 6:3-5) so that we could be born again into His resurrection life. "He who has died has been freed from sin… we have died with Christ (Romans 6:7-8)."   This operation of the cross was like a divine heart transplant.   When Jesus Christ died on the cross, God exchanged our terminally sin-sick heart with His Son's divine holy heart.   We were once sons of disobedience and children of wrath (Ephesians 2:1-2), but now that God has removed our sinful nature and put the Spirit of His Son into our hearts, we have become sons of obedience (Romans 6:6-20; Galatians 4:6; Colossians 2:11).

Since Christ has set us free from the kingdom of darkness, should we continue to practice sin? Absolutely not! "For you were called to be free, my brethren; only do not use your freedom to indulge sinful desires (Galatians 5:13)." Jesus Christ has set us free from sin for the very purpose that we would practice holiness (sanctification). "For God has not called us for the purpose of impurity, but to sanctification (1 Thessalonians 4:7)." The Bible says we have been freed from sin and have become enslaved to God (Romans 6:22). Many Christians think they can continue to willfully practice sin and still receive the benefits of salvation. Other Christians think that holiness is too strict a standard to keep.

By His Son's death on the cross, God has set us free to be His bondslaves.

Still other Christians think that spiritual freedom means you can do whatever you please, living lawlessly, and still be covered by the blood of Jesus. None of these are true. The apostle Paul said, "Should we sin because we are under grace? God forbid! (Romans 6:15)." And the apostle Peter said, "Act as free men and do not use your freedom as a covering for evil but use it as bondslaves for God (1 Peter 2:16)." Paul also wrote, "Keep yourself free from sin (1 Timothy 5:22)."

Even though we may be under grace, God has never changed His standard of holiness. Here is the divine truth: You are either a slave to sin or slave to God. "Do you not know that when you present yourselves to someone as slaves for obedience, you are slaves of the one whom you obey, either of sin resulting in death, or of obedience resulting in righteousness? (Romans 6:16)." Practicing obedience to God is essential because the Bible says "without sanctification no one will see the Lord (Hebrews 12:14)." Unless we walk by faith in this freedom from sin purchased by Christ's blood, we cannot know the Lord. The apostle John taught, "Everyone who sins breaks the law; in fact, sin is lawlessness. But you know that He appeared so that He might take away our sins. And in Him is no sin. No one who lives in Him keeps on sinning. No one who continues to sin has either seen Him or known Him (1 John 3:4-6)."

Jesus Christ died on the cross to set us free from the power of sin and death. If we do not use this priceless freedom to serve God as His bond-slaves, then Christ will have died needlessly for us. If we are not enslaved to God, we cannot be sanctified. And without sanctification, we cannot know God nor can we inherit eternal life (Romans 6:22).

"Now the Lord is the Spirit, and where the Spirit of the
Lord is, there is freedom."

2 CORINTHIANS 3:17

"It was for freedom that Christ set us free; therefore, keep standing firm
and do not be subject again to a yoke of slavery."

GALATIANS 5:1

CHAPTER TWELVE

The Obedience
of Faith

"Now to Him who is able to establish you according to my gospel and the preaching of Jesus Christ according to a revelation of the mystery which has been kept secret for long ages past, but now has been manifested, and by the Scriptures of the prophets, according to the commandment of the eternal God has been made known to all the nations, leading to obedience of faith."

ROMANS 16:25-26

Biblical faith is both rooted in and revealed by our obedience to Jesus Christ. This is what the apostle Paul called the obedience of faith (Romans 1:5; 16:26). God has revealed Himself clearly in His Son, Jesus Christ (Hebrews 1:1-3). Therefore, we demonstrate our faith and please God by believing and obeying His Son. "And without faith it is impossible to please Him (Hebrews 11:6)." Jesus said, "This is the work of God, that you believe in Him whom He has sent (John 6:29)." The Bible says, "He who believes in the Son has eternal life; but he who does not obey the Son shall not see life, but the wrath of God abides on him (John 3:36)."

True faith is inseparably linked with our willingness to be submitted to Christ's authority. This is the lesson of the centurion who asked Jesus to heal his servant (see Matthew 8:5-10). As the commander of one hundred Roman soldiers and under authority himself, he understood that Jesus was under God's authority, which then gave Jesus the ability to heal his servant. When Jesus heard this, He marveled and said, "Truly I say to you, I have not found such great faith with anyone in Israel (Matthew 8:10)."

Biblical faith is both rooted in and revealed by our obedience to Jesus Christ.

Just as faith is obedience to Christ, unbelief is disobedience and lawlessness (Hebrews 3:12-19). If we say we have faith but practice lawlessness, how can that faith save us? Faith without obedience is worthless and dead (James 2:14-26).

Jesus said, "Why do you call Me, 'Lord, Lord' and do not do what I say (Luke 6:46)?" The Bible says we cannot claim to know Christ and live lawlessly (1 John 3:4-9). Although Jesus died for the whole world, only those who obey Him will be saved (Hebrews 5:9). True obedience of faith does not produce a man-made morality. Even nonChristians can seemingly have "good" morals and "good" works. Professing Christians can practice religious, moral principles and still be lawless in their heart. What is lawlessness? If we habitually do not hear and obey Jesus' voice, we are lawless and not living under His authority. Jesus said, "My sheep hear My voice... and they follow Me (John 10:27)." Jesus Himself showed us the obedience of faith by doing nothing on His own initiative unless the Father told Him (John 5:19, 8:28; 12:49). Jesus said you cannot know Him unless you obey Him and only those who know Him will enter His kingdom (Matthew 7:21-23).

How can we possibly live a life of continual obedience to Jesus Christ? As anyone who has honestly tried can testify, we cannot live such a sanctified life in our own ability. If we could live such a devoted life through our own efforts, Jesus did not need to die on the cross for us. But God intended that the high standard of holiness and obedience he commanded in the Old Testament would be "a tutor to lead us to Christ (Galatians 3:24)." Then, to make such daily obedience possible, God included us in Christ's death on the cross, so that our sinful nature would be crucified, removed and buried forever (Romans 6:3-8). As the apostle Paul testified, "I have been crucified with Christ and I no longer live, but Christ lives in me; and the life I now live in the body I live by faith in the Son of God (Galatians 2:20)." Jesus Christ died in our place and He now wants to live in our place. *If we believe that our sinful nature is dead and gone, then Christ can begin to live through us. If we do not know that our* sinful nature has died with Christ on the cross, we will go on living as if we still enslaved to sin and in charge of our own life. However, a dead man no longer has any control over his life. He has lost the ability to decide what he wants and where he goes. If we do not know that we no longer have a sinful nature, we can try as hard as humanly possible to overcome besetting sins but we will always fail since we can only overcome sin by faith in the truth alone (Romans 7:14-25).

> *True faith is inseparably linked with our willingness to be submitted to Christ's authority.*

Faith comes from hearing and obeying the word of Christ (John 12:47-48; Romans 10:17). Jesus said, "If you continue in My word... you will know the truth and the truth will set you free... if the Son sets you free, you will be free indeed (John 8:32, 36)." God set us free from the power of sin when our sinful nature died with Christ on the cross (Romans 6:7). This is God's word of freedom to us but if we do not believe it and act on it, we will never experience its transforming power. Many Christians mistakenly think they are still wretched and held captive by a sinful nature (Romans 7:18-24). The Word of God is divinely powerful but it can only effectively work in you if you believe it (1 Thessalonians 2:13). The Bible says of those who do not believe: "The word they heard did not profit them because it was not united by faith in those who heard (Hebrews 4:2)." How can Jesus Christ live through us if we do not believe and act on the truth that His death freed us from sin's power?

"The righteous shall live by faith" means we believe and live based on what Jesus Christ accomplished for us on the cross: we believe Christ died for us; we also believe our sinful nature died with Christ so He might live through us. This is the foundation of enduring faith that results in our salvation and sanctification (Matthew 24:13; Hebrews 3:14). "For in just a very little while, He who is coming will come and will not delay. But My righteous one will live by faith; and if he shrinks back, I will not be pleased with him. But we are not of those who shrink back to destruction, but of those who have faith to the saving of the soul (Hebrews 10:37-39)." Jesus said, "When the Son of Man comes, will He find faith on the earth (Luke 18:8)?" When Christ returns, will He find us living in obedience under His authority by acting on the truth of His cross?

"Not everyone who says to Me, 'Lord, Lord,' will enter the kingdom of heaven, but only he who does the will of My Father who is in heaven."

MATTHEW 7:21-23

"This is love for God: to obey His commands."

1 JOHN 5:3

CHAPTER THIRTEEN

Receiving God's Promises

"He who overcomes shall inherit these things."

REVELATION 21:7

The Bible says God "has granted to us His precious and magnificent promises so that by them we might become partakers of His divine nature (2 Peter 1:4)." However, all of God's priceless promises are conditional upon our obedience. This is what the Bible calls the obedience that comes from our faith (Romans 1:5; James 2:26). We can only receive God's promises *if* we obey God's Word. We might call this the big *"if."* Even in the Old Covenant, the promises of God were conditional upon His people's faithfulness. God promised the Hebrews they would be a holy nation and a kingdom of priests to Him *if* they obeyed His voice and kept His covenant (Exodus 19:5-6).

In the New Covenant, the promises of God start with the new birth. God promised us salvation *if* we receive Jesus Christ as our Lord (Romans 10:9). Christ is able to save you forever *if* you draw near to Him (Hebrews

7:25). God promised to forgive our sins *if* we confess our sins and forgive others their sins (Matthew 6:14; 1 John 1:9). God promised to give us His Holy Spirit *if* we obey Him (Acts 5:32). God promised to give us His grace *if* we humble ourselves under His mighty hand and love Jesus with an undying love (Ephesians 6:23; 1 Peter 5:5-6). God promised us His love *if* we love and obey Him and we do not love the world (Daniel 9:4; 1 John 2:15). Jesus Christ promised we would be His disciples *if* we deny ourselves, carry our own cross, give up everything for Him and lose our life for His sake (Matthew 16:24-26; Luke 14:27-33). Jesus' teaching on discipleship reminds me of the time a young man excitedly said to me, "Isn't it great that salvation is free!" His face fell when I replied, "Yes, and it will only cost you your whole life." By this, I meant that God offers us His gift of salvation freely because His Son paid the price for our redemption. However, after we receive His gift, it will cost us everything to follow Christ.

> *All of God's promises are conditional upon our obedience. We can only receive God's promises if we obey God's Word. We might call this the big "if."*

Christ promised to reveal Himself to us *if* we keep His commandments (John 14:21). Christ promised to answer our prayers *if* we keep His commandments (1 John 3:22). God promised to meet our basic needs *if* we seek His Sovereignty in our life (Matthew 6:33). God promised we can know Him *if* we obey His commandments (1 John 2:3). Christ promised we would know His truth *if* we are willing to do God's will (John 7:17). Christ promised to set us free *if* we abide in His word (John 8:31-32). God promised we would be His Sons *if* we are led by His Spirit (Romans 8:14). Christ promised we would bear much fruit *if* we stay rooted in Him (John 15:5). Christ promised we will not see death, *if* we keep His word (John 8:51). God promised we would live in Him *if* we do not practice sin (1 John 3:6). God promised we would live and not die *if* by the

Spirit we are putting to death the sinful actions of our body (Romans 8:13). Christ promised we would enter the kingdom of heaven *if* we do God's will (Matthew 7:21).

God promised us His rest *if* we trust Him and cease from our works (Hebrews 4:1-11). God promised us His inheritance *if* we suffer with Christ (Romans 8:17). God promised that we would have fellowship with Him *if* we walk in His light (1 John 1:5-7). God promised us His reward *if* we endure affliction by faith (Hebrews 10:35-39). God promised we would be members of His household *if* we hold fast our confidence in Christ until the end (Hebrews 3:6). God promised us His kindness *if* we continue in His grace; otherwise, we would be cut off (Romans 12:22). God promised us His eternal life if we obey His Son (John 3:36). God promised we would reign with Christ *if* we endure and overcome with Him (2 Timothy 2:12; Revelation 2:26).

The Bible says only those who overcome will inherit these promises. But how can we possibly overcome the big *if?* It is impossible for us to overcome the big *if* in our own ability. Many have tried but all have failed. We cannot overcome the big *if;* only Jesus Christ can. The Bible says Christ died so that we might receive His eternal promises (Hebrews 9:15). The way we overcome the big *if* is *in Christ.* "For as many as are the promises of God, *in Christ* they are yes (2 Corinthians 1:20)." We receive the promises of God by abiding in Christ. How do we abide and live in Christ?

> *Believing and acting on the truth that we have died with Christ and that Christ now lives in us is the secret to receiving all the promises of God.*

The apostle Paul said, "Now *if* we have died with Christ, we believe that we shall also live with Him (Romans 6:8; also 2 Timothy 2:11)." The way to live in Christ is to know (believe and act) that we have already died in Christ. God has already overcome the big *if* for us by including us in

Christ's death. "Therefore, when one died, all died (2 Corinthians 5:12)." When Christ died, we died with Him and our sinful nature was removed from us (Colossians 2:11). "For we know that our old self was crucified with Him so that our body of sin *(our sinful nature)* might be done away with (Romans 6:6)." However, we must believe this divine truth in order to overcome the big *if.*

The Son of God died for us and He now wants to sovereignly live through us. As the apostle Paul declared, "I have been crucified with Christ and I no longer live but Christ lives in me, and the life that I live in the body, I live by faith in the Son of God who loved me and gave Himself up for me (Galatians 2:20). Believing and acting on the truth that we have died with Christ and that Christ now lives in us is the secret to fulfilling the big *"if"* and receiving all the promises of God.

"Behold, I stand at the door and knock; if anyone hears My voice and opens the door, I will come in to him and will dine with him and he with Me."

REVELATION 3:20

CHAPTER FOURTEEN

The Whole Gospel

*"For in the gospel a righteousness from God is revealed, a righteousness that is
by faith from beginning to end, just as it is written:
'The righteous will live by faith.'"*

ROMANS 1:16-17

Many professing Christians practice only part of the gospel: Christ's atonement for the forgiveness of sins. Although they know they are saved by faith, very few Christians know how to live by faith. Consequently, they trust Jesus as Savior and hope one day to go to heaven but, in between, they struggle vainly to live in this sin-sick world by the best of their ability and often mistake their self-effort for faith. This is not only tragic, it is alarming because God's people can be ignorant about a lot of things, but if they are ignorant about the meaning and power of the cross, they are in real trouble. As God said in Hosea 4:6: "My people are destroyed for lack of knowledge."

What is this Christian life that Jesus intended us to live? Jesus described it as a life of discipleship. As His disciples, Jesus commands us to deny ourselves and give up everything (Luke 9:23; 14:33). We are called to love just as He loves (John 13:34) and be holy just as He is holy (1 Peter 1:15). The more we read the Bible, we will realize forgiveness of sins is a gift (at Christ's expense) but discipleship will cost our entire life. We cannot genuinely profess to be Christians if we are not truly Christ's disciples. Jesus said, "Why do you call Me, 'Lord, Lord' and do not do what I say (Luke 6:46)?"

How can we live this life of spiritual purity, self-sacrifice and selfless love? The answer is we cannot. Jesus said, "Apart from Me you can do nothing (John 15:5)." It is impossible to follow Christ and truly obey His commands if we rely on our own morality and ability. But God has pro-vided the way through His Son's death on the cross. When Jesus died, He took our sin nature upon Himself so that our sinful nature died with Him (Romans 6:6). "God made Christ who knew no sin to be sin on our behalf so that we might become the righteousness of God (2 Corinthians 5:21)." We might call this a divine heart transplant by which God exchanged our terminally sin-sick heart with His Son's divine heart.

Many Christians trust Jesus as Savior and hope one day to go to heaven but, in between, they struggle vainly to live in this sin-sick world by the best of their ability and often mistake their self-effort for faith.

Since our sinful nature is now dead and gone, we can live the Christian life by faith in Christ who lives in us (Galatians 2:20).

Jesus has already borne our old sinful nature on His cross but He also said, "Whoever does not bear *his* own cross and come after Me cannot be My disciple (Luke 14:27)." A similar verse is found in Matthew 10:38: "Anyone who does not take *his* cross and follow Me is not worthy of Me." In the next verse (Matthew 10:39), Jesus then explains how we can bear our own cross: "Whoever finds his *life* will lose it, and whoever loses his *life* for My sake will find it." The Greek word used here for "life" is *psyche*, which means soul-life. Therefore, we bear our cross and prove we are His disciples by yielding our soul-life to Christ. God has made us spirit, soul and body (1 Thessalonians 5:23). When we were born again, our old sinful nature died and our regenerated spirit became one with Christ's Spirit (1 Corinthians 6:17). Our soul, however, is our natural personality - the sum of our individuality and the source of our natural temperament and talent. Because we retain free will, our soul does not automatically come under Christ's Sovereignty. However, once we know that we have died with Christ, we are capable of truly submitting to

Once we know that we have died with Christ, we are capable of truly submitting to Christ's authority so that God can transform and restore our soul.

Christ's authority so that God can transform and restore our soul (Psalm 19:7; Romans 12:1-2). God does not want to destroy our soul; He meant our soul to be a useful instrument just like our body. But now that we are in Christ, the important question we must face is, "Will we live by the power of His Spirit or the power of our soul?"

Each of us is endowed with soul-power. This is what we can accomplish by our natural personality. Until God has trained us by His Spirit, we will rely on our natural ability to do Christ's work and bear His fruit. Yet the power of our personality cannot reproduce Christ's life. Only Christ's Spirit in us can reproduce His life (John 6:63). When God shows us that we have died with Christ and we see the futility of our soul-power to bear His fruit, we will learn not to trust our natural zeal and ability to do God's work (Philippians 3:3). We may be born again but if we continue to live by the soul, we will quench and grieve the Holy Spirit in us. A brother in Christ once said if we live by the body, we become like beasts and if we live by the soul, we become rebels to God. The Bible says if we are led by the Spirit, we are sons of God but if we continue to be ruled by the soul, we are hostile to God (Romans 8:12). How can we know the difference between the Spirit and the soul so we can live under the sovereignty of the Spirit? Again, the answer is we cannot. Once again, we must ask Jesus to do in us what we cannot do ourselves. As we fix our eyes on Jesus who is Light, we have light (John 8:12) and the Spirit can show us when we act from out of our soul instead of being led by the Spirit (Hebrews 4:12-13).

Until we know we have died and our life is hidden in Christ (Colossians 3:3), our soul's driving need is for self-identity, self-preservation and self-fulfillment. Our self-identity may be as a Christian teacher, worker or minister. Since our self-esteem depends on our self-identity, fulfilling our soul-life becomes our aim. Tragically, much of what is done in Jesus' name is to satisfy this soulish drive for identity rather than finding our identity in Christ. The key to laying down our soul-life is to know the truth that we have already died and our sinful nature has been completely removed (Colossians 2:11). A dead man does not need an identity. If we know we have died in Christ, we are freed from soulish ambition (Galatians 6:14). We are then capable of dying daily to our soul-life so that Christ's life may be revealed in us to others (2 Corinthians 4:10-11). This is the whole gospel of God (Acts 20:27).

"Unless a grain of wheat falls into the earth and dies, it remains alone; but if it dies, it bears much fruit. He who loves his life loses it, and he who hates his life in this world will keep it to life eternal."

JOHN 12:24-25

CHAPTER FIFTEEN

Destined to Suffer
for Christ's Sake

"For to you it has been granted for Christ's sake, not only to
believe in Him, but also to suffer for His sake."

PHILIPPIANS 1:29

"For you yourselves know that we have been destined for this...
we kept telling you in advance that we were going to suffer affliction."

1 THESSALONIANS 3:3-4

Many Christians believe God is infinitely happy and that He also wants us to be happy. They believe the idea of sorrow and suffering is negative thinking and should be avoided. This is a false gospel. It ignores the whole counsel of God as revealed by His Word. Many people mistakenly believe that the pursuit of happiness is our God-given right. However, this directly contradicts the Bible, which declares the pursuit of holiness is our God-given obligation. Multitudes are now reaping the godless fruit of pursuing temporal, earthly happiness instead of seeking the righteousness of God that comes by faith and the church has been compromised by buying into this false gospel. The Bible is also clear we cannot pursue the holiness of God without suffering here on earth. In contrast to the false gospel of happiness, the Bible says Christ was "a man of sorrows and familiar with suffering (Isaiah 53:3)." Even though He was the Son of God, God perfected Jesus as the Son of Man, the author of our salvation, through sufferings (Hebrews 2:10; also 5:8)." Jesus Himself said, "The Son of Man must suffer many things (Mark 8:31)."

Jesus Christ could not have redeemed His bride without suffering, even to the point of suffering death on the cross. Similarly, the bride of Christ cannot be prepared for eternal union and co-rulership with Christ without also suffering. "If we suffer, we shall also reign with Him (2 Timothy 2:12)." Jesus told His disciples they could expect to drink from His cup of suffering (Matthew 20:22-23). The apostle Peter said, "For you have been called for this purpose, since Christ also suffered for you, leaving you an example for you to follow in His steps (1 Peter 2:21)." The apostle Paul said, "We must go through many hardships to enter the kingdom of God (Acts 14:22)." This suffering refers not to our initial salvation but to our sanctification and spiritual maturity. We are destined to suffer because we cannot possess our spiritual inheritance in Christ if we don't suffer for Christ's sake (Romans 8:17).

We are destined to suffer for Christ's sake because suffering produces Christian character and spiritual maturity.

Suffering is inseparably linked with knowing Jesus Christ. Paul said, "I want to know Christ... and the fellowship of sharing in His sufferings (Philippians 3:10)." We cannot resist sin and the carnal desires of our soul-life without suffering emotionally and physically. "Therefore since Christ has suffered in the flesh, arm yourselves with the same purpose, because he who has suffered in the flesh has ceased from sin, so as to live the rest of his time in the flesh no longer for the lusts of men, but for the will of God (1 Peter 4:1-2)." We cannot be God's legitimate sons if we are not willing to suffer the pain of His divine discipline (Hebrews 12:5-10). We cannot bear God's spiritual fruit if we are not willing to suffer the pain of His divine pruning (John 15:2). We cannot be Christ's soldiers if we are not willing to suffer hardship (2 Timothy 2:3).

We are destined to suffer for Christ's sake because suffering produces Christian character and spiritual maturity (Romans 5:3-4; James 1:2-4). Therefore, when we ask God to help us grow in Christ, we should not be surprised when we encounter hardship and suffering. God is Sovereign and God is Love. When we suffer, it is not by accident; it is by God's design. God has ordered our suffering according to His knowledge of our need and for our good. "And we know that God causes all things to work together for good to those who love God, to those who are called according to His purpose (Romans 8:28)."

The Son of God died in our place to forgive us from the penalty of sin; He now wants to live in our place to free us from the power of sin.

What is the mystery of suffering? Paul said, "We do not want you to be unaware, brethren, of our affliction... that we were burdened excessively, beyond our strength... so that we would not trust in ourselves but in God (2 Corinthians 1:8-9)." The Greek word for affliction is *thlipsis*. It is also translated as tribulation and simply means *pressure*. God has designed suffering to apply pressure on us until we are pressed beyond our natural ability. When we finally come to the end of ourselves, God will reveal the mystery of Christ's crucifixion to us. This is the divine revelation that God included us in His Son's death so that Christ might live in us (Romans 6:3-11; Colossians 1:27). The Son of God died in our place to forgive us from the penalty of sin; He now wants to live in our place to free us from the power of sin. God has made this possible by using Christ's death on the cross to remove our sinful nature and replace it with His Son's holy nature. This divine exchange is the secret to the overcoming Christian life. God has designed suffering to reveal and continually reinforce this divine truth in us. As Paul personally testified, "I have been crucified with Christ and I no longer live but Christ lives in me and the life I now live, I live by faith in the Son of God (Galatians 2:20)." This is the only way we can walk in holiness and suffer for Christ's sake.

Many Christians believe they are entitled to happiness rather than destined to suffer. This is a false gospel that will cause many to fall away from the faith during the coming tribulation and persecution. God has not called us to happiness but He has called us to holiness. There is no exception to this call for a Christian. Our reaction to affliction will determine whether our suffering produces God's divine objective – the joy of knowing Jesus Christ and being conformed to His image. Yielding to self-pity, anger and bitterness is a waste of our suffering. If we understand God's purpose in suffering, we can accept our affliction and trust in a wise and loving Almighty God. "Our present sufferings are not worth comparing with the glory to be revealed in us… for momentary, light affliction is producing for us an eternal weight of glory far beyond comparison (Romans 8:18; 2 Corinthians 4:17)."

"Therefore, those who suffer according to the will of God should entrust their souls to a faithful Creator in doing what is right."

1 PETER 4:19

CHAPTER SIXTEEN

They Loved Not
Their Lives

"And they overcame him by the blood of the Lamb and by the word of their testimony; and they loved not their lives unto the death."

REVELATION 12:10

In the final spiritual conflict of this age, a great persecution will come upon the church. The Bible says the body of overcomers who triumph over Satan during this intense warfare will have one distinguishing mark: "They loved not their lives" when faced with death. This indicates true Christians will die in this final conflict rather than forsake their bold testimony of Christ. It also indicates the final test of our faith in this end-time persecution will be our willingness to lose our lives for Christ's sake.

The Holy Spirit is calling this generation to prepare as soldiers of Christ for this end-time battle. However, we will only overcome Satan and his legions if we train in peacetime the way we will fight in wartime. Since our fight is not against mortal men but against the spiritual forces of evil, we will not win this battle with earthly weapons. Instead, we will overcome Satan by the blood of the Lamb. This is the basis for laying down our lives. This is the key to victory. The blood of the Lamb speaks of the triumphant work that Christ accomplished by His death on the cross. Just as Jesus Christ conquered Satan by laying down His life on the cross, we also will overcome the devil by laying down our lives by the power of the cross. Not only did Christ die on the cross for us (Romans 5:8), He also included us in His death (Romans 6:8). When Christ died, we died with Him (2 Corinthians 5:14). By the power of Christ's crucifixion, God removed our sinful nature and replaced it with His Son's life (Romans 6:6; 2 Corinthians 5:21; Colossians 2:11; 3:3). Therefore Satan no longer has any power over us to make us sin (Romans 6:7; 1 John 3:8).

If we believe this to be the gospel, then we should lay down our lives every day for Christ. This is how we can prepare for both the end-time conflict and the age to come when we will reign with Christ. Jesus said if we do not lose our own life and even hate it for His sake, we cannot be His disciples (Matthew 10:38-39; Mark 8:34-35; Luke 14:26-27). The Greek word for "life" used in these gospel accounts is *psyche*, which means soul-life. This is the life that originates from our natural personality and encompasses our attitudes, affections and abilities. What does it mean to lose our soul-life for Christ? It means we lay down our self-will and natural personality and preferences to Christ's authority. When we lay down our soul-life to Jesus Christ, we prove our faith in His Sovereignty and His completed work on the cross. We also demonstrate our love for the brethren (1 John 3:16). This is what the Lord meant when He said we must carry our own cross if we want to follow Him (Luke 9:23).

> *The blood of the Lamb speaks of the triumphant work that Christ accomplished by His death on the cross.*

Although the ultimate test of losing our soul-life may be to die for Christ (since this goes against the natural instinct of self-preservation), we will have many other daily opportunities to practice dying to self when Christ's authority crosses our natural desires. For example, we may be routinely challenged to lose our soul-life to serve our family. Or we may have to suffer a difficult affliction that presses us beyond our natural endurance. Or we may have to resist a temptation that is beyond our natural self-control. Or we may have to love a dedicated personal enemy who is impossible for us to naturally love. The only way we can triumph in these trials and temptations is to believe our sin nature has died and been removed by Christ's death. Then we can choose to overcome sin and die to our soul-life by faith in the power of Christ who lives in us.

Just as Jesus Christ conquered Satan by laying down His life on the cross, we also will overcome the devil by laying down our lives by the power of the cross.

There is yet another aspect to losing our soul-life for Christ's sake. When we know we have died with Christ, we will want to serve Him in the Spirit and not trust in our natural ability. This is what the apostle Paul meant when he said, "we are the true circumcision, who worship in the Spirit of God and glory in Christ Jesus and put no confidence in the flesh (Philippians 3:3). Unfortunately, many Christians are unwisely encouraged to use their natural talents to serve God without proper discipleship in losing their soul-life for Christ's sake. For example, believers with musical talents are urged to lead worship. Or those with natural leadership and speaking abilities are pressed into pastoring and preaching. However, most Christians have not been properly established in a foundation of Christ crucified *(we died with Christ so He might live in us).* Nor have they been properly trained in living by the power of the Spirit rather than the power of their soul (their natural personality). The tragic outcome is that many

Christians are fulfilling their soul-life through ministry rather than losing their soul-life to gain Jesus Christ. This is not just harmless; it is hostile to the Spirit of God (Romans 8:12-14; Galatians 5:17).

Many Christians also mistakenly think they can submit their natural man to Christ through self-discipline. But this only strengthens their soul-power (their natural personality) and separates them from the grace of God. It is impossible to lose your soul-life if you do not believe you have been crucified with Christ. But when you know your sinful nature is dead, God will reveal how your unsubmissive soul quenches the power of His Spirit. Then you will see the need to always identify by faith with Christ's death on the cross to receive His spiritual discipline and training.

The final conflict of this age is soon approaching. It is time for every Christian who hears the call of the Spirit to report for duty to our Commander-in-Chief, Jesus Christ, for spiritual warfare training. Our Lord Jesus has already secured the victory for us by including us in His death. If we know we have died with Christ, let us train by laying down our lives now so we will be ready to lay down our lives for Him in the coming war against the saints.

"Suffer hardship with us like a good soldier of Christ Jesus. No one serving
as a soldier entangles himself in everyday life,
so that he may please his commanding officer."

2 Timothy 2:3-4

CHAPTER SEVENTEEN

Christ is All and in All

"Christ is all and in all."

COLOSSIANS 3:11

The overriding theme of the New Testament is Jesus Christ. This is particularly true of the apostle Paul's letter to the Colossians, which reveals Christ more than any other letter in the New Testament. Paul wrote this short letter around A.D. 62 from his imprisonment in Rome to the Christian community of house churches in Colossae, a city in what is now western Turkey. In his letter, Paul unfolds the gospel to the "saints and faithful brethren in Christ at Colossae" to help them see the majesty and power of the Son of God. In just the first chapter of Colossians alone, Paul speaks of Christ thirty times.

Paul starts his letter by stating that God's kingdom is "the kingdom of the beloved Son (Colossians 1:13)." Paul follows this by declaring that Jesus Christ is eternal God. "He is the image of the invisible God... for in Christ all the fullness of the Deity lives in bodily form... He is before all things and in Him all things hold together (Colossians 1:15, 17; 2:9)." Paul then reveals Christ as the Creator. "For by Him all things were created, both in the heavens and on earth, visible and invisible, whether thrones or powers or rulers or authorities – all things have been created through Him and for Him (Colossians 1:16). Paul further reveals Christ as the Redeemer. "For the Father was pleased to have all His fullness dwell in Him, and through Him to reconcile all things to Himself, having made peace through the blood of His cross, whether things on earth or things in heaven (Colossians 1:19-20)."

Paul proclaims that Jesus Christ is Lord of heaven and earth. "He is the head over all rule and authority (Colossians 2:10)." Paul declares Christ's headship and authority in the church. "He is also head of the body, the church... so that in everything He might have the supremacy (Colossians 1:18)." Paul also reveals Jesus Christ's preeminent role in the new creation, which is His church, the body of Christ. "He is the beginning, the first born from the dead... He has now reconciled you in His fleshly body through death, in order to present you before Him holy and blameless and beyond reproach (Colossians 1:18; 22)." Paul tells them the Old Covenant feasts and the Sabbath are a "mere shadow of the things that were to come – the reality is found in Christ (Colossians 2:16-17)." Paul declares that Christ, by His death on the cross, conquered Satan and

By linking Old Covenant circumcision with New Covenant baptism, Paul leaves no doubt that the death and removal of our sinful nature, as symbolized by circumcision, is also portrayed by the burial stage of water baptism.

his forces of darkness. "And having disarmed the powers and authorities, He made a public spectacle of them, triumphing over them by the cross (Colossians 2:15)." Paul reveals that Christ is the mystery of God "in whom are hidden all the treasures of wisdom and knowledge (Colossians 2:2-3)." Paul tells the Colossians that Christ, who is the fullness of God and Creator, Redeemer and Sovereign Lord, now lives in them. Paul declares the mystery of God is "Christ in you, the hope of glory (Colossians 1:27)."

Yet Paul does not leave the Colossians with only doctrine about Christ. Paul wants them to know Christ and be complete in Christ. "We proclaim Him, admonishing every man and teaching every man with all wisdom, so that we may present every man complete in Christ (Colossians 1:28)." Paul exhorts them, "As you have received Christ as Lord, so live in Him (Colossians 2:6-7)." How did they first receive Christ? By faith in Christ's completed work on the cross. Then how do they live in Christ? Once again, by faith in Christ's completed work in the cross! Paul warns them that man-made religion with its rules and regulations has no power to stop them from sinning (Colossians 2:20-23). Paul proclaims the only way they can experience Christ's life is to stay connected to Christ their head (Colossians 2:19). He reminds them this is entirely possible if they know (believe and act) on the truth that they have died with Christ. "For you have died and your life is hidden with Christ (Colossians 3:3)."

Paul uses the picture of circumcision to teach the Colossians that Christ removed their sinful nature from them when they were saved. "In Him you were also circumcised with a circumcision made without hands, in the *removal of the sinful nature,* by the circumcision of Christ (Colossians 2:11)." Paul then shifts in the very next verse (Colossians 2:12) from the Old Covenant seal of righteousness (circumcision) to the New Covenant seal of righteousness (baptism) in order to further show that their old sinful nature was removed from them when they were born again. Paul explains that since their old sinful nature died and was removed (verse 2:11), it was then disposed of by burial: "Having been *buried with Him in baptism* and raised with Him through your faith in the power of God, who raised Him from the dead (verse 2:12)." By linking Old Covenant circumcision with New Covenant baptism, the apostle Paul leaves no doubt that the death

If we believe and act on the divine truth that God has exchanged our sinful nature with His Son's nature, then Christ will be all and in all.

and removal of our sinful nature, as symbolized by circumcision, is also portrayed by the burial stage of water baptism. Paul's point is that baptism confirms (just as circumcision did) that our old sinful nature not only died with Christ but was also removed from us through Christ's death on the cross. Having established this truth, Paul exhorts the Colossians to "put to death" the carnal attitudes and actions of their unconverted soul-life (Colossians 3:5) since they "have put on the new man who is being renewed to a true knowledge according to the image of their Creator – a renewal in which… Christ is all and in all (Colossians 3:10-11)."

Jesus Christ is the alpha and omega – the beginning and the end. Christ is the head and we are His body. Christ is the fullness of God and we have been given fullness in Him. God's desire is for Christ to be *all* sovereign in *all* His body. This is the goal of the gospel and God's eternal purpose. If we believe and act on the divine truth that God has exchanged our sinful nature with His Son's nature, then Christ will be all and in all.

"Therefore if you have been raised up with Christ, set your hearts on the things above, where Christ is seated at the right hand of God. Set your minds on things above, not on earthly things. For you have died and your life is hidden with Christ in God. When Christ, who is your life, is revealed, then you also will be revealed with Him in glory."

COLOSSIANS 3:1-4

CHAPTER EIGHTEEN

Not I but Christ

"I have been crucified with Christ and
I no longer live but Christ lives in me,
and the life which I now live in the body, I live
by faith in the Son of God who loved me and
gave Himself up for me."

GALATIANS 2:20

This simple but profound statement sums up the promise of the New Covenant, the purpose of Christ's Atonement and the power of Christ's gospel. This is the gospel that Jesus Christ revealed to the apostle Paul and this is the gospel that Paul spent his life proclaiming (see 1 Corinthians 1:17-2:5; Galatians 1:11-16; Ephesians 3:8-10; and Colossians 1:25-29). In the middle of this verse, Paul defines the Christian life as "I no longer live but Christ lives in me." This can be summarized as "not I but Christ." Take a moment to reflect on these four words "not I but Christ." Such a life is the clearest witness of Jesus Christ the world could ever see. This should be the Christian life we aspire to live. Here Paul declares not only can Christ fully live His life in us, he provides two conditions for us to experience this divine life.

The first condition is found at the beginning of the verse and the second one is at the end. The first condition is to know "I have been crucified with Christ." This is the secret to living the Christian life. Before we can hope to live such a life, we must know our sinful nature has been crucified with Christ (Romans 6:6). This is crucial. We needed forgiveness from the penalty of our sins but we also needed deliverance from the power of our sin nature. Christ's death has provided full provision for both our forgive-

God's way to permanently deal with our sins was to remove the sinner (the sin factory) from within us and substitute Christ in his place.

ness and our deliverance. Since we came into sin by birth, we could only be freed from sin by our death (Romans 6:7). However, we could not put ourselves to death; therefore God has crucified us with Christ. When Christ died, we died and God performed a divine heart transplant and replaced our terminally sin-sick heart with His Son's divine heart. However, the death of our sinful nature will never become real to us by our will or effort but only when we believe we have already died in Christ. Our sinful nature has once and for all time been executed and removed. That wretched self-centered "I" whom we loathed has died and been buried (Romans 6:3-6). This is the Biblical truth. But if we don't know the truth, then we cannot be set free from sin (John 8:32). That's why Paul said, "Do you not know you have died to sin... for he who has died has been freed from sin (Romans 6:2-3, 7)."

The knowledge that we have died with Christ can only be seen by God's divine revelation opening our spiritual eyes. If we do not know that our sinful nature has already died with Christ, we will mistakenly try to live the Christian life by the best of our ability. We may think God will honor our dedication and meet our effort halfway to help us. However, God's way is not to help our natural man do the work of the Spirit. Jesus said, "That which is born of the flesh is flesh and that which is born of the Spirit is spirit (John 3:6)." Only the Spirit gives life; our soul has no power to overcome sin (John 6:63). God's way to permanently deal with our sins was to remove the sinner (the sin factory) from within us and substitute Christ in his place. When we know we have died, then who is left? Only Christ is left. Just as Paul said, "I no longer live but Christ lives in me." Christ has now become our identity (Colossians 3:3-4).

The second condition for experiencing God's ordained life of "not I but Christ" is found at the end of the verse: "The life which I now live in the body I live by faith in the Son of God." Faith is the substance of things hoped for, the evidence of things not yet seen (Hebrews 11:1). Although we know our salvation required no work on our part, we often mistakenly think our sanctification depends on our best effort. However, the Christian life is not one of trying but of trusting, for the Bible says,

> *The Christian life is not one of trying but of trusting, for the Bible says, "The righteous will live by faith."*

"The righteous will live by faith (Romans 1:17)." By faith, we work out our salvation and substantiate God's truth that we have died in Christ and Christ now lives in us. We are freed from sin's power the same way we know our sins are forgiven - by believing God's Word. "In the same way, count yourselves dead to sin but alive to God in Christ Jesus (Romans 6:11)."

Knowing we have already died in Christ, we acknowledge we are inadequate and incapable. We no longer try to live the Christian life by our own strength but we trust Jesus Christ to live His life in us. We believe Jesus is all we need - He has become our wisdom, our righteousness, and our sanctification and redemption (1 Corinthians 1:30). We stand firm by faith in the glorious truth that our old man of sin is gone and Christ now lives in us despite the accusing lies of that deceiver, the devil. The Holy

Spirit then confirms and establishes this powerful liberating reality in our life until Christ is fully formed in us (Galatians 4:19; 1 Peter 5:8-10). Knowing we have died and Christ lives in us, we present ourselves each day as a living and holy vessel for God's use (Romans 12:1-2). We gladly yield our soul-life (our natural attitudes, affections and abilities) to His Sovereignty so His life might be manifest in us (Mark 8:34-35). For the joy of knowing Christ and the desire to lay down our lives for the brethren and by faith in what He has done, we resist the carnal desires that wage war against our soul (1 Peter 2:11; 4:1-2). We refuse to act independently apart from Christ's authority (John 5:19, 30; 15:5). Instead, we rest by faith in Christ's completed work on the cross. We then wholeheartedly take whatever action Jesus Christ initiates in us by relying on "His power that works in us (Ephesians 3:20)."

Jesus Christ died in our place and since we also died in Him, He now wants to live in our place. Thus the first step for us to experience a life of "not I but Christ" is to know we have died in Christ. The next step is to trust Jesus Christ to sovereignly live in us. May God give us divine revelation to know the Son of God and all He has accomplished on the cross so we might experience and express the fullness of Christ (Ephesians 4:13).

"For to me, to live is Christ."

PHILIPPIANS 1:21

Chapter Nineteen

The King is Coming!

"Rejoice greatly, O daughter of Zion! Shout in triumph, O daughter of Jerusalem! Behold your King is coming to you!"

ZECHARIAH 9:9 (SEE ALSO MATTHEW 21:5)

Jesus Christ is King! The prophets heralded the coming Messiah King (Isaiah 9:6-7; Daniel 7:13-14). The wise men hailed Christ's birth as King (Matthew 2:2). Jesus Himself said, "I am a King... for this reason I have come into the world (John 18:37)." The disciples declared Jesus was King (John 1:49; Luke 19:38). The apostles "upset the world" when they boldly proclaimed "King Jesus (Acts 17:6-7)." The angels in heaven worship Jesus as the King of kings (Revelation 17:14). At Calvary, Jesus proved He is a King worthy of our devotion (Revelation 5:12). Jesus Christ is God the Savior King who came not only to die for His Kingdom but to reign over His Kingdom (Philippians 2:8-11). The Kingdom was at the heart of Jesus' ministry (Mark 1:14-15). Jesus told His disciples to seek His Kingdom, pray for His Kingdom and proclaim His Kingdom (Matthew 6:10, 6:33; 24:14). Since God the Father has appointed Jesus as King, the Kingdom of God is the realm of Christ's Sovereign rule (Ephesians 1:22).

The Kingship of Christ is not an option for Christians. Jesus said, "Why do you call Me, 'Lord, Lord,' and not do what I say (Luke 6:46)?" God wants to give us His Kingdom but we cannot receive it unless Christ is our King (Luke 12:32; Acts 4:12). We cannot receive Christ's Spirit apart from Christ's Sovereignty. The focus of the early disciples was on Christ their risen King and His Sovereign Kingdom. They knew when they were born again they had changed kingdoms; God had rescued them from Satan's dominion and transplanted them into Christ's Kingdom (Colossians 1:13). They did not just outwardly change their old worldly lifestyle for a new "Christian" lifestyle. They knew Christianity meant Christ reigned in their lives. They knew discipleship meant they were bondslaves of Jesus Christ because He had ransomed them with His own life (Romans 6:22; 1 Peter 2:16; 1 Corinthians 6:20).

The Kingship of Christ is not an option for Christians. God wants to give us His Kingdom but we cannot receive it unless Christ is our King.

Jesus told His disciples a parable of a king who was far away and whose servants did not want him to return and reign over them (Luke 19:11-27). As long as the king remained away, his sovereignty did not threaten them. In the same way, many professing Christians want Jesus to remain a far off King so they can honor Him with their lips from a safe distance but not be threatened by His Sovereign demands on their life. They want to enjoy the benefits of belonging to Christ's Kingdom without the cost of losing their soul-life to serve Christ the King (Matthew 10:38-39). At the end of the parable, Jesus said when the king finally returned, he ordered all those who rejected his reign over them to be slain. This is really a story of the end of the age. When Christ returns, He will gather out of His Kingdom all those who practiced lawlessness and never made Him King and throw them into the eternal fire of hell (Matthew 7:21-23; 13:36-50; 25:41).

The desire to submit to Christ's Kingship should motivate every child of the Kingdom. But who could free us from our soul's primal need for self-preservation, self-autonomy and self-fulfillment? We cannot possibly free ourselves from our sinful nature; only Jesus Christ is able (Romans 7:24-25). If we think we are able, in our natural strength, to be Christ's bondslaves in spirit, soul and body, it is because we have never honestly tried. It is impossible for us in the natural to turn away from preserving and promoting our soul-life and live a life of absolute surrender to Christ. First, we must acknowledge this truth. Next, God must open the eyes of our heart to see what Jesus Christ has already fully accomplished for us by His death on the cross.

The revelation of the cross of Christ is the secret to coming under the Kingship of Christ. When we see that God has included us in His Son's death on the cross, we are freed to be Christ's bondslaves (Romans 6:6-22). When we know our old sinful nature has been crucified with Christ, then Christ our King can fully reign in us (Galatians 2:20). If we do not know we have died with Christ, we will never fully experience Christ's Sovereignty. Christ will not force His Sovereignty on us if we are busy trying to be good "Christians" and fulfill ourselves in "Christian" ministry. The Kingdom and the cross are inseparable; we cannot know the King and possess His Kingdom except by the cross. But

The revelation of the cross of Christ is the secret to coming under the Kingship of Christ.

God will not share His precious revelation of the cross of His Son if we still want to maintain self-control and self-sovereignty over our lives. As long as we still think we are able in our own strength to do Christ's work, we will be blinded by our own self-confidence to the power of the cross of Christ. God will only reveal the truth of the cross to us when we finally come to the end of ourselves and are truly ready to receive His Son's Sovereignty in our lives.

Jesus said His Kingdom would be given to a people who produce its fruit (Matthew 21:43). He compared His Kingdom to planting a seed (Mark 4:14-20). When we first receive the word of Christ's Kingship into our heart, it is only a small seed. If His seed doesn't find a heart of faith in us, it shrivels and dies in the heat of affliction and persecution or is choked out by the pleasures and worries of this world. However, if the word of Christ's Sovereignty finds a heart of faith in us, it grows like a mustard seed into a mature tree. It takes over the whole garden of our life and bears much fruit. Christ our King died for us and included us in His death so He might sovereignly live in us. If we know we have died with Christ, let us now suffer with Christ in this life so that we might also reign with Him in the age to come (2 Timothy 2:12; Revelation 20:6). Let us lay down our lives and prepare the way for the coming of our King! Come soon King Jesus!

"Now to the King eternal, immortal, invisible, the only God, be honor and glory forever and ever. Amen."

1 TIMOTHY 1:17

CHAPTER TWENTY

The Triumph
of the Cross

*"Thanks be to God, who always leads us in triumph in Christ, and manifests
through us the sweet aroma of the knowledge of Him in every place."*

2 CORINTHIANS 2:14

The precious phrase, *"in Christ,"* is found over eighty times in the
New Testament to describe our glorious spiritual inheritance in Jesus
Christ. God has made us joint-heirs *in Christ* (Romans 8:17). He has blessed
us with every spiritual blessing in the heavenly places *in Christ* (Ephesians
1:3). He has predestined us to spiritually reign *in Christ* (Romans 5:17).
According to the Bible, this should be our normal Christian experience *in
Christ.*

But first, how do we get *"in Christ?"* There is nothing we could possibly
do to put ourselves *in Christ.* This is a miraculous work only God Himself
could do. The moment we received Jesus Christ as our Lord and Savior and
were born again of the Holy Spirit (John 3:5-7), God placed us *in Christ*
(1 Corinthians 1:30). The Bible says that we were spiritually immersed

into Christ. This is the true spiritual significance of baptism, which means immersion in the Greek *(baptisma).* "For all of you who were baptized *(immersed) into Christ* have clothed yourselves with Christ (Galatians 3:27)." A brother in Christ once used the analogy of inserting a piece of paper into a book to describe this event. Then whatever happened to the book also happened to the paper in the book. If the book was immersed under water, the paper was also immersed under water. This is what spiritually happened to us when we were immersed *into Christ.*

Christ's redemption (His death, burial and resurrection) was an eternal event in the spiritual realm. Because we have been immersed into union with Christ (1 Corinthians 6:17), we have been spiritually incorporated into every aspect of Christ's redemption. Our union with Christ starts at the cross when we were immersed into His death. "Or do you not know that all of us who have been baptized into Christ Jesus have been baptized into His death? (Romans 6:3)." When Christ died, our old sinful nature died *in Christ* and was buried (removed) *in Christ* (Romans 6:6; Colossians 2:11).

What does it mean to triumph in Christ? It means that in Christ we are able to overcome the power of Satan and sin.

When Christ was made alive and raised from the dead, we were made spiritually alive and raised *in Christ* (Romans 6:4-11; Ephesians 2:5-6). Since Christ has been seated in the heavenly places, we are also seated in the heavenly places *in Christ* (Ephesians 2:6). Because Christ has triumphed over the world through the cross, we have also triumphed over the world *in Christ* (Romans 8:37; 2 Corinthians 2:14).

What does it mean to triumph *in Christ?* It means that *in Christ* we are able to overcome the power of Satan and sin. By His death on the cross, Christ triumphed over sin (John 1:29; Romans 8:1-2). Because we are *in Christ,* we have also overcome sin (Romans 6:11; 1 John 3:9; 5:4-5).

When Christ died, God freed us from the power of sin by including us in His Son's death (see Romans 6:3-7). Before we died *in Christ*, Satan had power over our sinful nature (Ephesians 2:2). However, since our sinful nature has been crucified and removed by Christ's death (Romans 6:6), we have been freed from sin (Romans 6:7) so that sin no longer has power over us (Romans 6:14). Thus, by His death on the cross, Jesus Christ removed our sinful nature and thereby disarmed the power of the devil to make us sin (Hebrews 2:14; 1 John 3:8). "And having disarmed the powers and authorities, He made a public spectacle of them, triumphing over them by the cross (Colossians 2:15)." Because Christ has triumphed through the cross, all spiritual powers and authorities are subject to Him (Ephesians 1:20-22; 1 Peter 3:22).

Since we are *in Christ*, we have also overcome the devil, the enemy (1 John 4:4; 5:18-19). When Jesus sent His disciples out to preach the gospel, He gave them power and authority over all the demons and to heal the sick (Luke 9:1-2). He told them, "Behold, I have given you authority to tread on serpents and scorpions, and over all the power of the enemy and nothing shall injure you (Luke 10:19)." Because we are *in Christ*, we also have authority over the power of the enemy.

> *By His death on the cross, Christ removed our sinful nature and thereby disarmed the power of the devil to make us sin.*

How do we triumph *in Christ*? We overcome the same way we received forgiveness of sins. We believe what God says is true and act on it. If we are *in Christ*, we believe that God has forgiven us because of Christ's sacrifice on the cross (Ephesians 1:7). In the same manner, if we are *in Christ*, we believe that God has made us overcomers because of Christ's triumph on the cross (1 John 5:4-5). Christ has already done everything for us. Christ, who lives in us, has become our Savior and He has also become our

Overcomer. Salvation did not depend on our self-effort. We receive God's grace, Christ's forgiveness of sins, because of His sacrifice on the cross. In the same way, overcoming does not depend on our self-effort. We receive God's grace, Christ's overcoming life, because of His triumph on the cross. This leads to good works born from faith in Christ's completed work on the cross. There is no other way to bear true fruit.

If we are still trying to overcome sin and Satan by our own ability, we will be defeated. If overcoming depended on us, we would never make it. However, since we have died *in Christ*, we no longer have a sinful nature. Our sinful nature has been crucified and removed *in Christ*; therefore, we do not have to keep trying harder to overcome. Instead, we can depend on the power of the cross of Christ by which we have been crucified to the world and the world has been crucified to us (Galatians 6:14). In our natural strength, we cannot overcome the devil and sin, but now we can look with confidence to our Lord Jesus Christ who overcomes through us. What is victory? Victory is fixing our eyes by faith on Jesus Christ who has already triumphed on the cross (Hebrews 12:2)! God has immersed us *in Christ's* victory! This is the triumph of the cross and the truth that sets us free!

"But thanks be to God, who gives us the victory through our Lord Jesus Christ."

1 CORINTHIANS 15:57

CHAPTER TWENTY-ONE

Living by the Spirit

"So I say, live by the Spirit, and you will not carry out the desire of the flesh."

GALATIANS 5:16

If we want to experience Christ's life, we must learn how to live by the Spirit. The Bible says that *if* we live by the Spirit, we overcome sin and are the sons of God. We may be born again, but if we do not practice living by the Spirit, then Christ will not be revealed in us and through us. What does it mean to *"live by the Spirit?"* To live by the Spirit means we practice a lifestyle of being governed by the Spirit. How can we do that? The answer is found in Christ's death on the cross. The Bible says that, before we were saved, we were all *in Adam* (1 Corinthians 15:22). This means we had all inherited Adam's sinful nature, which led to spiritual death (Romans 5:19). However, when we were born again, God put us *in Christ* (Romans 6:3; 1 Corinthians 1:30). This means God spiritually immersed us into Christ's death and, by the divine operation of the cross, He removed our sinful Adam nature and replaced it with Christ's holy nature (Romans 6:4-11).

Then what can prevent us from living by the Spirit? It certainly is not the sinful Adam nature. That issue has already been settled by Christ's death on the cross. Now that we are born again, we do not have a sinful nature (Colossians 2:11). The question then is no longer whether we are *in Adam* or *in Christ*. Now that we are *in Christ*, the question is whether we will be governed by the *Spirit* or by the *flesh* (our unconverted soul). The chief obstacle to our living by the Spirit is no longer our old Adam nature but our Adam way of thinking (our unrenewed mind), which needs to be transformed by the truth of God's Word. The apostle Paul said, "Do not be conformed to this world, but be transformed by the renewing of your mind, so that you may prove what the will of God is... (Romans 12:2)." When we believe and act on the central New Covenant provision of Christ's death on the cross *(our sinful nature no longer lives, but Christ lives in us),* then we will live

The chief obstacle to our living by the Spirit is no longer our sinful Adam nature but our Adam way of thinking (our unrenewed mind), which needs to be transformed by the truth of God's Word.

by the Spirit (Galatians 2:20). However, if we do not believe and act on the truth of Christ's death on the cross, we have no alternative than to vainly struggle to live the Christian life by the best of our natural or carnal *(fleshly)* ability and mistake our self-effort for faith. It may surprise you that carnal Christian behavior (what the Bible calls "deeds of the flesh") can be expressed in two very different ways. The first way is obvious. "Now the deeds of the flesh are evident, which are immorality, impurity, sensuality... (Galatians 5:19)." But the second way is more disguised. "No wonder, for Satan disguises himself as an angel of light. Therefore, is it not surprising if his servants also disguise themselves as servants of righteousness (1 Corinthians 12:14-15)." The carnal lifestyle of a Christian is obvious if they are practicing immorality; however, if they are practicing *outward* morality even while they are *inwardly* lawless and unsubmitted to Christ, it can be more difficult to discern their carnality.

There is a great difference between a Christian who overcomes sin by believing and acting on what Christ has accomplished by His death on the cross and a Christian who tries to "overcome" sin by faith in his own natural ability and willpower. The apostle Paul described people who practice this kind of outward moral behavior as "those who take pride in appearance (2 Corinthians 5:12)" and "want to make a good impression outwardly (Galatians 6:12)." Jesus described them as "hypocrites" and "people who trusted in themselves that they were righteous (Luke 13:15; 18:9)." Any religious morality that is derived apart from faith

We now have the obligation and privilege as Christ's disciples to carry our own cross and "put to death" our old way of thinking (the unrenewed mind).

in the power of Christ's crucifixion is a bastard holiness that is the offspring of the flesh (man's strength) and not the fruit of the Spirit. If a professed Christian persists in habitually practicing this kind of false religious morality, it is not harmless; it is hypocritical and hostile to God because it is not of true faith (Romans 14:23; Galatians 5:17).

Although most Bible translations confusingly use the term "flesh" for both the sinful nature and the unconverted soul (the unrenewed mind), there is a crucial difference. Our unrenewed mind is not like the sinful nature, which was a powerful entity - a "sin factory" within us that continuously produced sinful attitudes and actions and, therefore, had to be destroyed by Christ's death on the cross. Now that we no longer have a sinful nature, we are not captive to sin and our unrenewed mind can be transformed and submitted to Christ's sovereignty by believing the Word of God. Since Christ's death on the cross has already dealt with our sinful nature, we do not have to put it to death every day over and over again. Instead, we now have the obligation and privilege as Christ's disciples to carry our own cross and "put to death" our old sinful way of thinking (the unrenewed mind or unconverted soul). This means we are now able *by faith* to put off our old way of thinking and put on the mind of Christ (Ephesians 4:22-24; 1 Corinthians 2:26). By faith in Christ's completed work on the cross, we are able to exchange our carnal attitudes and affections for Christ's attitudes and affections. This is what the apostle Paul called "taking every thought captive to the obedience of Christ (2 Corinthians 10:5)." Paul taught the first century church, "If you are living according to the flesh *(the unconverted soul-life)*, you will die; but if by the Spirit, you are putting to death the misdeeds of the body, you will live... now all those who belong to Christ Jesus have put to death on the cross the flesh *(the unconverted soul-life)* with its passions and desires (Romans 8:13; Galatians 5:24)."

Living by the Spirit is not some emotional or mystical experience. It means we are living by faith in the truth of what Christ has accomplished on the cross *(Christ died for us and included us in His death so He might sovereignly live in us)*. Our faith will be genuine and our fruit evident if we take up our own cross, putting to death the carnal desires and deeds of our unconverted soul-life for Christ's sake and His body's sake. Then the fullness of Christ's life will be revealed in us.

"For all who are being led by the Spirit of God, these are the sons of God."

ROMANS 8:14

CHAPTER TWENTY-TWO

The Fellowship of the Cross

"Have you forgotten that all of us, when we were baptized into fellowship with Christ Jesus, were baptized into fellowship with His death?"

ROMANS 6:3 (CONYBEARE TRANSLATION)

Jesus bore our sinful nature on His cross but He also said we must bear our own cross. "Whoever does not bear his own cross and follow Me, cannot be My disciple (Luke 14:27)." Therefore the work of the cross is not just His; it must by faith become ours. This is how we "work out" our salvation and prove we are His disciples. "Work out your salvation with fear and trembling; for it is God who is at work in you, both to will and to work for His good pleasure (Philippians 2:12-13)." How do we bear our own cross? Some Christians believe they still have a sinful nature, which they must put to death daily through self-suppression, self-discipline and self-denial. However, this is not what Jesus meant. He knew our will-power would never be strong enough to overcome the power of sin. He died on the cross for us so that just as we received Him by faith, we might now walk in Him and overcome sin by faith (Colossians 2:6-7). How did we first receive His Spirit? Was it by our self-discipline? No, it was by faith in Christ and what He had done on the cross. How do we now walk in His Spirit and bear our own cross? Is it by our self-denial? No, once again it is by faith in Christ and what He has accomplished on the cross (Galatians 3:1-2).

Bearing our own cross does not mean we now try to crucify our sinful nature. It is impossible for self to kill self. If we are born again, we have already died with Christ (Romans 6:8). Our sinful nature (that sin factory that produced sins) has already been destroyed and done away with (Romans 6:6). Because our sinful nature has died, we have already been crucified to the world (Galatians 6:14). By faith in God's Word, we can now count ourselves dead to sin (Romans 6:11). Therefore, bearing our own cross means believing God's Word: when Christ died we also died with Him (2 Corinthians 5:14). Bearing our own cross means we stand firm in the truth that our sinful nature is dead and gone.

Jesus bore our sinful nature on His cross but He also said we must bear our own cross. Therefore the work of the cross is not just His; it must by faith become ours.

When we know we have already been crucified with Christ, we have the ability to no longer act on our own self-initiative. We can look to Christ who indwells us as the source of our life and direction (Galatians 2:20). As we persevere by faith in the divine fact that our sinful nature is gone (in spite of what we feel or see), the Holy Spirit will confirm and establish this divine truth in our life until Christ is formed within us (Galatians 4:19; 1 Peter 5:10).

Jesus Christ has already done the work for us. He has already won the struggle against sin. He bore our sinful nature on His cross so that when He died, we died with Him. However, there is a price to follow Jesus Christ and prove we are His disciples. The cost is bearing our own cross and losing our soul-life for Christ's sake. Jesus said, "If anyone wishes to come after Me, he must deny himself, and take up his cross and follow Me. For whoever wishes to save his soul-life will lose it; but whoever loses his soul-life for My sake will find it (Matthew 16:24-25)." Our soul-life is our individual personality and encompasses our attitudes, affections and abilities. Our flesh (the Greek is *sarx,* which means body and soul in this context) will suffer when we turn away from our natural desires and yield to Christ's Sovereignty. This is our cooperation with the daily

There is a price to follow Jesus Christ and prove we are His disciples; the cost is bearing our own cross and losing our soul-life for Christ's sake.

inworking of His death to our soul-life. This is our fellowship in Christ's sufferings (Philippians 3:10). "Since Christ has suffered in the flesh, arm yourselves also with the same purpose, because he who has suffered in the flesh has ceased from sin so as to live no longer for the lusts of men but for the will of God (1 Peter 4:1-2)."

Our sinful nature has already been crucified with Christ but now the work of the cross must begin to touch our soulish attitudes and affections. This process is what the Bible calls "sanctification," without which no one will see the Lord (Hebrews 12:14). This is the goal of our faith and the reason why the holy seed of Christ was planted in us – so that we might bear fruit for God. If this process of sanctification does not take place in our lives, we are bastards and not legitimate sons of God (Hebrews 12:8). Therefore, bearing our own cross is not an option, it is essential if we are to know Christ and receive our eternal inheritance in His kingdom.

Bearing our own cross is what the apostle Paul called "being conformed to His death (Philippians 3:10)." As we bear our cross daily, the Holy Spirit will train us to turn away from being governed by our soul-life (Luke 9:26-33; John 12:24-25). The cross will work in us a godly detachment in spirit from everything of man's interests and bring us into an attachment to God's interests. God uses the inward revelation of His Word and the external pressure of His trials to bring about this transformation. God made our soul to be good and useful; therefore, the work of the cross will not destroy our soul. We will still possess our soul and its faculties. But when the mark of the cross is imprinted on our soul, we will no longer persist in independently asserting ourselves apart from Christ; we will be yielded and fruitful vessels of our Lord Jesus Christ (Romans 12:2).

When we see the cross for what it is - a place of death, our "unconverted" soul-life may wish for self-preservation and we may hesitate to choose the fellowship of the cross. But glory to God! Jesus Christ has given us His victory over this desire for self-preservation through the power of His crucifixion! We have already died with Jesus Christ to the world. As we bear our cross by faith each day, we will experience the power of His resurrection life. "We always carry around in our body the death of Jesus, so that the life of Jesus may also be revealed in our body (2 Corinthians 4:10)." Let us now fix our eyes on Jesus, the author and finisher of our faith, and endure "the loss of all things" for the sake of the gospel and the even greater joy of knowing Him. Let us gladly identify with His sufferings so that we might know Jesus Christ and His love.

"I want to know Christ and the power of His resurrection and the fellowship of His sufferings, being conformed to His death."

PHILIPPIANS 3:10

CHAPTER TWENTY-THREE

Put on the Armor of Light

"The night is nearly over; the day is almost here. So let us put aside the deeds of darkness and put on the armor of light."

ROMANS 13:12

We are living in the last days when deep spiritual darkness covers the earth. The final spiritual conflict of this age is fast approaching and it is time for every believer to put on the armor of light to be ready for that day. "Put on the full armor of God, so that you will be able to stand firm against schemes of the devil. For our struggle is not against flesh and blood, but against the rulers, against the authorities, against the powers of this dark world and against the spiritual forces of evil in the heavenly realms (Ephesians 6:11-12)." God's armor of light can stop all the enemy's weapons and protect every true believer in time of danger.

The armor of light contains the belt of truth, the breastplate of right-eousness, the shoes of the gospel, the shield of faith, the helmet of salvation and the sword of the Spirit, which is the Word of God (Ephesians 6:14-17).

Without this armor, no Christian can hope to defeat the devil's forces of darkness. His aim is to deceive and devour weak and vulnerable souls in this final conflict. However, with God's armor of light, every Christian can stand in the heat of battle and triumph over the devil. "And they overcame him *(the devil)* by the blood of the Lamb and by the word of their testimony, and they did not love their lives even when faced with death (Revelation 12:11)."

In order for God's armor of light to effectively protect us in battle, two actions are necessary. The first action required of us is *repentance.* Every soldier of Christ must repent from any deeds of darkness. The Bible warns us, "Do not give the devil a foothold (Ephesians 4:27)." Any Christian who continues to practice sin will have holes in his armor and the enemy will use these openings to snare and defeat him. "Be on the alert. Your enemy the devil prowls around like a roaring lion looking around for someone to devour (1 Peter 5:8)." Some Christians think they can practice sin each day but then quickly grab their armor when the spiritual combat gets intense.

We were saved by faith in Christ's sacrifice on the cross and we now overcome by faith in Christ's victory on the cross.

But if you have a habit of practicing sin, you will not be ready when the enemy comes upon you. You will not be able to put on the armor of light to protect you during the time of greatest danger. You must practice righteousness now so you can wear the armor of light when you need it. "God is light... if we walk in the light as He Himself is in the light... the blood of Jesus His Son purifies us from all sin (1 John 1:5-7)."

The second action required of us is *faith.* Every soldier of Christ must have faith in His Commander Jesus Christ. It is crucial for us to believe that God, through Jesus Christ, has already totally defeated the devil. The Bible says Christ disarmed Satan's forces of darkness and triumphed over them through the cross (Colossians 2:16). "So that by His death He might destroy him who holds the power of death - that is, the devil – and free those who all their lives were held in slavery... (Hebrews 2:14-15)." When Christ died, God included us in Christ's death so that our sinful nature died with Him and was removed from us (Romans 6:6). When Christ rose from the dead, God included us in His resurrection so that His Son might live in us (Ephesians 2:4; Colossians 1:27). Because we no longer have a sinful nature, we are freed from the power of sin and the devil can no longer cause us to sin (Romans 6:7). "The one who practices sin is of the devil; for the devil has sinned from the beginning. The Son of God appeared for this purpose, to destroy the works of the devil (1 John 3:8)."

We must never lose sight of Christ's triumph on the cross. "Let us fix our eyes on Jesus, the author and perfecter of our faith, who for the joy set before Him endured the cross... (Hebrews 12:2)." We were saved by faith in Christ's sacrifice on the cross and we now overcome by faith in Christ's victory on the cross. The cross is the secret to our overcoming. Christ conquered Satan and sin on the cross. Through the cross of Christ, we have been crucified to the world and the world has been crucified to us (Galatians 6:14). We are now seated with Christ in the heavenly places far above all rule and

We do not have to fight to gain victory over sin; instead we fight from a secure position of victory over sin because of Christ's victory!

authority and power and dominion (Ephesians 1:20-21; 2:6). Jesus Christ commands us to stand firm and occupy the spiritual ground of victory He has already conquered for us (Romans 8:37). Therefore, we do not have to fight to gain victory over sin; instead we fight from an already secure position of victory over sin because of Christ's victory!

We are involved in a spiritual battle with the forces of darkness in which the devil is waging an all-out war to capture the hearts and minds of the human race. "The god of this world has blinded the minds of the unbelieving so that they might not see the light of the gospel of the glory of Christ (2 Corinthians 4:4)." Therefore, when we put on the armor of light, we must also put aside all worldly pursuits and pleasures that divide our devotion to Christ. "No soldier in active service entangles himself in the affairs of everyday life, so that he may please his commanding officer (2 Timothy 2:4)." Through His triumph on the cross, Jesus has enabled us and expects us to lay aside all activities and associations that compromise us.

But that is not all. Jesus died on the cross to deliver each one of us from our own prison of darkness, so that God's light could shine through us to a world sick with sin. We were redeemed from Satan's dominion not merely for ourselves, but for countless others who languish under sin's power. Therefore, putting on the armor of light is not an option; it is a necessity. "The weapons of our warfare are not worldly but divinely powerful to demolish strongholds… we take every thought captive to make it obedient to Christ (2 Corinthians 10:4-5)." By putting on the armor of light, we ensure we are ready to hear and carry out Christ our Commander's orders!

"Therefore put on the full armor of God, so that when the day of evil comes, you may be able to stand your ground, and after you have done everything, to stand firm."

EPHESIANS 6:13

CHAPTER TWENTY-FOUR

The Work of the Cross

"Now having been freed from sin and enslaved to God, you derive your benefit, resulting in sanctification, and the outcome eternal life."

ROMANS 6:22

I n this verse, the apostle Paul reveals the progressive work of the cross of Christ in the life of a believer. In order to examine the complete work of the cross in this verse, we will start at the end, which is also the purpose of Christ's death. Paul declares the outcome of Christ's death on our behalf is *eternal life*. The Greek word for *"life"* used here is *zoe,* which means God's divine life. Therefore, the objective of Christ's death on the cross was to bring us into God's eternal, divine life, not only in the age to come, but into His divine life here on earth. Paul also addresses what is necessary for us to receive this eternal life.

Paul declares that *sanctification* is required. The Greek word for sanctification is *hagiasmos,* which means holiness or spiritual and moral purity. It is evident from this context that Paul is not speaking about our initial sanctification when we were saved by Christ; he is speaking about the need for us to live a sanctified or holy life in Christ. Paul teaches here that sanctification, which results in eternal life, is the fruit of being God's bondslave. We have now reached a crucial point in Paul's unfolding of the complete word of the cross. How can we serve God with a pure heart and remain unstained by the sin of the world? Here, Paul gives us the divine answer: we are able to be God's bondslaves when we are freed from sin. "And having been freed from sin, you have become slaves of righteousness… for when you were slaves to sin, you were free in regard to righteousness (Romans 6:18 & 20)."

Previously, in Romans 6:6-8, Paul explained how God freed us from sin. Since we were born into sin, we could only be freed from sin through death. "For he who has died has been freed from sin (Romans 6:7)." Therefore, when we were born again, God spiritually included us in the death of His Son. Paul wrote, "Do you not know that when you were baptized *(immersed)* into Christ, you were baptized *(immersed)* into His death (Romans 6:3)?" Knowing and believing this divine truth is so critical to receiving the full benefit of Christ's Atonement and inheriting eternal life that Paul repeats this fact several times in Romans Chapter Six. When Christ died, we died with Him (Romans 6:8). When Christ was crucified, our sinful nature was crucified with Him (Romans 6:6). When Christ was buried, our sinful nature was buried with Him. "Therefore we have been buried with Him through baptism *(immersion)* into death (Romans 6:4)."

If you do not believe to the point of acting on the divine truth that you have died with Christ, you cannot experience freedom from sin and unbroken fellowship with God.

If you do not believe to the point of acting on the divine truth that you have died with Christ, you cannot experience freedom from sin and unbroken fellowship with God. It was essential for God to remove our sinful nature. The purpose of Christ's death on the cross was to reconcile us to God. However, this reconciliation is only possible if we no longer have a sinful, unholy nature. Therefore God used the death of His Son to exchange our sin nature with His holy nature. "God made Him who had no sin to be sin on our behalf so that we might become the righteousness of God in Him (2 Corinthians 5:21)."

We have now seen how Paul presented a progressive series of divine facts in his teaching on the doctrine of our co-crucifixion with Christ. Let us review these facts:

- Christ died for us and spiritually included us in His death;
- Therefore when Christ died, our sinful nature died with Him;
- Since we no longer have a sinful nature, we have been freed from the power of sin;
- Since sin is no longer master over us, we are now free to be God's bondslaves; and
- As we present ourselves daily as slaves to God, our lives will yield the fruit of sanctification and we will inherit His eternal life.

In order for us receive this full provision of Christ's crucifixion on our behalf, these divine facts must be linked together by the bond of true faith, which is an acting faith, not just an assenting faith. "For in the gospel a righteousness from God is revealed, a righteousness that is by faith from first to last, just as it is written: 'The righteous will live by faith.' (Romans 1:17)." Therefore, if we do not believe (and act on) the truth of these divine facts, then Christ's death will be of no benefit to us. "For we have also had the gospel preached to us, just as they did; but the word they heard did not profit them because it was not united by faith in those who heard (Hebrews 4:2)."

We cannot claim to believe without corresponding action. When we act on what we believe, we bear fruit and prove we are Christ's disciples.

For example, we must believe (and act on) the truth that Christ died for us so that we can experience salvation and forgiveness of sins. We must also believe (and act on) the truth that our sinful nature died with Christ so that we can experience deliverance from the power of sin. We must then believe (and act on) the truth that we are freed from sin so that we can be God's bondslaves. And we must believe (and act on) the truth that we are God's bondslaves or we will not experience sanctification without which we cannot know the Lord and inherit eternal life (Hebrews 5:9; 12:14)." This is the gospel that Paul preached and practiced: "I have been crucified with Christ and I no longer live but Christ lives in me; and the life that I now live in the body, I live by faith in the Son of God (Galatians 2:20)."

Paul declares that he "lives by faith" in Christ and this truth that he preaches. Again, this is an acting faith, not merely assenting. In fact, without action, our faith is dead (James 2:26). We cannot claim to believe without corresponding action. When we act on what we believe, we bear fruit and prove we are Christ's disciples (John 15:8). This is what it means to believe that we have been freed from sin and enslaved to God, which results in our sanctification. Our knowledge of the truth must result in our acting on the truth. This is real faith and only then is eternal life possible.

"God has chosen you from the beginning for salvation through the sanctifying work of the Spirit and through faith in the truth. It was for this He called you through our gospel, that you may gain the glory of our Lord Jesus Christ."

2 THESSALONIANS 2:13-14

CHAPTER TWENTY-FIVE

Restoring the Gospel

"He (Christ) must remain in heaven until the time comes for God to restore everything, as He promised long ago through His holy prophets."

ACTS 3:21

Five centuries ago, the Protestant Reformation dawned when God gave divine revelation to a Catholic monk named Martin Luther that "the just shall live by faith (Romans 1:17)." The truth of the gospel, which had been obscured for nearly one thousand years, became the torch that spread the fires of evangelism around the world. Yet the Reformation restored only a part of the gospel; certainly a major part, but something very crucial was still missing from the gospel.

In practice, the Protestant Reformation restored the gospel of "the just shall be saved by faith," but never restored the whole gospel of how "the just shall live by faith." There is a vast difference. As a result, each generation of believers since then has known their sins were forgiven but has struggled unsuccessfully against the power of sin. This is the great dilemma that has challenged Christians to this day: After Christ saves us, how can we be His witnesses in the world without being overcome by the world? Unless we find God's divine solution, each generation of believers that is added to the church starts their Christian life by the Spirit but ends up vainly trying to overcome sin by their natural ability. It is evident that the body of Christ desperately needs the *whole* gospel.

Through the centuries, many Christians have looked to the Bible to solve this dilemma. In the 1500s, a band of believers thought they had found the answer. They advocated a return to practicing adult water baptism by immersion. They believed this Biblical truth would restore the whole gospel by insuring there were true converts to the church. Yet as time passed, it became apparent that something significant was still missing from the practice of the gospel. In the 1600s and 1700s, companies of Christians once again thought they had found the answer to the dilemma. They championed a return to holiness as the way to restore the gospel. Yet as time passed, once again it became apparent that something significant was still missing from the gospel since a zeal for holiness was not enough to sustain true sanctification.

This is the great dilemma that has challenged Christians to this day: After Christ saves us, how can we be His witnesses in the world without being overcome by the world?

In the 1800s, dedicated Christians once again thought they had found the answer to the dilemma and called for a return to the church's mission of world evangelism. Millions of new believers were brought into the church through this vast and noble undertaking. Yet as time passed, once again it became apparent that something significant was still missing from the gospel as many if not most of these new believers drifted away from the true faith. Then, in the early 1900s, a group of Christians thought they had finally found the answer to the dilemma. They believed the baptism in the Holy Spirit would give Christians all the power they needed to be Christ's witnesses in the world. Yet as time passed, once again it became evident that something significant still needed to be restored to the gospel in order for the church to become the pure bride ready for Jesus Christ's return.

In our present time, many sincere Christians are returning to a simpler, more Biblical model of practicing church. Of course, other groups of believers in the past have also attempted to practice a New Testament pattern of church with the aim of restoring the whole gospel. All of these - water baptism, the baptism in the Holy Spirit, the pursuit of holiness, global evangelism and a return to simple and organic church – are important parts of God's plan to restore everything before Jesus Christ returns. Yet none of these, in themselves, will enable the church to overcome Satan and his evil forces during these dark and perilous last days.

The answer to the church's centuries old dilemma is found in the cross of Christ. The mystery of the cross is like the centerpiece of a divine jigsaw puzzle that is the key to understanding the whole gospel of Jesus Christ. When we see the full meaning of Christ's crucifixion, the whole Bible and all its truths fit together to form the eternal purpose of God in Jesus Christ. God knew we needed forgiveness for our sins; He also knew we needed deliverance from our sin nature. Otherwise, we could not overcome sin. Therefore, when Jesus died, He not only bore our sins on the cross; He also bore our sin nature on the cross. Since our bondage

> *When we see the full meaning of Christ's crucifixion, the whole Bible and all its truths fit together to form the eternal purpose of God in Jesus Christ.*

to sin came when we were born sinners; our deliverance from sin came when God included us in His Son's death. When Christ died, God performed a divine heart transplant and replaced our sinful heart with His Son's divine heart. Therefore, we no longer have a sinful nature; we now have Christ's holy nature.

Thus Christ not only died in our place; He now wants to sovereignly live in our place. The cross of Christ is the secret to the victorious Christian life. When we know we have died with Christ, we can live by faith in the Son of God who lives in us. The gospel of the cross is the power of God to not only save the elect but to sanctify the church to be the bride of Christ. This is the *whole* gospel.

God has given us His Son to be our hiding place during the coming tribulation. This is a great promise but if we don't know Christ as our hiding place, we won't be able to experience God's provision when we need it. Jesus Christ becomes our hiding place when we know (believe and act) that we died with Christ and our life is now hidden with Christ in God. Therefore, the only way to prepare for the trouble ahead is to believe we have been crucified with Christ and enthrone Him in our hearts everyday as our Lord and King. If we practice living out this truth of the cross, Christ will be our shelter in the coming great storm. When God divinely reveals the mystery of the fullness of His Son's crucifixion to the church, she will overcome the world. Then our Lord Jesus Christ will return to crush Satan and claim His bride.

"And I saw another angel flying in midair, having an eternal gospel
to preach to those who live on the earth, and to every nation
and tribe and tongue and people."

REVELATION 14:6

CHAPTER TWENTY-SIX

The Stumbling Block of the Cross

"But we preach Christ crucified: a stumbling block."

1 CORINTHIANS 1:23; SEE ALSO GALATIANS 5:11

The message of Christ crucified is a stumbling block because it strikes at the root of man's self-righteousness and rebellion toward God. To receive Jesus Christ as our Lord and Savior, we must humble ourselves and acknowledge our unrighteousness before God. By faith, we then depend on Christ and His atoning sacrifice on the cross for our righteousness. This is what is called saving faith. Unbelievers reject the message of Christ crucified because they do not want to acknowledge God and give up their soul-life by submitting to the sovereignty and righteousness of Jesus Christ. "He who does not take his cross and follow after Me is not worthy of Me. And he who has found his soul-life will lose it, and he who has lost his soul-life for My sake has found it (Matthew 10:38-39)."

The message of the cross confronts each person with a spiritual crisis - a decisive moment in their life to choose whether to give up their self-identity, self-life and self-righteousness and submit to Christ's authority. Many people are so fiercely determined to protect and control their soul-life (self-rule) that the Holy Spirit cannot convict them of their unrighteousness and their need for Jesus Christ to save them. Anyone who wants to maintain their own self-righteousness and self-sovereignty instead of submitting to Christ's righteousness and sovereignty will stumble over the cross of Christ (see Romans 9:30-10:4). The Bible says, "He who believes in the Son has eternal life; but he who does not obey the Son will not see life, but the wrath of God abides on him (John 3:36)."

However, the word of the cross goes far beyond just cleansing us from sin. Christ's death on the cross not only provided us forgiveness for sins; His death also provided us deliverance from sin's power. Christ not only bore our sins on the cross, He bore our sin nature on the cross with Him. If we believe in Christ, then when Christ died we died with Him. Since our sinful nature has died with Christ and been removed from us, we have been freed from sin's power (Romans 6:6-7). Jesus Christ not only died in our place, He now wants to live in our place. This is Christ's complete provision for us as a result of His crucifixion. But why is this complete truth of the cross a stumbling block to even many Christians? Why don't more Christians want to embrace the exchanged life that is provided for us in Christ? Why would any Christian be satisfied with a life that is just an outward cultural or moral change?

The message of the cross is only a stumbling block if you do not want to submit to Christ's Sovereignty.

Once again, the cross strikes at the root of our self-identity, self-righteousness and self-will. The real crux of the matter is whether we are willing to lose our soul-life and submit to Christ's authority. In order to "see" that you have died with Christ so that He can live in you, you must be willing to completely surrender your whole life to Jesus Christ.

The exchanged life means you give up control of your soul-life in return for Christ's Sovereignty and His divine life. You cannot enter into the experience of Christ's exchanged life unless you are willing to give up your soul-life (your natural attitudes, affections and abilities) for Christ's attitudes, affections and abilities. Jesus said, "He who loves his soul-life loses it, and he who hates his soul-life in this world will keep it to life eternal (John 12:25)."

This means when Christ becomes your life, you died to the right to run your own life. Knowing and acknowledging the truth that you have been crucified with Christ will affect all of your life's decisions, such as whom you marry, which friends you choose, what job you have, how you spend your money, where you live and how you live. "Whoever does not carry his own cross and come after Me can-not be My disciple... none of you can be My disciple who does not give up everything he has (Luke 14:27 & 33)." Submitting wholeheartedly to Christ's Sovereignty will impact every area of your life - spirit, soul and body. "If anyone wishes to come after Me, he must deny himself and take up his cross and follow Me (Matthew 16:24). Christ's Lordship will completely pervade your daily life and all your pursuits, activities and associations. Christ's Sovereign Spirit will ultimately transform even your natural temperament and your affections and attitudes.

If you are willing to lose your soul-life for Christ's sake, then the gospel of Christ crucified is great news!

If knowing Christ and submitting to His Sovereignty is what you really desire, then entering into the knowledge that you died with Christ is liberating. However, if you do not want to wholeheartedly submit to Christ's authority, then the message of the cross will offend you. Tragically, many so-called "Christians" love their soul-life too much to give it up for Jesus Christ and misuse God's grace as an excuse to practice sin. Just as the apostle Peter warned, "Do not use your freedom as a cover for evil (1 Peter 2:16)."

Some Christians sincerely want to surrender completely to Christ, but they do not know how and their experience makes them feel that they will always fail. The gospel of Christ crucified is indeed good news for these people. For the Word of God teaches us that because Jesus surrendered His life to God (to the point of death), we are capable by faith of doing the same thing because we no longer have a sinful nature and Christ now lives in us. If you are willing to lose your soul-life so that you can find it, you do not need to suffer from defeat anymore. Jesus said, "If you continue in My word, then you are truly disciples of Mine; and you will know the truth, and the truth will set you free… so if the Son sets you free, you will be free indeed! (John 8:31-32, 36)." The message of the cross is only a stumbling block if you do not want to submit to Christ's Sovereignty. If you are willing to lose your soul-life for Christ's sake, then the gospel of Christ crucified is great news!

"This is the judgment, that the Light has come into the world, and men loved the darkness rather than the Light, for their deeds were evil. For everyone who does evil hates the Light, and does not come to the Light for fear that his deeds will be exposed. But he who practices the truth comes to the Light, so that his deeds may be manifested as having been wrought in God."

JOHN 3:19-21

CHAPTER TWENTY-SEVEN

True Discipleship

"If anyone would come after Me, he must deny himself and take up his cross daily and follow Me. For whoever wants to save his life will lose it, but whoever loses his life for Me will save it."

LUKE 9:23-24 & MARK 8:34-35

By this statement, Jesus defined discipleship and what it means to be a Christian. There is no way around what Jesus said. We must take up our cross daily and lose our life for His sake or we cannot follow Him. The Greek word for life used here is *psyche,* which means our soul-life. Our soul-life is based on our natural personality and includes our natural attitudes, affections and abilities. At this point, we must strongly reinforce that the only way we can lose our soul-life is to know what Jesus Christ has already accomplished for us on the cross. When Jesus Christ died, we died with Him (Romans 6:8; 2 Corinthians 5:14). Our sinful nature was crucified with Him and removed from us (Romans 6:6). Therefore, by Christ's death, we have already died to the soulish life of this world (Galatians 6:14). This is a divine fact that only God can reveal to you.

Since God created our soul, He does not want to destroy our soul. However, He does want to restore our soul to its proper place and use. When Adam fell, man began to live independently by the power of his soul rather than by the life of God. But then, two thousand years ago, through the death of His only Son, God "undid" the fall and laid the foundation for restoring man to His purpose and fellowship. Now that we are born again, we no longer have Adam's sinful nature within us; instead, we have Christ's Spirit indwelling us (Romans 6:6; Galatians 2:20). But now that we are in Christ, the question is, "Will we continue to be governed by the strength of our soul or will we be governed by the power of His Holy Spirit?"

When we live by the soul, our life is controlled by our natural preferences and capabilities. The Son of God also had a human soul but He never acted from his soul's initiative; He only acted according to His Father's will (John 5:19; 30; 8:28). When we live by faith in Christ who lives in us, our soul is submitted to His Spirit and is a holy vessel for His use. However, if we live by the power of our personality, then our soul is hostile to Christ's Spirit and is of no use to Him. Therefore, in order for Jesus Christ to be able to use us as His bondservants, we must die to living based on our soul-life (our natural desires and abilities). This is what it means to be conformed to Christ's death (Philippians 3:10).

Every disciple who identifies with Christ's death has the mark of the cross on their soul.

Tragically, most professing Christians today are governed by the power of their soul rather than by the life of Christ. Even if we lead an admirable "moral" life based on our natural self-discipline, our witness is limited to the power of what our natural man can accomplish. This is no Christian witness at all. The reason for this dilemma is that most Christians do not know (believe and act on) the truth that they have died with Christ. As a result, they remain captive to their natural temperament and rely on their natural ability to serve God. If we are particularly naturally gifted and talented, we may impress others with our Christian ministry but we won't impress God. Nor will we have any impact on Satan if the source of our ministry is our own soul-power.

How can we be governed by the power of God's Spirit rather than our soul-life? First, we must know with certainty that we have been crucified with Christ. This is the only basis for losing our soul-life. Unless we have divine revelation that God included us in Christ's death, we will try to change our soul-life by our own willpower and effort, which only leads to pride and further sin. Next, we must apply the cross to our soul-life by identifying with Christ's death daily (when Christ died, we died with Him). This *When the mark of the cross is imprinted on our soul, we will stay submitted to Christ rather than independently asserting our will.* means we will often have to go against the voice of our soul and our natural temperament. There is only one way we can resist gratifying our soul's natural desires and reject fulfilling our soul's natural potential. This is by always reminding ourselves that we have died with Christ and He is now our life.

This is the secret to overcoming sin and losing our soul-life for Christ's sake. When we stay rooted by faith in Christ's death, His resurrection life will be formed in us. There are two ways God helps us abide in Christ's death so He might transform our "unconverted" soul. First, God sends us His Word, the sword of the Spirit, to expose and separate any impure soulish mixture in our faith (Hebrews 4:12). For example, we may think we love sharing the gospel until the Holy Spirit shows us that we love hearing ourselves speak. And we may think we love ministering to others until the Holy Spirit shows us that we love fulfilling our natural talent. Next, God sends us trials as a "sentence of death" to our natural strength so we will only rely on the life of His Son in us (2 Corinthians 1:8-9). When our confidence in our natural ability is broken, we will no longer trust in ourselves to overcome but only trust in what Jesus Christ has accomplished on the cross.

Every disciple who identifies with Christ's death has the mark of the cross on their soul. The work of the cross won't destroy our soul; we will still possess our soul and its faculties. But when the mark of the cross is imprinted on our soul, we will stay submitted to Christ rather than independently asserting our will. We will also not depend on the power of our soul to do Christ's work. The only way we can restore our soul is to lose it for Christ's sake (Matthew 16:25). This is true discipleship that leads to eternal life. How can we possibly restore the church to its right place in Christ if our own soul is not restored to its right place in Christ? May God open our eyes to see what His Son has fully accomplished for us on the cross so we can follow Him with all our heart and soul. This is what it means to come under Christ's Sovereignty and be His true disciples and bondservants.

"Whoever does not carry his own cross and come after Me cannot be My disciple. . . the man who loves his soul-life will lose it, while the man who hates his soul-life in this world will keep it for eternal life."

LUKE 14:27 & JOHN 12:25

CHAPTER TWENTY-EIGHT

The Kingdom
and the Cross

"Being found in appearance as a man, He humbled Himself by becoming
obedient to the point of death, even death on a cross. Therefore God exalted
Him to the highest place and gave Him the name that is above every name, that
at the name of Jesus every knee should bow, in heaven and on earth and under
the earth, and every tongue confess that Jesus Christ is Lord."

PHILIPPIANS 2:8-11

The word of the kingdom and the word of the cross are inseparably linked. Together, they form the eternal gospel of Jesus Christ. The word of the kingdom is the message that God the Father desires for Christ to reign as absolute King in our life. The word of the cross is the message that Christ died for us to make this possible. Coupled together, these two divine truths can be expressed as: Christ died for us and included us in His death so He might sovereignly live in us.

The kingdom and the cross are one gospel. We cannot have the kingdom without the cross nor can we have the cross without the kingdom.

The kingdom of God is the Kingship of Christ, but Christ can only rule as King in our life if we embrace the transforming power of His cross. All of us were naturally born with a rebellious and lawless sinful nature. "Through the one man's *(Adam's)* disobedience the many were made *(constituted)* sinners (Romans 5:19)." Therefore, when we were born again of the Spirit, God performed a divine heart transplant. God used the death of His only Son to translate us from *Adam* into *Christ*. When Christ died on the cross, God exchanged our sinful heart with His Son's holy heart. This divine exchange has made it possible for God to now reign in us through Jesus Christ. This was the apostle Paul's personal testimony: "I have been crucified with Christ and I no longer live but Christ lives in me; and the life I now live in the body, I live by faith in the Son of God who loved me and gave Himself up for me (Galatians 2:20)."

> *The word of the kingdom and the word of the cross are one gospel.*

It is impossible for us to spiritually embrace the cross of Christ unless we also embrace His Kingship. God will not share the precious truth of the cross of His Son with us unless we are willing to submit wholeheartedly to His Son's authority. Our heartfelt prayer is for anyone who desperately struggles with besetting sins because of spiritual ignorance concerning the divine exchange of the cross. However, we also need to be aware that there is a counterfeit Christianity that gives lip service to the kingdom and the cross. Many so-called Christians who claim that Jesus is their Lord are not even born again. And many of those who are "born again" are willful enemies of the cross of Christ because they love their soul-life too much to give it up for Christ. Jesus said, "If anyone wishes to come after Me, he must deny himself, and take up his cross and follow Me. For whoever wishes to save his soul-life will lose it; but whoever loses his soul-life for My sake will find it… whoever does not carry his own cross and come after Me cannot be My disciple (Matthew 16:24-25; Luke 14:27)."

Anyone who professes to be a Christian but does not carry his own cross, deny himself and lose his soul-life for Christ's sake is practicing lawlessness and does not truly know Jesus Christ. Jesus said, "Why do you call Me, 'Lord, Lord,' and do not do what I say? (Luke 6:46)." He also said, "Many will say to Me on that day, 'Lord, Lord, did we not prophesy in Your name, and in Your name cast out demons, and in Your name perform many miracles?' And then I will declare to them, 'I never knew you; depart from me, you who practice lawlessness (Matthew 7:22-23).'"

There are many false teachers today who profess to know the cross of Christ. However, anyone who chooses to govern himself instead of submitting to the power of Christ's Spirit is practicing a counterfeit Christianity. Anyone who does not bear the fruit of the cross, which is sanctification, is not a true disciple. Jesus said, "You shall know them by their fruit." He did not say, "You shall know them by their gifts and ministries." Anyone who is trying to fulfill their soul-life through ministry instead of losing their soul-life for Christ's sake is walking in darkness. The Bible says, "If we say we have fellowship with Him and yet walk in the darkness, we lie and do not practice the truth (1 John 1:6)." The Bible also says of such people, that they hold to "a form of godliness, although they have denied its power; avoid such men of these (2 Timothy 3:5)" and "What fellowship can light have with darkness? ... therefore, come out from them and be separate... and I will be a Father to you and you will be My sons and daughters (2 Corinthians 6:14-18)."

> *The kingdom of God is the Kingship of Christ, but Christ can only rule as King in our life if we embrace the transforming power of His cross.*

Everyone who is destined for eternal salvation as the bride of Christ will wholeheartedly embrace the gospel of the cross and the King. Every child of God that wants Jesus Christ to reign in their life will rejoice to learn that God has removed their sinful nature by Christ's death on the cross. Knowing that we have been crucified with Christ, we are now free to lose our soul-life for His sake (Galatians 6:14). We gladly submit all our attitudes, affections, associations and activities to Christ's Sovereignty so that He might rule our soul-life. We present ourselves each day as a living and holy sacrifice to God so He might transform our soul and conform us into His Son's image. We joyfully give up trying to fulfill our soul-life in this world so that we might be eternally joined to our beloved bridegroom Jesus in the age to come. "Now this is eternal life, that they may know You, the only true God, and Jesus Christ whom You have sent (John 17:3)."

When we are ready to submit ourselves to Christ's Sovereignty and lose our soul-life for His sake, God will reveal to us the mystery of the cross, which is also the mystery of the gospel. Then God will be glorified since we will no longer live for ourselves but for Christ the King who lives in us. "One died for all, therefore all died; and He died for all, so that they who live might no longer live for themselves, but for Him who died and rose again on their behalf (2 Corinthians 5:14-15)." This is the eternal gospel of Christ.

"Do not be afraid little flock, for your Father has chosen gladly to give you the kingdom."

LUKE 12:32

CHAPTER TWENTY-NINE

God Causes the Growth

"The kingdom of God is like a man who casts seed upon the soil; and he goes to bed at night and gets up by day, and the seed sprouts and grows — how, he himself does not know. The soil produces crops by itself; first the blade, then the head, then the mature grain in the head. But when the crop permits, he immediately puts in the sickle, because the harvest has come."

MARK 4:26-29

Since farming was commonly practiced in Israel, Jesus often used examples of planting and harvesting to teach His disciples about the kingdom of God. In this parable, Jesus compared the kingdom of God to *a seed* that once deposited in the soil grows and produces a harvest apart from man's effort. Of course, the condition of *the soil* is also important and we will look at that shortly. The spiritual lesson of this parable is that God, not man, causes the growth in His kingdom. "So then neither the one who plants nor the one who waters is anything, *but God who causes the growth* (1 Corinthians 3:6)." This is an important Biblical truth that many Christians do not understand. Although they know their salvation depended on God's mercy and not their own deeds, many Christians mistakenly think their spiritual growth now depends on their self-effort.

After we are saved, what should we do to grow as Christians? To answer this question, we need to look at another one of Jesus' parables. Jesus told a story of seed being sown on different kinds of ground (see Matthew 13:3-23; Mark 4:2-20; Luke 8:4-15). In this parable, the seed once again represents the kingdom of God and the soil represents the con-

Although they know their salvation depended on God's mercy and not their own deeds, many Christians mistakenly think their spiritual growth now depends on their self-effort.

dition of our heart. Just as the condition of the soil determines how much fruit that the seed can produce, the condition of our heart determines how much spiritual fruit God can produce in us. Jesus said the seed was sown on four kinds of ground but only the last one yielded any fruit. "Other seed fell on good soil. It came up and yielded a crop, a hundred times more than was sown (Luke 8:8)." Jesus then said, "The seed in good soil, these are the ones who have heard the word in an honest and good heart, and hold it fast, and bear fruit with perseverance (Luke 8:15)."

The lesson of this parable is that the gospel of the kingdom must be received in an honest and good heart to bear fruit. What is an "honest and good" heart? God said, "But to this one I will look, to him who is humble and contrite of spirit, and who trembles at My word (Isaiah 66:2)." With this in mind, the apostle Peter wrote, "Humble yourselves, therefore, under God's mighty hand (1 Peter 5:6)." Based on these and many other Scriptures, we can conclude that, from God's point of view, a good and honest heart is a *humble* heart. The apostle James said, "In *humility* receive the word planted in you, which is able to save your souls (James 1:21)."

Just as we were saved when we received Christ with a humble heart full of faith, we must now live in Christ the same way. The apostle Paul taught, "So then, just as you received Christ Jesus as Lord, continue to live in Him, rooted and built in Him, strengthened in the faith as you were taught (Colossians 2:6-7)." Therefore, after we are born again, the next baby steps we take are very important. We know we were not able to save ourselves; however, after we are saved, we may wrongly conclude we can grow as Christians by trying our very best. This is a common trap that even the early Christians fell into. The apostle Paul admonished the Galatians for this wrong thinking, "Are you so foolish? Having begun by the Spirit, are you now trying to perfect yourselves by your human effort (Galatians 3:3)?" All Christians through the centuries have faced this same dilemma. What is the work of God that we should do? When Jesus was asked this question, He replied, "This is the work of God, that you believe in Him whom He has sent (John 6:29)." The work that God requires of us is always the work of faith - to believe in Jesus Christ and His completed work on the cross (1 Corinthians 2:2).

The work that God requires of us is always the work of faith - to believe in Jesus Christ and His completed work on the cross.

This does not diminish the purpose and value of Bible study, prayer, fellowship, and acts of service. However, we will never spiritually grow and bear fruit unless we learn to abide (stay rooted by faith) in Christ and His death and resurrection (John 15:4). The Bible says that when Christ died, we died with Him and our sinful nature was removed from us (Romans 6:6). God can deal with our sins but He cannot deal with our unbelief. If we do not believe Christ died for us, Christ's death cannot save us. In the same way, if we do not believe our sinful nature has died in Christ, Christ's life cannot bear fruit in us. Just as we could not save ourselves, we cannot spiritually grow apart from faith in the cross of Christ.

Jesus Christ said, "He who abides in Me and I in him, he will bear much fruit (John 15:5)." When we were born again, God planted us in Christ (Romans 11:16-24). Our responsibility is to now stay rooted by faith in Christ and in what He accomplished for us by His death on the cross. We must strongly resist the urge to try harder outside of faith. It is impossible for us to grow in Christ no matter how hard we try. The Bible says "It does not depend on man's desire or effort, but on God's mercy (Romans 9:16)." Just as faith was the key to our salvation and new birth, faith is also the key to our sanctification and spiritual growth. If we abide (stay rooted by faith) in the truth of Christ's death, God will cause Christ's life to be formed in us. "For if we have become united with Him in the likeness of His death, certainly we shall also be in the likeness of His resurrection (Romans 6:5)."

In another parable, Jesus compared the kingdom of God to planting a mustard seed. When sown into good soil, the seed grew into a tree larger than everything else and took over the whole garden. If we know we have died in Christ and we no longer have a sinful nature, then let us fix our eyes on Jesus. He is not only the author of our faith; He is the perfecter of our faith and His divine life will continue to grow within us until He takes over our whole life.

Jesus said, "How shall we picture the kingdom of God, or by what parable shall we present it? It is like a mustard seed. . . though it is smaller than all the seeds that are upon the soil, yet when it is sown, it grows up and becomes larger than all the garden plants."

MARK 4:30-32

CHAPTER THIRTY

Stand Firm in Liberty

"It was for freedom that Christ has set us free. Stand firm, then, and do not let yourselves be burdened again by a yoke of slavery."

GALATIANS 5:1

Jesus Christ died to set us free from sin – not only from the penalty of sin but also from the power of sin. When Christ died, God included us in His Son's death. Because our sinful nature died with Christ, we have been eternally freed from bondage to sin. "For we know that our old self was crucified with Him in order that our sinful nature might be done away, so that we would no longer be slaves to sin. For he who has died has been freed from sin (Romans 6:6-7)." This is our glorious victory over sin in Christ!

After we have experienced this great salvation, what's next? We must be careful to avoid the mistake of the Galatian Christians, whom the apostle Paul chastised, "Are you so foolish? Having begun by the Spirit, are you now trying to perfect yourselves by your human effort? (Galatians 3:3)." The Galatians experienced this miraculous born again experience but were then deceived into thinking they must sanctify themselves by their own effort. Paul reminded them that all their effort would never set them free from sin. Only Christ's death on the cross sets us free from sin. We could not crucify ourselves and we cannot sanctify ourselves apart from the cross of Christ. Because of Christ's death on the cross, we no longer have an old Adam nature; however, if we still have an unrenewed mind (the old Adam way of thinking), we will have a natural tendency to think we can be righteous because of our own merit and that we can resist sin by our own strength. Even after the Holy Spirit gives us divine revelation that only Christ's death on the cross gave us freedom from the power of sin, our natural habit (especially under stress) will be to fall back on our own strength to try to master sin.

Trying to sanctify ourselves this way is not only burdensome; it is impossible. We need to stand firm by faith in the liberty we have in Christ and resist the inclination to do anything by our own self-effort, knowing it would be fruitless. The work of God never changes – it is always the work of faith. Jesus said, "This is the work of God – that you believe in Him whom He has sent (John 6:29)." Now that Christ has completely delivered us from our sinful nature and the power of sin, our work of faith is to keep our eyes fixed on Jesus and His finished work on the cross. This is how we live the Christian life. Many Christians think now that Jesus has saved us, we should try hard to sanctify ourselves. But we must remember that Jesus is not only the author of our faith *(our salvation)*; He is also the perfecter of our faith *(our sanctification)* (Hebrews 12:2).

Whenever we step out of God's work of faith and enter into our own effort, we take the burden for our sanctification out of God's hands and put it in our own hands.

Whenever we step out of God's work of faith and enter into our own efforts, we take the burden for our sanctification out of God's hands and put it in our own hands. This prevents God from doing the sanctifying work of the Spirit in us that comes only from faith. It also produces ungodly anxiety and stress since we have decided (in unbelief) that the work of God now depends on our own effort. This yoke of unbelief is an awful burden to bear. The Bible calls it "the yoke of *slavery.*" This man-made yoke is in marked contrast to Jesus' yoke. He said, "Come to Me, all who are weary and heavy-laden, and I will give you rest. Take My yoke upon you... My yoke is easy and My burden is light (Matthew 11:28-30)."

Now that we are saved, we can "count ourselves to be dead to sin but alive to God in Christ Jesus (Romans 6:11)." The Greek word used here for count is *logizomai,* which is an accounting term meaning "credit to the account." The language of mathematics is precise and certain. All over the world, one plus one equals two. This Scripture means we can count on the fact that we are dead to sin with absolute certainty just as we can count on the fact that one plus one equals two. Now that we have died with Christ and

We can count on the fact that we are dead to sin with absolute certainty just as we can count on the fact that one plus one equals two.

we no longer have a sinful nature, we should present ourselves each day as a living and holy sacrifice to God. As we do this, God will renew our minds and transform our souls by His Word (Romans 12:1-2; see also Ephesians 4:23)."

It is important to remember that faith is always active – not passive. We cannot just forget about what Jesus has done on the cross and then expect God to transform us. Many Christians have drifted away from the faith because they unwisely practiced this kind of "passive faith," which is really not faith at all. True faith actively believes by acting on the divine facts. If we never actively believed that Jesus Christ, the Son of God, died on the cross for *our sins,* we would never be saved. In the same way, if we do not actively believe that Jesus Christ included us in His death to remove *our sinful nature* and free us from sin's bondage, we will never experience freedom from chronic and entangling sins.

We need to stand firm by faith in the spiritual freedom Christ has purchased for us on the cross. Whenever we find ourselves afraid and overcome by sin, it is a sign that we have stepped out of this place of faith. At that point, we should repent and return to fixing our eyes on Jesus Christ – who He is and what He has done for us on the cross. Whenever we are overwhelmed by a sense of failure, it reveals we are trying to sanctify ourselves in our own strength instead of fixing our eyes on Jesus Christ. Whenever we become religiously merciless with ourselves and with others around us, it is an indication that we have stepped out of that place of faith in Christ. Christ's burden is easy and His yoke is light and where the Spirit of the Lord is, there is spiritual liberty and mercy; not carnal severity.

We cannot sanctify ourselves and we cannot sanctify others; only Christ can accomplish His sanctification in each one of us. Therefore, we must remember to always stand firm on the sure foundation of faith in Christ and His completed work on the cross, by which He has given us spiritual liberty and rest.

"Now the Lord is the Spirit, and where the Spirit of the Lord is, there is liberty."

2 CORINTHIANS 3:17

"So if the Son sets you free, you will be free indeed."

JOHN 8:36

CHAPTER THIRTY-ONE

What Counts is a New Creation

"Therefore, if anyone is in Christ, he is a new creation; the old has gone, the new has come!"

2 CORINTHIANS 5:17

There are three New Testament verses that start with the phrase: "Neither circumcision nor uncircumcision means anything, what counts is…" Each of these three verses completes the ending of this phrase with a different statement: 1) what counts is *a new creation;* 2) what counts is *faith working through love;* and 3) what counts is *obeying God's commands.* When considered together in logical order, these three form a progression of truth that reveal how God works His eternal purpose in us for His glory.

Let's consider the first verse: "Neither circumcision nor uncircumcision means anything; what counts is *a new creation* (Galatians 6:15)." The Bible discounts circumcision and anything else man can do to achieve righteousness. Only a righteousness based on God's new creation counts for anything. The new creation is the heart of the New Covenant and the basis of our new birth and salvation. The old creation began in Adam. The new creation began in Christ. God's new creation is the body of Christ, His church. But before God could make His new creation, He had to first deal with the old creation, our Adam nature. God had to take care of not only its fruit *(our sinful actions)*; He had to also remove its very root *(our sinful nature)*.

Therefore, Jesus Christ died not only to forgive us for our sins; He also died to free us from our sinful nature. Since we were born into sin, we had to die to be freed from sin. God accomplished this by including us in His Son's death. When Christ was crucified, our sinful nature died with Him (Romans 6:6). When Christ was raised from the dead, we were raised with Him as a new creation (2 Corinthians 5:17; Ephesians 2:5-6). Jesus Christ now lives in us (2 Corinthians 13:5; Colossians 1:27). Thus God used the death of His only Son to perform a divine heart transplant by which He replaced our terminally sin-sick heart with His Son's holy heart. This is the mystery of the gospel and the foundation of God's new creation – His church.

> *God's new creation is the body of Christ, His church. But before God could make His new creation, He had to first deal with the old creation, our Adam nature. God had to take care of not only its fruit (our sinful actions); He had to also remove its very root (our sinful nature).*

Now let's consider the second verse: "In Christ Jesus neither circumcision nor uncircumcision has any value. The only thing that counts is *faith working through love* (Galatians 5:6)." Faith, which is motivated by love, is the way we work out our salvation. "We know love by this, that He laid down His life for us; and we ought to lay down our lives for the brethren (1 John 3:16)." This is the way faith works. If we lay down our soul-life (our natural attitudes and abilities) for Christ's sake and the brethren's sake, we abide in God's love and true faith. If we do not lay down our soul-life for the brethren, we do not abide in God's love and we don't know Him (1 John 4:8). If we try to live the Christian life by dying to self through our own willpower and moral strength, we quench the power of Christ's Spirit from working in us. Therefore, having begun by the Spirit when we were born again, we now refuse to rely on our natural strength to live the Christian life (Galatians 3:3; Philippians 3:3).

Knowing we have died with Christ, we now live by faith in the Son of God who lives in us (Galatians 2:20). As we abide (remain united) in the power of Christ's death, He abides in us with the power of His resurrection life (John 15:4). "For if we have been united with Him like this in His death, we will certainly also be united with Him in His resurrection (Romans 6:5)." Thus faith in Jesus Christ and His completed work on the cross is not only

Since we were born into sin, we had to die to be freed from sin. God accomplished this by including us in His Son's death.

the basis for our spiritual birth (our salvation); it is also the only basis for our spiritual growth (our sanctification). This is the true gospel. "For in the gospel a righteousness from God is revealed, a righteousness that is by faith from first to last, just as it is written: 'The righteous will live by faith (Romans 1:17)."

Finally, let's now consider the third verse: "Circumcision is nothing and uncircumcision is nothing; what counts is *obeying God's commands* (1 Corinthians 7:19)." Obeying God's commands is the outcome of our sanctification and the confirmation of our faith. Our obedience springs from our faith in Christ's triumph on the cross – when Christ died; we also died to the world (Galatians 6:14). Do you really want to know Jesus? Jesus Christ said He would reveal Himself to you *if* you obey Him (John 14:21).

"We know that we have come to know Him *if* we obey His commands (1 John 2:3)." Everyone who obeys God's commands abides in Him and He in them; everyone who does not obey God's commands does not know Him (1 John 3:6 & 24). "For just as the body without the spirit is dead, so also faith without works is dead (James 2:26)." This is what the apostle Paul called "the obedience that comes from faith (Romans 1:5)."

It is possible for us to obey God commands because of God's divine heart transplant, by which He made us a new creation in Christ. "Because everyone who has died has been freed from sin (Romans 6:7)." Everyone who is born of God is able to obey His commands and overcome sin because Christ who lives in us is greater than Satan, the ruler of this world (1 John 3:9; 4:4). "But now having been freed from sin and enslaved to God, you derive your benefit, resulting in sanctification, and the outcome, eternal life (Romans 6:22)." The Bible says that everyone who obeys Jesus Christ inherits eternal life. "He is the source of eternal salvation for all who obey Him (Hebrews 5:9)."

If we are trying to be moral apart from faith in the cross of Christ, we are practicing a counterfeit Christianity that is not based on God's new creation. "Are you so foolish? After beginning by the Spirit, are you now trying to attain your goal by your human effort (Galatians 3:3)?" God's new creation in Christ is the only foundation for the true Christian life and the true church of Christ.

"For we are the true circumcision, who worship in the Spirit of God and glory in Christ Jesus and put no confidence in the flesh (our natural ability)."

PHILIPPIANS 3:3

124

CHAPTER THIRTY-TWO

The Works of Faith

"For just as the body without the spirit is dead,
so also faith without works is dead."

JAMES 2:26

The Bible says that faith must produce works. Very few Christians understand the relationship between faith and works or which works are acceptable to God and which are not acceptable. What does the Bible mean by "faith" and "works?" Faith is "what we believe" and works are "what we do." The Bible says we are saved solely by faith in Jesus Christ because there are no works which could ever earn us righteousness. "For by grace you have been saved through faith… not by works, so that no one can boast (Ephesians 2:8-9; see also Titus 3:5)." But once we are saved, the Bible says we must then express our faith by our works; otherwise our faith is not valid. "Faith apart from works is inactive and ineffective and worthless (James 2:20)." Therefore, salvation is not a result of our good works, but good works should result from our salvation if our faith in Jesus Christ is real.

At this point, it is important to note the difference between what the Bible calls "dead works" and "good works." In the early church, new Christians received discipleship training on the need to repent from dead works in order to serve the living God (Hebrews 6:1; 9:14). From a Biblical perspective, "dead works" include anything we do to establish a religious or moral identity outside of faith in Christ. Many works of service done by Christians today fall under this category. Dead works have three distinguishing features that separate them from what the Bible calls "good works." The source, the power and the outcome of dead works are different than the source, the power and the outcome of good works. Dead works are initiated by our natural mind, are empowered by our natural ability, produce what we can achieve and get man's approval. Good works are initiated by the mind of God, are empowered by the Spirit of God, produce what only God can achieve and always result in God's approval.

The Son of God is the perfect example of someone who always did good works. Jesus Christ never did any works independently of God's will. "Truly, truly, I say to you, the Son can do nothing of Himself, unless it is something He sees the Father doing... I can do nothing on My own initiative... because I do not seek My own will, but the will of Him who sent Me (John 5:19 & 30). By His good works, Jesus showed us that the work of God is God Himself at work. Jesus said, "The Father abiding in Me does His works (John 14:10)." Even though Jesus was the Son of Man, He never did any works that sprang from the strength of his human soul. Jesus showed us the only works acceptable to God are those initiated and empowered by the Spirit of God. "For all who are being led by the Spirit of God, these are the sons of God (Romans 8:14)." All good works must spring from true faith in Jesus Christ. When some people asked Jesus what they must do to do

Salvation is not a result of our good works, but good works should result from our salvation if our faith in Jesus Christ is real.

the works of God, He replied, "This is the work of God, that you believe in Him whom He has sent (John 6:29)."

If God Himself is not doing the work, it is not the work of God. If we can do a work without relying on God's wisdom and power, then such a work is likely to be natural and void of the Spirit. Since dead works are not authorized by God, they are disobedient works. For this reason, it is crucial for Christians to hear and obey the Holy Spirit in order to do good works and not dead works. We simply cannot do good works if we cannot hear God's voice. Jesus emphasized this truth when He said, "He who has an ear, let him hear what the Spirit says to the churches… My sheep hear My voice and they follow Me." If we cannot hear the Holy Spirit, we will naturally do dead works that spring from our soul but mistakenly think they are good works.

The Son of God is the perfect example of someone who always did good works. Jesus Christ never did any works independently of God's will.

They may even appear to be "Christian" works but they are still dead works if the Spirit of God did not initiate them. Many Christians are doing dead works because so few are able to discern the difference between the spirit and the soul (Hebrews 4:12). If we are used to living by the strength of our soul and being led by our soul (our natural personality and ability), we will be deceived into doing dead works. In fact, others may even encourage us to do them.

The Bible says we must stop doing our own works to enter into God's rest and His works (Hebrews 4:10). The only way we can stop doing dead "Christian" works and enter into God's works is if we believe the truth of the cross. If we believe that we have been crucified with Christ and our sinful nature is dead and gone (Romans 6:6), then we can hear and obey Jesus Christ who will initiate and do His good works through us (Galatians 2:20). "For we are God's workmanship, created in Christ Jesus to do good works, which God prepared in advance for us to do (Ephesians 3:10)."

At the end of this age, every Christian will appear before the judgment seat of Christ (2 Corinthians 5:10). On that day, Christ will assess our works and allot our rewards and responsibilities for the age to come (Matthew 25:21; Luke 19:17). The works we have done on earth will not only be judged for their quantity but also for their quality (1 Corinthians 3:10-15). Every good work we have done in obedience to the Holy Spirit will be treated as gold, silver and precious stones. But every dead work we have done will be treated as wood, hay and straw and be burned up.

On that day, Christ will judge the hidden motives of everyone's heart (Romans 2:19). If your dead works were done out of spiritual ignorance, your works will be rejected but you will still be saved. But if your dead works were done lawlessly for selfish ambition and personal profit, you will be rejected. The angels of God will cast you out of Christ's presence and you will face God's judgment and eternal punishment with the rest of the hypocrites and unbelievers (Matthew 7:21-23; 13:41-42; 25:26-30). Knowing then the kindness and severity of God, we should do the works of true faith to make sure we are doing the true works of God.

"So then, my beloved. . . work out your salvation with fear and trembling; for it is God who is at work in you, both to will and to work for His good pleasure."

PHILIPPIANS 2:12-13

CHAPTER THIRTY-THREE

Restoring the City of God

"And I saw the holy city, new Jerusalem, coming down out of heaven from God, made ready as a bride adorned for her husband."

REVELATION 21:2

In Revelation 21 and 22, we see a glorious vision of a great city, the new Jerusalem. This city is the consummation of God's eternal purpose through the ages - the full expression of Jesus Christ in His church, His bride. The old Jerusalem was but a shadow and symbol of this heavenly Jerusalem. The old Jerusalem was the capital of Israel, the only kingdom that God had thus far established on the earth. It was called the city of David since within its walls were the throne of David and the tabernacle of David. For King David not only made Jerusalem the royal city from which he ruled; he also made it the holy city by installing God's Ark of the Covenant on Mount Zion in Jerusalem.

The new Jerusalem is the city of God. This is the heavenly city whose architect and builder is God and whose foundation is Jesus Christ (Hebrews

11:10; 1 Corinthians 3:11). This divine city is the body and bride of Christ, the church of the living God. "But you have come to Mount Zion, to the heavenly Jerusalem, to the city of the living God... to the church of the first born whose names are written in heaven (Hebrews 12:22-23)." Jesus the Messiah King is the fulfillment of God's covenant with David (Isaiah 9:7; Luke 1:31-33). For the throne of David foreshadowed Christ's Sovereignty over His church and the tabernacle of David foreshadowed Christ's Presence in His church. God's intent that Christ's Sovereignty and Presence would be preeminent in His church is clearly revealed by the apostle Paul: "God placed all things under His *(Christ's)* feet and appointed Him to be head over everything for the church, which is His body, the fullness of Him who fills all in all (Ephesians 1:22-23).

When God's people were not faithful to Him, the city of David was over-run by its enemies and its foundations and walls fell into ruin. Just as the old Jerusalem was destroyed, the new Jerusalem, the church of the living God, also fell into ruin. Within just a few genera-tions after our Lord ascended to heaven, the church began to lose its spiritual connection to Christ its sovereign head (Colossians 2:19). More concerned with outward order and form than the reality of Christ's Sovereign Presence, the city of God fell into disrepair. Its spiritual foundations and walls finally collapsed and lay desolate for centuries. Yet God has always preserved for Himself a remnant of survivors or overcomers.

> *The new Jerusalem is the consummation of God's eternal purpose through the ages - the full expression of Jesus Christ in His church, His bride.*

After a long period of physical desolation, God raised up Ezra and Nehemiah from His band of faithful survivors to rebuild the old Jerusalem. In the same way, God is raising up His body of overcomers to restore the new Jerusalem. In the first century, the apostle James addressed the Council of Jerusalem to this end, "With this the words of the prophets agree, just as it is written, 'After these things I will return and I will rebuild the tabernacle of David which has fallen and I will rebuild its ruins and I will restore it (Amos 9:11; Acts 15:15-16).'" Isaiah also prophesied of this glorious restoration, "Those from among you will rebuild the ancient ruins; you will raise up the age-old foundations; you will be called the repairer of the breach; the restorer of the streets in which to dwell (Isaiah 58:12 & 61:4)."

In restoration, the foundations have the priority. Everything else in the city - its walls, its gates and streets - rests on its foundations. If the foundations are not properly laid, everything else is askew. Five centuries ago, God began to restore His beloved city, His church, when He gave divine revelation to Martin Luther that the just are saved by faith. The foundation of justification by faith in Christ and His completed work on the cross began to be laid anew (1 Peter 2:6). Since then, much has been added to this beginning foundation to rebuild the church. However, the church's complete foundation has not yet been fully restored.

For the past five hundred years, the church has acted on only half of the gospel - the just are saved by faith. Yet the whole gospel is "the just shall live by faith."

Because we have built on an incomplete foundation, the entire structure is now at risk (1 Corinthians 3:10-13). The city's walls may outwardly appear impressive, but they are inwardly compromised and weak. God's watchmen, His prophets, are now warning the city to restore its ancient foundations; otherwise its walls will be breached and overrun by the enemy.

What crucial part of God's sure foundation is missing? For the past five hundred years, the church has acted on only half of the gospel - the just are *saved* by faith. Yet the whole gospel is "the just shall *live* by faith (Romans 1:17)." God's people know they are saved by faith but they do not know how to live the overcoming Christian life by faith. Yet Christ's death on the cross not only provided us salvation by faith; His death also provided us sanctification by faith. For Christ not only died to forgive us from the penalty of our sins; He also died to deliver us from the power of sin by removing our sinful nature (Romans 6:6). God's people need to believe not only that Christ has died for their sins (Romans 5:8), they also need to believe and act on the Biblical truth that they have died with Christ (Romans 6:8). They need to know *(believe and act)* that they are no longer slaves to sin (Romans 6:7). Then they will not try to live as Christians by the best of their natural ability and mistake their self-effort for Biblical faith (Galatians 3:3).

In ancient times, the prophet Daniel effectively interceded for the old Jerusalem when God revealed the city's restoration was close at hand. In these last days, God's watchmen are sounding the trumpet once again to restore the full foundation of the new Jerusalem, the bride of Christ. When God's faithful remnant believe and act on the truth that they have died with Christ, they will overcome the world by the power of Christ who indwells them. Then Jesus Christ will triumphantly return for His holy bride, the glorious city of God (Revelation 19:6-16; 21:2-11).

"On your walls, O Jerusalem, I have appointed watchmen; all day and all night they will never keep silent. You who remind the Lord, take no rest for yourselves; and give Him no rest until He establishes and makes Jerusalem a praise in the earth."

ISAIAH 62:6-8

CHAPTER THIRTY-FOUR

Come Out of Babylon

"Fallen, fallen is Babylon the great! She has become a dwelling place of demons and a prison of every unclean spirit and. . . come out of her, my people, so that you will not share in her sins and receive her plagues."

REVELATION 18:2-4

The new Jerusalem is the holy city of God, the bride of Christ and the kingdom of heaven. In dark contrast, Babylon is the abominable city of Satan, the mother of harlots and the kingdom of the world (Revelation 17 & 18). Yet many of God's people are not only doing business in Babylon, they are living in Babylon and loving Babylon. This is appalling since God's intention was, by His Son's death, to rescue us from the dominion of darkness and bring us into the kingdom of His beloved Son (Colossians 1:13).

The English word "church" is derived from the Greek word *kuriakos*, which means "to belong to the Lord." In the New Testament, however, "church" is directly translated from the Greek *ekklesia*, which means congregation, but its root meaning is "to call out from." Based on the Greek words *kuriakos* and *ekklesia,* the church comprises those people who belong to the Lord and whom He has called out from the world. However, after we are saved, the Bible says if we do not come out of Babylon, we will be judged with Babylon.

Salvation is only the beginning and not the end of God's eternal purpose for His people. The power of Christ's gospel is intended to not only save you from Babylon; it is intended keep you *(sanctify you)* from ever returning to Babylon. On the eve of His crucifixion, Jesus prayed to the Father on behalf of His disciples, "I do not ask you to take them out of the world, but to keep them from the evil one. They are not of world, even as I am not of this world. Sanctify them in the truth; Your word is truth (John 17:15-17)."

Salvation is only the beginning and not the end of God's eternal purpose for His people.

The apostle James warned God's people to keep themselves "unpolluted by the world (James 1:27)." The apostle John wrote, "Do not love the world nor the things in the world. If anyone loves the world, the love of the Father is not in him. For all that is in the world, the lust of the flesh and the lust of the eyes and the boastful pride of life, is not from the Father, but is from the world (John 2:15-16)." The apostle Paul further exhorted, "No soldier in active service entangles himself in the affairs of everyday life, so that he may please the one who enlisted him (2 Timothy 2:4)."

Many professing Christians say they want to avoid the mark of the Beast, but tragically they already have the mark of Babylon on them. Jesus said, "Where your treasure is, there your heart will be also (Matthew 6:21)." Your heart cannot be divided between two cities – the new Jerusalem and Babylon. "Either you will hate the one and love the other, or you will be devoted to the one and despise the other (Matthew 6:21-24)." Babylon is the kingdom of this world. When you seek to fulfill your soul-life with the riches and pleasures of Babylon, you are an enemy of the new Jerusalem. Everyone who is not born again already belongs to Babylon but every Christian who is governed by his unconverted soul-life (and not the Holy Spirit) remains captive to Babylon. The Bible says that Babylon is a dwelling place for every kind of demonic spirit (Revelation 18:2). You may be born again, but if your soul-life is not submitted to Christ's Sovereignty, you can be deceived and snared by Babylon's demonic forces (James 3:15). If you are habitually seeking comfort, companionship and fulfillment in Babylon, you are hostile to God. James warned, "You adulterous people, don't you know that friendship with the world is hatred toward God? Anyone who chooses to be a friend of the world becomes an enemy of God (James 4:4)." Paul admonished, "I warn you, as I did before, that those who live like this will not inherit the kingdom of God (Galatians 5:21)."

How can you escape from the tentacles of Babylon and God's wrath to come? If you are a born again Christian, begin to believe and act on what Christ has accomplished for you on the cross. Only the cross of Christ can save you and deliver you from the kingdom of this world. The Bible says that when Christ was crucified, your sinful nature was not only crucified with Him; it was removed from you (Romans 6:3-11). Therefore, Christ's death on the cross has fully delivered you from the power of Babylon. Since you no longer have a sinful nature, Babylon should no longer have any foothold in you. As Paul testified, "May I never boast except in the cross of the Lord Jesus Christ, through which the world has been crucified to me and I to the world (Galatians 6:14)."

The power of Christ's gospel is intended to not only save you from Babylon; it is intended keep you from returning to Babylon.

Babylon rules and corrupts the world – politically, economically, and religiously. The false church belongs to Babylon. This false church comprises everyone who practices a form of godliness but, by their deeds, they deny the power of Christ's crucifixion (2 Timothy 3:5). Whereas the true church is the bride of Christ, the false church is the harlot of Satan.

Everyone who is born again must come out of the false church before God's wrath is poured out on Babylon.

When our hearts are set on the world and we are indulging ourselves in the things of the world, we prove ourselves to be enemies of the cross of Christ (Philippians 3:18-19). If we lose sight of Christ and His completed work on the cross, then the desire to follow Him, suffer with Him and come out of the world loses its focus and becomes pathetically dim. If we allow ourselves to be seduced by Babylon, we will lose our rightful identity as Christ's bride. "Therefore, since Christ has suffered in the flesh, arm yourselves with the same purpose, because he who has suffered in the flesh has ceased from sin, so as to live the rest of the time in the flesh no longer for the lusts of men, but for the will of God (1 Peter 4:1-2)."

The time is coming when God will judge Babylon. Every child of God should judge themselves now and, if convicted of sin, you must repent resolutely and come out of Babylon so you will not be judged and condemned with the world.

"We know that we are the children of God, and that the whole world is under the control of the evil one."

1 JOHN 5:19

"Therefore, come out from their midst and be separate," says the Lord... "And I will be a Father to you, and you shall be sons and daughters to me."

2 CORINTHIANS 6:17-18

CHAPTER THIRTY-FIVE

Suffering –
God's Crucible

*"Beloved, do not be surprised at the fiery ordeal among you, which comes upon
you for your testing, as though some strange thing were happening to you; but to
the degree that you share the sufferings of Christ, keep on rejoicing, so that also
at the revelation of His glory, you may rejoice with exultation."*

1 PETER 4:12-13

The prophet Malachi foretold that the Messiah would purify His chosen people as a refiner purifies gold and silver. "But who can endure
the day of His coming? And who can stand when He appears? For He is
like a refiner's fire... He will purify the sons of Levi and refine them like
gold and silver, so they may present to the Lord offerings in righteousness
(Malachi 3:2-3)." Zechariah also prophesied the Lord would purify the sur-
viving remnant of His people like gold and silver are refined. "And I will
bring the third part through the fire, refine them as silver is refined, and
test them as gold is tested (Zechariah 13:9)." In Proverbs, King Solomon
described the Lord as the refiner of His people. "The melting pot is for

silver and the crucible is for gold, but it is the Lord who tests the hearts of men (Proverbs 17:3)."

In Biblical times, when the metal smith or refiner wanted to purify gold or silver, he would put the precious metals in a refining pot called a crucible. He would then build a fiery furnace under the crucible. When the gold or silver had melted in the crucible, the refiner would skim off the dross or impurities that rose to the surface. The refiner would then repeat this process until he could see his own image reflected in the molten surface of the crucible. Trials, afflictions and persecutions are the crucible that Christ uses to purify His church until He sees His image reflected in us. "Behold, I have refined you, but not as silver; I have tested you in the furnace of affliction (Isaiah 48:10)." Gold or silver that passed the test of the furnace was called "refined" and had precious value. "Take away the dross from the silver and there comes out a vessel for the smith (Proverbs 25:4)." Those metals that failed to pass the test were rejected. In Jeremiah 6:29-30, God calls Israel "rejected silver" because He tried in vain to refine them.

Trials, afflictions and persecutions are the crucible that Christ uses to purify His church until He sees His image reflected in us.

This crucible of suffering is also called the baptism of fire (Luke 3:16). God has designed His crucible of fire and suffering to humble us and reveal the fullness of His Son in us. Affliction, loneliness, heartbreak and persecution are all intended to bring us to the end of ourselves and into Christ's fullness. For as long as we think we have any spiritual life or strength in ourselves, Christ's life cannot be fully manifested in us. Therefore, suffering is intended to bring us to the point where we no longer trust in our own strength (2 Corinthians 1:8-9). God will then reveal the power of His Son's crucifixion in us so that we see that Christ not only died for us (Romans 5:8), but that we died with Christ (Romans 6:8). When we know we have been crucified with Him and our sinful nature has been removed (Romans 6:6), we will no longer rely on our natural ability to serve Christ. When we know this divine truth with certainty, we are able to trust Christ to live in us (Galatians 2:20). Jesus Himself suffered God's humbling of His soul. "Although He was a Son, He learned obedience from the things He suffered (Hebrews 5:8)."

In the Book of Revelation, we see the new Jerusalem, the holy city, made of pure gold (Revelation 21:18). This heavenly vision reveals the bride of Christ will be like gold purified by fire and clearly reflect the image of Christ in her. This is what Jesus meant when He told the church of Laodicea to buy refined gold (Revelation 3:18). What will it cost the church to buy Christ's pure gold? God has never changed the price: The cost is always our soul-life. Jesus said, "He who has found his soul-life will lose it, and he who has lost his soul-life for My sake will find it (Matthew 10:39)." God does not want to destroy our soul; He wants to transform our soul

When God's crucible of suffering has removed the dross of unbelief from us, we will be dressed in faith as Christ's bride.

into His Son's image if we will allow His crucible of suffering to humble us. The apostle Paul said suffering produces character (Romans 5:3-4). The Greek word used here for character is *dokime* whose root meaning is "proven and tested," just as gold and silver has been tested in the crucible. In other words, God's suffering produces Christ's character in us that has been proven under fire.

We may be surprised and think it is strange when we encounter fiery trials as a Christian. Yet Peter assures us this testing is essential to purify our faith in Christ just as fire is necessary to refine gold (1 Peter 1:6-7; 4:12-13). Job went through this fiery crucible when he said, "Though He slay me, yet will I trust in Him... when He has tested me, I will come forth as gold (Job 13:15; 23:10)." We cannot expect to reign with Christ as His bride if we have not suffered with Him (2 Timothy 2:12). When God's crucible of suffering has removed the dross of unbelief from us, we will be dressed in faith as Christ's bride. Christ's life will have been forged in us like gold refined by fire and we will reign with Him as vessels of honor fit for the Master's use. More importantly, we will truly know Him.

The apostles understood God's purpose in suffering was to prepare the church to be Christ's bride and eternal companion. That is why they rejoiced in suffering. Peter said, "To the degree that you share the sufferings of Christ, keep on rejoicing (1 Peter 4:13)." James said, "Consider it pure joy, my brothers, whenever you face trials of many kinds… blessed is the man who perseveres under trial; for once he has been approved, he will receive the crown of life which the Lord has promised (James 1:2, 12)." Our joy in suffering is motivated by our longing to know Him despite the humiliation that suffering brings. If we allow suffering to obtain its divine objective, we will become lovesick and, like the bride of Solomon, come up from the wilderness of suffering, leaning on our Beloved (Song of Songs 5:8; 8:5).

*"In this you greatly rejoice, though now for a little while you may have had to
suffer grief in all kinds of trials. These have come so that your faith —
of greater worth than gold, which perishes even though refined by fire —
may be proved genuine and may result in praise, glory and honor
when Jesus Christ is revealed."*

1 PETER 1:6-7

CHAPTER THIRTY-SIX

Anointed for Burial

*"There came a woman with an alabaster vial of costly perfume of pure nard;
and she broke the vial and poured it over His head. . . Jesus said, 'She has
anointed My body beforehand for burial. Truly I say to you, wherever the
gospel is preached in the whole world, what this woman
has done will also be spoken in memory of her.'"*

MARK 14:3-10

What is the meaning of this story that Jesus said should be told
wherever the gospel is preached? The details of this event, which
occurred just before the Lord's crucifixion, can also be found in Matthew
26:6-13 and John 12:1-8. From these accounts, we read that Mary, whose
brother Lazarus had been raised from the dead by Jesus, poured a vessel of
costly ointment, worth nearly a year's wages, on the Lord's head. Some disciples considered this extravagant and Judas led them in complaining that
her actions were a waste. "The disciples were indignant when they saw this
and said, 'Why this waste?' For this perfume might have been sold for a
high price and the money given to the poor (Matthew 26:8-9)." But Jesus

said, "Leave her alone... she has done what she could. She has anointed My body beforehand for burial (Mark 14:6-8)."

This story reveals the cost of the gospel and the worth of Christ. Jesus said, "If anyone wishes to come after Me, he must deny himself, and take up his cross and follow Me. For whoever wishes to save his soul-life will lose it, but whoever loses his soul-life for My sake and the gospel's will save it (Mark 8:34-35). In other words, the gospel of Christ will cost us our whole life. The goal of the gospel is not just to save sinners. Salvation is just the beginning and not the end of God's purpose. This is why God included us in His Son's death so that His risen Son might sovereignly live in us. "Do you not know that all of us who have been baptized (*immersed*) into Christ Jesus have been baptized (*immersed*) into His death (Romans 6:3)?" Just as Jesus was anointed for burial so that, by His death, He might bear much fruit; He has also included us in His death and anointed us in His Spirit so that we too might bear much fruit. The Bible says, "We have been buried with Him through baptism into death (Romans 6:4)."

To the carnal-minded, losing our soul-life for the sake of the gospel is a terrible waste. However, you only entertain the idea of waste when you underestimate the Lord's worth.

How do we produce this fruit? Jesus said, "Truly, truly, I say to you, unless a grain of wheat falls into the earth and dies, it remains alone; but if it dies, it bears much fruit. He who loves his soul-life loses it, and he who hates his soul-life in this world will keep it to life eternal (John 12:24-25)." We must take up our cross and lose our soul-life to bear spiritual fruit. "For if you are living according to the flesh (*the unconverted soul-life*), you will die; but if by the Spirit, you are putting to death the misdeeds of the body, you will live... all those who belong to Christ Jesus have put to death on the cross the flesh (*the unconverted soul-life*) with its passions and desires (Romans

8:13; Galatians 5:24)." The only possible way we can carry our cross and lose our soul-life *by the Spirit* is to believe we have died with Christ. Why is this? The Bible says that when Christ was crucified, our sinful nature was crucified with Him and removed from us (Romans 6:6; Colossians 2:11). When we take up our cross, we are identifying by faith with Christ's death so that His death becomes our death. The apostle Paul testified, "I have been put to death on the cross with Christ and I no longer live, but Christ lives in me and the life I now live in the body, I live by faith in the Son of God (Galatians 2:20)." Exercising faith in this Biblical fact enables us to overcome the power of sin and produce fruit.

When we give ourselves wholeheartedly to Christ's sovereignty in this way, some may say we are wasting our life and we could do so much more with our talent. To the carnal-minded, losing our soul-life for the sake of the gospel is a terrible waste. However, you only entertain the idea of waste when you underestimate the Lord's worth. Jesus is the "Pearl of Great Price" worth selling everything for, so that we might know Him (Matthew 13:46). When God opens our eyes to see His Son's worth, we will gladly lose our soul-life for Him. "Worthy is the Lamb who was slain, to

> *By including us in His Son's death, God also intended that His risen Son would sovereignly rule in our lives.*

receive power and wealth and wisdom and strength and honor and glory and praise! (Revelation 5:12)." Paul said, "I count all things to be loss in view of the surpassing value of knowing Christ Jesus my Lord, for whom I have suffered the loss of all things, and count them but rubbish so I may gain Christ (Philippians 3:8)."

God has always intended that the preaching of the gospel would produce a people wholly devoted to His Son, a people rich in good works (1 Timothy 6:18), which spring from faith in the truth that believers are "dead to sin but alive to God (Romans 6-11)." By including us in His Son's death, God also intended that His risen Son would sovereignly rule in our lives. This means we become bondslaves of the Lord in everything we think and do. This is the fruit of the gospel that God has, from the beginning of time, desired to express through us, which is the fruit of our sanctification to Him (Romans 6:22).

The end of the age is almost upon us. Many true believers will be poured out as a sacrificial offering for the sake of Christ and His gospel (Philippians 2:17; 2 Timothy 4:6). Jesus Christ has already anointed us for burial by including us in His death and giving us His Holy Spirit. Let us pray that the fragrance of His anointing will be poured out through our lives. As Paul wrote, "We always carry around in our body the death of Jesus, so that the life of Jesus may also be revealed in our body. For we who are alive are always being given over to death for Jesus' sake, so that His life may be revealed in our mortal body (2 Corinthians 4:10-11)." Therefore, knowing that we have died with Christ and we have been anointed for burial by the Holy Spirit, let us proclaim the Lord's worth to all heaven and earth by "wasting" our lives on Him!

"But thanks be to God, who always leads us in triumph in Christ, and manifests through us the sweet aroma of the knowledge of Him in every place. For we are a fragrance of Christ to God among those who are being saved and among those who are perishing; to the one an aroma from death to death, to the other an aroma from life to life."

2 CORINTHIANS 2:14-16

CHAPTER THIRTY-SEVEN

Unveiling the Bride

*"Hallelujah! For the Lord our God, the Almighty reigns. Let us rejoice
and be glad and give the glory to Him. For the marriage of the Lamb
has come and His bride has made herself ready."*

REVELATION 19:6-7

In these last days, God is preparing a bride for His Son (Revelation 21:2).
Who is this bride? The image of the bride begins in the Old Testament
with Eve (Genesis 2:18-24) who is a type of the church (Ephesians 5:22-
32). In the New Testament, John the Baptist calls Jesus Christ the bridegroom and His disciples the bride (John 3:29). Later, Jesus also refers to
Himself as the bridegroom in relation to His disciples (Luke 5:34-35). For
just as God created Eve out of Adam's body, God created the church out
of Christ's body (Ephesians 5:30). For when Christ willingly gave up His
body and died on the cross for us, God performed a divine heart transplant and exchanged our sinful heart with His Son's divine heart (Romans
6:3-11).

Just as there was a betrothal period in Biblical times between the bride
and bridegroom until their wedding ceremony, so the body of Christ is now

145

betrothed to Jesus Christ (2 Corinthians 11:2). Through water baptism, new believers declare their betrothal to their bridegroom, Jesus Christ, and their union with His death, burial and resurrection. According to Biblical custom, this betrothal is a binding commitment or covenant that can only be broken by infidelity. And by Biblical tradition, the bride remains veiled until her marriage. After the second coming of Christ, the bride will be revealed, the wedding feast will take place and the eternal union of the Lamb of God and His bride will be consummated.

However before this wedding can take place, the bride must make herself ready (Revelation 19:7; 21:2). Jesus Christ made a number of promises to the seven churches in the book of Revelation (Chapters 2-3). These promises were not only for those early churches, they are for the church today. Like all of God's promises, these too are conditional upon the obedience of our faith. Christ said those who by faith obey His Spirit and overcome Satan would inherit His promises. He promised those who overcome would have their names written in the Book of Life and be ready

After the second coming of Christ, the bride will be revealed, the wedding feast will take place and the eternal union of the Lamb of God and His bride will be consummated.

for their marriage and eternal union with Him (Revelation 2:26; 3:5 & 21). Although the entire nation of Israel was called to be God's chosen people, most were unfaithful to Him. When that occurred, God no longer called them His bride; He called them a harlot (Isaiah 1:21). But God's covenant promises were still fulfilled through His remnant of survivors or overcomers (Isaiah 37:31-32). Many Christians think because of God's grace they can love the world and have Jesus too (Matthew 6:24; James 4:4; 1 John 2:15). They are deceived. Jesus Christ will not marry a harlot. God's covenant promises to the church will only be fulfilled through His faithful bride of overcomers (see 1 John 4:4, 5:4; Revelation 21:7).

How can we become Christ's overcoming bride? It is not enough for us to zealously desire to be His bride. It is impossible for us to overcome Satan and sin by our own willpower and natural strength and zeal. If overcoming depended on us, we would be defeated. "But thanks be to God! He gives us the victory through our Lord Jesus Christ (1 Corinthians 15:57)." The Bible says we overcome Satan by the blood of the Lamb and by the word of our testimony (Revelation 12:11). The blood speaks of the triumphant work that Christ has accomplished by His crucifixion. On the cross, Jesus destroyed Satan's power over God's elect (Colossians 2:15; Hebrews 2:14; 1 John 3:8). By His death, Jesus redeemed us

The bride of Christ who crushes Satan wears the full armor of God under her wedding dress.

from both the penalty of sin and the power of sin. The secret to overcoming is knowing we have died in Christ. When Christ died, our sinful nature died with Him and was buried (removed) with Him (Romans 6:4-6). Christ lives in us! (Colossians 1:27). We are now raised with Christ and seated with Him in victory (Ephesians 2:4-6). Therefore, the power of Christ's blood shed on the cross silences all of Satan's accusations and lies. The blood of Christ nullifies Satan's power to accuse us of sin; it also nullifies Satan's power to arouse us to sin.

The bride of Christ who crushes Satan wears the full armor of God under her wedding dress (Ephesians 6:10-17). When Satan accuses Christ's bride of failing God (Revelation 12:10), she stops his lies with the shield of faith and proclaims there is no condemnation in Christ (Romans 8:1). When Satan tempts Christ's bride to love her soul-life (John 12:25), she uses the sword of the Spirit to make him flee and proclaims she is dead to the world through the cross of Christ (Galatians 6:24). The bride who overcomes Satan knows she has died with Christ and is full of the Spirit and testimony of Jesus, her bridegroom (Matthew 25:1-13). This is the bride who conquers Satan by the word of her testimony and by the blood of the

Lamb and she does not love her life even when faced with death (Revelation 12:11). "Now have come the salvation and the power and the kingdom of our God, and the authority of His Christ. For the accuser of our brothers, who accuses them before God day and night, has been hurled down (Revelation 12:10)."

On His wedding day, Jesus will unveil His bride clothed in white wedding clothes without stain or blemish - holy and blameless (Ephesians 5:27). These wedding clothes are the righteous acts that spring from our faith in Jesus Christ and His victory on the cross (Revelation 19:8). This is the bride who has proven herself worthy by her undying love and faith in Jesus Christ and His cross. When Jesus Christ returns and is revealed, this is the bride who will be revealed with Him in glory (Colossians 3:4). This is the glorious bride of Christ who will be joined in heavenly marriage and eternal union to her true love and Lord, the Lamb of God, Jesus Christ.

"In that day the Lord of hosts will be a beautiful crown and a glorious diadem to the remnant of His people... and as the bridegroom rejoices over his bride, so your God will rejoice over you"

ISAIAH 28:5; 62:5

"And the Spirit and the bride say, 'Come.' He who testifies to these things says, 'Yes, I am coming quickly.'"

REVELATION 22:17 & 20

CHAPTER THIRTY-EIGHT

The Wedding Clothes

"The kingdom of heaven may be compared to a king who gave a wedding feast for his son. And he sent out his slaves to call those who had been invited to the wedding feast... and the wedding hall was filled with guests. But when the king came in to see the guests, he noticed a man there who was not wearing wedding clothes. 'Friend,' he asked, 'how did you get in here without wedding clothes?' The man was speechless. Then the king told the attendants, 'Tie him hand and foot, and throw him into the darkness, where there will be weeping and gnashing of teeth.'"

MATTHEW 22:1-13

This parable is really a commentary on Christ's own wedding to His bride at the end of this age. There is one thing certain about this wedding: God will not allow anyone to participate in His Son's marriage unless they are wearing the right wedding clothes. Now let us take a look at Christ's heavenly wedding from the perspective of the Book of Revelation. "I heard what sounded like a great multitude, like the roar of rushing waters and like loud peals of thunder shouting, 'Hallelujah! For the Lord our God the Almighty reigns. Let us rejoice and be glad and give the glory to Him, for the marriage of the Lamb has come and His bride has made herself ready. *It was given to her to clothe herself in fine linen, bright and clean; for the fine linen stands for the righteous acts of the saints.'* Then he said to me, 'Write, 'Blessed are those who are invited to the marriage supper of the Lamb (Revelation 19:6-9).'" Again, the Bible is clear you cannot participate in Christ's wedding feast unless you have the right wedding clothes. The Bible also says these wedding clothes signify our sanctified works done in faith.

In these last days, many professing Christians are not wearing these wedding garments. They think they are spiritually dressed to meet Christ when they are actually stark naked. Jesus said, "You do not know that you are naked. Buy from Me white garments so that you may clothe yourself and the shame of your nakedness will not be revealed (Revelation 3:17-18)." It is important to note here

For two thousand years, God has never changed the price that the bride of Christ must pay for her wedding clothes. The cost is always the same — the price is our soul-life.

that Jesus was speaking to those in the church and not to unbelievers. Here Jesus declared we must buy our *own* wedding clothes. For two thousand years, God has never changed the price that the bride of Christ must pay for her wedding clothes. The cost is always the same – the price is our soul-life. Jesus said, "If anyone wishes to come after Me, he must deny himself and take up his cross and follow Me. For whoever wishes to save his soul-life will lose it, but whoever *loses his soul-life for My sake and the gospel's will find it* (Mark 8:34-35)."

Therefore, we can only buy our wedding clothes if we pay for them with *our soul-life.* Nothing else will suffice. What does it mean to lose our soul-life for Christ's sake? God has made us spirit, soul and body (1 Thessalonians 5:23). When we were born again, our sinful nature died and our regenerated spirit became made one with Christ's Spirit (1 Corinthians 6:17). Our soul, however, is our individual personality – our will, intellect and natural temperament. Because we retain free will, our soul does not automatically come under Christ's Sovereignty. However, once we know that we have already died with Christ, we are capable of submitting our whole being to Christ's authority so that God can transform and restore our soul. God does not want to suppress or destroy our soul. He made the human soul and meant it to be a useful instrument, just like our body. But now that we are in Christ, the important question is this: Will we live according to the power and desire of God's Spirit within us or will we quench the Spirit and live according to the strength of our soul and our natural desires?

Losing our soul-life means we give up our whole being completely to Christ's Sovereignty. It means we exchange our own attitudes, affections and abilities for Christ's attitudes, affections and abilities. This is what it means to walk in sanctification. "Present your bodies a living and holy sacrifice acceptable to God... and do not be conformed to this world, but be transformed by the renewing of your mind so that you may prove what the will of God is... (Romans 12:2)." This is what Paul meant when he exhorted believers to "be made new in the attitude of your minds... and take captive every thought to make it obedient to Christ (Ephesians 4:23; 2 Corinthians 10:5)."

The issue is one of ownership. Will we continue to be enslaved to our soul's natural desires, or will we be enslaved to God in sanctification?

Jesus compared the kingdom of God to a pearl of great price. He said when a man found such a pearl, he sold all he had to buy it (Matthew 13:46). Therefore, we prove we are Christ's disciples by yielding ourselves by faith to Christ's Sovereignty so that His thoughts become our thoughts and His actions become our actions. Jesus said, "If anyone comes to Me and does not hate... his own *soul-life*, he cannot be My disciple (Luke 14:26)." The issue is one of ownership. Will we continue to be enslaved to our soul's natural desires, or will we be enslaved to God in sanctification? Every Christian who lays down their soul-life to Christ will overcome sin, the world and the devil. Everyone who overcomes will be dressed in wedding clothes ready for the marriage supper of the Lamb. Jesus Christ said, "You have a few people... who have not soiled their clothes. *They will walk with Me, dressed in white, for they are worthy. He who overcomes will, like them, be dressed in white.* I will never blot out his name from the book of life, but will acknowledge his name before My Father (Revelation 3:4-5)."

Losing our soul-life for Christ's sake is only possible *if* we believe that our sinful nature has already died and been removed by Christ's death on the cross. Why is this? Because when God included us in His Son's death in this way, He made it possible for us to walk in sanctification by faith and wear wedding clothes as the bride of Christ. Tragically, many professing Christians are not ready for the marriage supper of the Lamb. If they do not buy their wedding clothes soon, they will be speechless when God throws them out of His Son's wedding, for they will have proven themselves unworthy and shamefully unclothed.

"Behold, I come like a thief! Blessed is he who stays awake and keeps his clothes with him, so he may not go naked and be shamefully exposed."

REVELATION 16:15

CHAPTER THIRTY-NINE

The Pearl of Great Price

"The kingdom of heaven is like a merchant seeking fine pearls, and upon finding one pearl of great price, he went and sold all that he had and bought it."

MATTHEW 13:44-46

J esus Christ is the Pearl of Great Price! The Bible says that "Christ is the radiance of God's glory (Hebrews 1:3)... in whom are hidden all the treasures of wisdom and knowledge (Colossians 2:3)." When we really see Jesus Christ and who He is, we will want to sell all we have in order to know Him - the Pearl of Great Price. How much will it cost us to "sell all" for Christ? For two thousand years, the price has always been the same. Even if there are only a few "buyers," God has never lowered the price. The cost of knowing Christ is to believe in Him to the point that we want to give up our whole life for Him. Jesus said, "If anyone wishes to come after Me, he must deny himself and take up his cross and follow Me. For whoever wishes to save his soul-life will lose it, but whoever loses his soul-life for My sake and the gospel's will save it (Mark 8:34-37)."

What does it mean to give up our soul-life for Christ and how do we do this? It means we give Jesus Christ complete control over our lives and become His bondslaves out of love. We then exchange our desires, interests and abilities for His desires, interests and abilities so that He can motivate us and work through us. We let the mind of Christ totally permeate our entire being because we want to know Him and love Him more than we want anything else in this world. And we do this by faith "for he who comes to God must believe that He is and that He is a rewarder of those who seek Him (Hebrews 11:6).

Jesus said, "Whoever loses his soul-life for My sake will find it to life eternal (John 12:24)." The only way we will want to give up our soul-life is if we see that the Pearl of Great Price is worth far more than anything we have to give up. We first begin to see Jesus Christ clearly when we are born again into His kingdom. Jesus said, *When we really see Jesus Christ, we will want to sell all we have in order to know Him - the Pearl of Great Price.* "Truly, truly, I say to you, unless one is born again he cannot see the kingdom of God (John 3:3)." If we do not see Jesus is the Pearl of Great Price, we will not be able to "sell all" for His sake. If we do not see the eternal value of knowing Christ, we will not be able to lose our soul-life here on earth for His sake. Without seeing the Pearl of Great Price, the magnetic pull of the sin of the world is irresistible.

Why do so few people give up their soul-life for Jesus Christ? Many never see the Pearl of Great Price. "The god of this world has blinded the minds of the unbelieving so that they might not see the light of the gospel of the glory of Christ, who is the image of God (2 Corinthians 4:4). In the case of others who once were saved but now live only to fulfill their soul-life in this world, they have lost sight of the Pearl of Great Price. They now simply love their soul-life too much to give it up for Christ. They are like

Esau who sold his inheritance for a bowl of beans (Genesis 25:27-34). "But what will it profit a man if he gains the whole world and forfeits his soul? Or what will a man give in exchange for his soul? (Matthew 16:26)."

Here is the glorious truth: It is possible for us to give up this world and all its pleasures because God, through the death of His Son, destroyed our sinful nature and removed it from us. When Christ died, God performed a divine heart transplant and exchanged our sinful heart with His Son's holy nature (Romans 6:3-11). Because our sinful nature died with Christ, we have died to the world (Galatians 6:14). We no longer have to practice sin. "No one who is born of God will continue to sin because God's seed *(Christ)* abides in him, and he cannot go on sinning because he is born of God (1 John 3:9)."

Gaining Jesus Christ is worth far more than everything we have to sell. Knowing Jesus is worth far beyond anything we have to lose. When Jesus told His disciples they must bear their own cross, deny themselves and lose their soul-life for His sake, what did He give them in return? He gave them Himself – the Pearl of Great Price. "This is eternal life, that they may know You, the only true God, and Jesus Christ whom You have sent (John 17:3)." If we underestimate the worth of Jesus Christ and overestimate the value of what we have to lose, we will feel sorry for ourselves because we have to give up so much. We will have lost sight of the Pearl of Great Price. How

Gaining Jesus Christ is worth far more than everything we have to sell. Knowing Jesus is worth far beyond anything we have to lose.

much we "sell all" is in direct proportion to how much we see Christ. As we obey Jesus Christ and His Word, He will increasingly reveal Himself to us. "Whoever has My commands and obeys them, he is the one who loves Me. He who loves Me will be loved by My Father, and I too will love him and disclose Myself to him (John 14:21)." Giving up your whole life for the One you love and the One who loves you is the most beautiful experience you can have in this life. We lose our soul-life so we might gain the indescribable experience of close companionship and deep communion with Jesus.

How did Moses endure ill-treatment and resist the passing pleasures of sin? How could Moses consider disgrace for Christ of greater value than the treasures of Egypt? The Bible says Moses endured "by seeing Him who is unseen (Hebrews 12:25-27)." This was also the apostle Paul's testimony: "Whatever things were gain to me, those things I have counted as loss for the sake of Christ. More than that, I count all things to be loss in view of the surpassing value of knowing Christ Jesus my Lord, for whom I have suffered the loss of all things, and count them but rubbish so that I might gain Christ (Philippians 3:7-8)."

So let us fix our eyes on Jesus and, like Moses and Paul, see Him who is unseen, for He is the author and finisher of our faith. Let us endure this race to the end so that we might receive the crown of glory He has for us. Nothing on this earth can compare to seeing Him and knowing Him – He is true riches! He is worth far more than anything we might lose, even our very lives. Jesus Christ died to make it possible for us to see Him and know Him. Let us sell all to buy the Pearl of Great Price!

"The kingdom of heaven is like a treasure hidden in the field, which a man found and hid again; and from joy over it he goes and sells all that he has and buys that field."

MATTHEW 13:44-45

CHAPTER FORTY

God's Glorious Church

*"Christ loved the church and gave Himself up for her to make her holy...
to present her to Himself as a glorious church."*

EPHESIANS 5:25-27

The Bible uses several terms to describe the church: the city of God, the temple of the Spirit, and the body of Christ. However, the *"bride of Christ"* may best describe the divine relationship God is preparing the church to have with His Son. This divine union is the eternal purpose of God the Father. It was in God's heart from before time to obtain a bride and holy companion for His Son. The apostle Paul knew God's desire when he declared, "I betrothed you to one husband, so that to Christ I might present you as a pure virgin (2 Corinthians 11:2)." It was also God's intention to manifest His divine power and wisdom through the church. God accomplished His will through His Son. "He made known to us the mystery of His will, according to His kind intention which He *purposed in Him... that is, the summing up of all things in Christ*, things in the heavens and things on the earth (Ephesians 1:9-10)." Paul declared that God's grace was given to him "to bring to light... the mystery, which for ages was hidden in God who created all things; so that the manifold wisdom of God might now be made known *through the church* to the rulers and authorities in the heavenly places, *according to His eternal purpose which He accomplished in Christ Jesus our Lord* (Ephesians 3:9-11)."

From the beginning to the end of the Bible, God's eternal purpose for man is evident. In the Book of Genesis, we see God created Adam in His image to have fellowship with man and to have man rule over the earth (Genesis 2:27-28; 3:8). In this way, Adam would express God's wisdom and power to a heavenly audience. But instead of preserving his friendship with God and his dominion over the earth, Adam disobeyed God and fell under Satan's domain. Adam's rebellion against God affected all mankind and the entire human race inherited his sinful spiritual nature (Romans 5:19). Yet despite Adam's fall, God did not change His divine plan. At the right time, God sent His Son, born as a man, to destroy Satan's power and restore mankind to Himself and to His eternal purpose.

Jesus Christ came to earth with one overriding mission - to die on the cross in order to rescue us from Satan's rule and reconcile us to God. Christ's crucifixion is, therefore, the most momentous event in history and the triumph of the ages. Through His death on the cross, Jesus Christ redeemed us from both the penalty of sin and the power of sin. On the cross, Jesus drank the cup of God's wrath for our sin so we might drink His cup of salvation. God used the death of His only Son to perform a divine heart transplant and save us from certain doom. When Jesus died on the cross, God exchanged our terminally sin-sick heart with His Son's divine heart (Romans 6:1-11; Colossians 2:11-3:4). God then raised Jesus Christ from the dead and exalted Him as the eternal King of

> *From His Son's death and resurrection, God has created a people in His Son's image - the body of Christ, the church, who is destined to fulfill His eternal purpose.*

glory (Philippians 2:9-11). Thus God included us in His Son's death so that His risen Son might sovereignly live in us (Romans 6:5; Galatians 2:20; Colossians 1:27).

From His Son's death and resurrection, God has created a people in His Son's image - the body of Christ, the church, who is destined to fulfill His eternal purpose (Romans 8:29-30). What Adam lost for mankind by his diso-bedience, Christ regained for us by His obedience to the death. For as a husband loves his wife, Christ loved the church and gave His life for her. Just as Eve was cre-ated from Adam's body to be his bride and

The "bride of Christ" may best describe the divine relationship God is preparing the church to have with His Son.

glory, God created the church from Christ's body to be His bride and glory. And as Eve was created as Adam's helpmate to reign over the earth, God cre-ated the church as Christ's helpmate to reign with Him in the age to come.

By the cross, our Lord Jesus Christ destroyed Satan's power to keep the church captive to sin and death (Colossians 2:10; Hebrews 2:14; 1 John 3:8). However, the church has, in the past, chiefly failed to enforce Christ's victory because she has tried to do, in the power of her soul, what she can only do through the power of Christ's death and resurrection. "And they overcame him *(Satan)* because of the blood of the Lamb and because of the word of their testimony, and they did not love their life even when faced with death (Revelation 12:11)." The blood speaks of the triumphant work that Christ has accomplished by His crucifixion. When the church knows (and acts on) the divine truth that she has died with Christ, the gates of hell will not be able to prevail against her fulfilling God's eternal purpose.

When the church realizes she no longer has a sinful nature inherited from Adam and she is a holy new creation in Christ, she will not only vanquish Satan, she will fulfill her divine destiny. "Now the salvation, and the power, and the kingdom of our God and the authority of His Christ have come, for the accuser of our brethren has been thrown down (Revelation 12:10)." When the church puts no confidence in her natural morality and ability and by faith trusts solely in Christ to overcome through her, she will be ready to reign with Him (Philippians 3:3). "Hallelujah! For the Lord our God, the Almighty reigns. Let us rejoice and be glad and give the glory to Him, for the marriage of the Lamb has come and His bride has made herself ready (Revelation 19:6-7)."

Under the Old Covenant, when Solomon completed building God's temple, the glory of God filled the temple, which was His house (2 Chronicles 7:2). Now, under the New Covenant, when the Holy Spirit has completed building the body of Christ into God's temple, the glory of God will once again fill His house, which is the church (Ephesians 2:19-22). "'And the latter glory of this house will be greater than the glory of the former house,' says the Lord (Haggai 2:9)."

God's divine plan is to have an eternal companion and co-regent worthy for His Son and a heavenly family for Himself so that Christ would be all and in all forever and ever. God chose the church for this celestial purpose before the foundation of the world. God birthed the church from out of His Son's death and He will glorify and magnify His risen Son through the church. When the body of Christ has fulfilled God's mission of ushering in His kingdom, Christ our King will return and crush Satan under His feet, which is the church. Then the bride of Christ, the glorious church, will reign in eternal union with her divine Lover and Lord, the Lamb of God.

"To Him be the glory in the church and in Christ Jesus
to all generations forever and ever. Amen."

Ephesians 3:21

Do Christians Have Two Natures?

This is one of the devil's lies that has greatly bewitched and weakened the church. Many born again Christians believe this satanic lie that they have two natures within them, a new nature and an old nature, which war against each other. They believe that their new nature loves God and wants to practice righteousness but that their old nature loves sin and wants to practice lawlessness. They think that their Christian life reflects whichever of their two natures they yield themselves to the most. This lie is one of the greatest deceptions the devil has foisted on the church. Many Christians have become hopelessly discouraged and are overcome by sin because they have swallowed this lie; while others are deceived by self-pride that they can overcome the old nature.

OUR SINFUL NATURE WAS PUT TO DEATH ON THE CROSS WITH CHRIST

The Bible says that every person is born with a fallen spiritual nature which we inherited from our ancestor Adam. This inner sinful nature, which the Bible also refers to as the old man or the old self, is hostile and rebellious to God. Since this is man's inward nature before he is born again of the Spirit, it controls man's attitudes and actions and compels man to sin. This sinful nature is like a "sin factory" inside unregenerate man that continuously produces sinful thoughts and behavior that are alien and hostile to God. Since we were born into sin and were, therefore, sinners by nature, God's plan of redemption was to spiritually include us in His Son's death so that we could be freed from sin. Therefore, when we were born again, God spiritually immersed us into Christ's death (Romans 6:3). The Scriptures clearly state that when Christ died, we died with Him (Romans 6:8; 2 Corinthians 5:14; Colossians 2:20; 3:3).

Contrary to the faulty theology currently taught in many churches today, born again believers do not have two natures. "For we know that our old man was crucified with Him in order that our body of sin *(our sinful nature)* would be done away with so that we would no longer be slaves to sin (Romans 6:6)." Our old man of sin (that sin factory) was destroyed with Christ's death and buried with Him and our sinful nature was removed from us. The apostle Paul taught that since our old sinful nature has died and been removed, we have been freed from the power of sin. "For he who has died has been freed from sin (Romans 6:7)." This Biblical fact is so fundamental to our Christian faith that God has ordained the practice of water baptism for new believers to always remind the church of this powerful truth of Christ's Atonement. When we are buried (or immersed) under water during baptism, this outwardly demonstrates that our old man of sin (our sinful nature) was done away with and removed from us. "Therefore we have been buried with Him through baptism into death (Romans 6:4)."

THIS IS BASIC CHRISTIANITY

This is basic Christianity. However, if we do not believe to the point that we *act* on the Biblical truth of Christ's Atonement, we will not experience the divine provision that Christ died to give us. For example, if we do not believe and *act* on the Biblical truth that Christ's death has completely freed us from the penalty of our sins, we will not experience freedom from condemnation of sin. In the same way, if we do not believe and *act* on the Biblical truth that Christ's death has completely freed us from our sinful nature, we will not experience freedom from the power of sin. "For we also have had the gospel preached to us, just as they did; but the word they heard did not profit them, because it was not united by faith in those who heard (Hebrews 4:2)."

OTHER DEVILISH VARIATIONS TO THIS BIG LIE

Since Romans 6:6 plainly states that our old sinful nature was crucified and *done away with* through Christ's death on the cross, the devil has fabricated two other deceptive variations to this lie to try to subvert this truth and power of the cross of Christ. The first devilish variation of this lie alleges that even if a Christian's sinful nature has died, it was never completely destroyed and removed from him when he was born again. In other words, this devilish fabrication promotes the false idea that a Christian's sinful nature is not irrevocably dead and extinct but instead resides in a Christian like a dormant volcano, which can spontaneously erupt into life and cause destruction and havoc at any time.

This falsehood is aimed at keeping Christians fearful and captive to sin so that they cannot walk in the fullness of Christ's life and power. There are a dozen Scripture verses that state we have died with Christ. The New Testament Greek word used in many of these verses is *apothnesko*, which means expired or died and conveys a sense of finality – of being very dead. For example, in Romans 6:7-8, the apostle Paul declared, "Because anyone who has *died* has been freed from sin… we have *died* with Christ (see also Colossians 3:3)." Based on the New Testament Greek, this is clearly not just a figurative or symbolic or merely positional death. Our sinful nature, which was central to who we were and at the very core of our self-identity, actually died when we received Christ into our heart; it was not merely rendered "inactive" or "dormant."

THE PRESENCE AND POWER OF SIN DOES NOT DWELL IN A CHRISTIAN

There is yet a second variation to the lie that born again Christians have two natures. This second devilish fabrication alleges that even if a Christian no longer has a sinful nature, he still has the presence and power of sin dwelling in his physical body. This falsehood is also aimed at keeping Christians captive to sin. Some Christians are confused when they read Romans Chapter Seven and think perhaps the person being described in this passage is a Christian who has two natures – a good and evil nature. However, Paul wrote this particular chapter to his fellow Jewish brethren (see Romans 7:1) to convince them that in Christ, they died not only to sin; they also died to the Old Covenant Mosaic Law. In this chapter, Paul describes the frustration and anguish of a person who wants to obey God but cannot do so because of his sinful nature. Finally, at the end of Chapter Seven, this pitiful person cries out, "I am a wretched man! Who will set me free from this body of death *(this sinful nature)?* (Romans 7:24)." Based on his own personal experience, Paul then triumphantly reveals who has freed us from our sinful nature. Paul declares, "Thanks be to God through Jesus Christ our Lord! (Romans 7:25).

When reading Romans Chapter Seven, it is important to remember that Paul wrote the Epistle to the Romans in the Greek language, a precise and expressive language which often strategically uses the *present* tense to dramatically describe a *past* action and experience. In Chapter Seven, Paul made effective use of this *historical present* tense, as it is called in the Greek language, to vividly describe the futility and misery of a person who wants to serve God but finds himself continually frustrated and sabotaged by his rebellious sinful nature because he is not born again. In writing this chapter, Paul drew from his own past personal experience as a devout Pharisee before He became a born again Christian. We should also point out that if a person is born again but mistakenly believes he still has a sinful nature, then he will also think that he is still under the power of sin and inwardly think of himself as a hopeless sinner.

MAN'S SINFUL NATURE WAS HIS ACHILLES HEEL

God knew that man's sinful nature was his Achilles heel, which Satan could use to continually snare him in sin. This is why the Old Covenant could not accomplish God's eternal purpose since man's sinful nature prevented him from truly obeying God's commandments. Therefore, what the Mosaic Law was powerless to do because of our sinful nature; God did in the New Covenant by sending His Son who perfectly fulfilled the Law and became sin on our behalf when He was crucified so that we might become the righteousness of God in Christ (Romans 8:3; 2 Corinthians 5:21). Not understanding the purpose and meaning of Romans Chapter Seven, some Christians cite Romans 7:17 ("sin… dwells in me") to justify their belief that the presence and power of sin still resides in a Christian's physical body. However, as we said earlier, Paul was describing a person who is not born again, yet wants to obey God and cannot do so because of his sinful nature. Also we must ask: where does sin dwell in our physical body after we are born again? Is it in our hands and feet? Jesus said, "If your hand or foot causes you to stumble, cut it off and throw it from you; it is better for you to enter life crippled or lame, than to have two hands or two feet and be cast into the eternal fire (Matthew 18:8)." However, Jesus did not mean that sin resides in our physical body and we must now amputate our hands and feet to become free of sin. Jesus meant we must decisively stop practicing sin if we want to be His disciples and enter the kingdom of heaven.

GOD'S DIVINE HEART TRANSPLANT

Jesus revealed where sin resides in unregenerate man when He said, "From within, *out of the heart of men,* proceed evil thoughts, fornications, thefts, murders, adulteries, deeds of coveting, and wickedness, as well as deceit, sensuality, envy, slander, pride and foolishness. All these evil things proceed from within and defile the man (Mark 7:21-23)." Once again, Jesus did not mean that sin resides in our physical heart; otherwise we would need a physical heart transplant to be freed from sin. Jesus meant that sin dwells in unconverted man's spiritual heart. Everyone is born with a heart of sin; this was our spiritual condition before we were born again. Therefore, God's solution was to perform a divine heart transplant to save man from the power of sin. When His Son died on the cross, God exchanged our terminally sin-sick heart with His Son's divine heart. "God sent the Spirit of His Son into our hearts (Galatians 4:6)." By this divine exchange, God completely delivered us from all indwelling sin and Christ now dwells in us. Although our physical body will age and die because of sin's effect upon the human race, this does not mean that evil now indwells our body as a malignant power that can cause us to sin. The Bible emphatically declares that sin does not indwell the body of a born again believer. The Scriptures testify that we are now a "new man, which in the likeness of God has been created in righteousness and holiness (Ephesians 4:24)."

THEN WHY DO CHRISTIANS STILL SIN?

One of the main reasons why Christians mistakenly think they still have a sinful nature is because they continue to practice sin. Since our sinful Adam nature is dead and gone, then why do we continue to sin? The Bible says the reason why Christians continue to sin is because their minds have not yet been renewed by the truth of God's Word. Although our *Adam sinful nature* is dead, our *Adam way of thinking* (our unrenewed mind) will still continue in the habit of worldly thinking and sinning until it is transformed by God's Spirit of truth. More specifically, our mind needs to be transformed by God's Word to the point that we act on this truth that our sinful nature has already died with Christ and we have been freed from sin. The apostle Paul taught, "Do not be conformed to this world, but be transformed by the *renewing of your mind*, so that you may prove what the will of God is (Romans 12:2)." He also exhorted believers to "*be made new in the attitude of your mind* (Ephesians 4:23)." In other words, our unbelieving, sinful attitudes need to be exchanged for Christ's attitudes. The Bible calls this process of "putting off" or "putting to death" our soulish attitudes and "putting on" the mind of Christ the work of "sanctification." As we present ourselves each day to God as a living and holy sacrifice and immerse ourselves in His Word, the Holy Spirit will accomplish this sanctifying work of transformation in our soul-life.

THE GREAT DIFFERENCE BETWEEN THE SINFUL NATURE AND UNRENEWED MIND

We should always remember that there is a great difference between the sinful nature and the unrenewed mind. The unrenewed mind does not have the same power as the sinful nature. Our old sinful nature was like a continuously operating "sin factory" that had to be destroyed by Christ's death on the cross before we could be set free from slavery to sin.

The unrenewed mind or unconverted soul, on the other hand, is simply our soulish mindset, which the Holy Spirit within us can transform now that we no longer have a sinful nature. Since we have become united with Christ in His death and resurrection, we no longer have the presence and power of sin indwelling us; we now have the presence and power of Christ indwelling us. If we believe and act on this divine truth of Christ's completed work on the cross, we will no longer practice sin because we have been freed from sin. "No one who is born of God will continue to sin, because God's seed abides in him; he cannot go on sinning, because he has been born of God (1 John 3:9)."

The devilish lie that Christians still have the presence of sin residing somewhere in their natural body is just another deceptive way of saying Christians still have a sinful nature. Those who mistakenly think that a born again Christian still has a sinful nature sometimes justify their opinion by focusing on the interpretation of the Greek word, *katargeo,* as it appears in Romans 6:6: "For we know that our old self was crucified with Him, in order that our body of sin (our sinful nature) might be *done away with (katargeo)*, so that we would no longer be slaves to sin." In this verse, the New American Standard Bible translates the Greek word *katargeo* by the phrase, "done away with." This is an appropriate translation within this Scriptural context since our old man (our sinful nature) died and was buried (done away with) by our baptism (immersion) into Christ's death. The King James Version translates *katargeo* in this verse as *"destroyed,"* which also fits this Scriptural context since our sinful nature (the sin factory) was destroyed by Christ's death on the cross. However, those who mistakenly believe that the sinful nature still resides within a Christian think the word *katargeo* should be translated as "idle" or "unemployed." In other words, they think the sinful nature is just sitting "idle" in a Christian and that a Christian can unwittingly "reemploy" and "reactivate" their old sinful nature whenever they sin.

"Katargeo" Means Destroyed and Removed

However, this interpretation is neither Scriptural nor logical. A careful review of the twenty-seven times that *katargeo* is used in New Testament reveals that *"done away with"* or *"destroyed"* is the proper translation of *katargeo* in Romans 6:6. In fact, *katargeo* might be accurately and more clearly translated as *"removed."* This is exactly how *katargeo* is translated in 2 Corinthians 3:14 to describe how the Old Covenant veil that blinds Jews to seeing Jesus as their Messiah is removed *(katargeo)* whenever someone turns to Christ. This veil certainly is not rendered just idle or unemployed; it is forever taken away! With this in view, the Old Covenant prophet Ezekiel foretold of the divine heart transplant that God would perform in the New Covenant: "Moreover, I will give you a new heart and put a new spirit within you; and I will *remove* your heart of stone and give you a heart of flesh (Ezekiel 36:26)." The Bible here does not need any subjective interpretation; it is very clear. God, through His prophet Ezekiel, declared our heart of stone (our sinful nature) would be *removed* through the New Covenant!

Our Sinful Nature Was Removed and Buried with Christ

The Bible says we have died with Christ (Romans 6:8; 2 Corinthians 5:14; Colossians 2:20; 3:3); we were buried with Christ (Romans 6:4; Colossians 2:12); and we were raised with Christ (Ephesians 2:6; Colossians 2:12; 3:1). Consider this divine fact: resurrection means to be raised from the dead. Just as Christ was raised from the dead, we were raised from the dead with Him. Therefore, we had to die and be buried before we could be raised from the dead. Water baptism outwardly demonstrated this divine truth when we were buried in a watery "grave." But when we died with Christ, who died and was then buried? Was it our physical body? No. We know that our physical body did not die when we received Christ. Was it our soul? No. We know that our soul (our personality - our will, intellect and emotions) did not die when we received Christ. Yet, the Bible clearly states that we died with Christ when we were born again. Then who died? According to the Bible, our sinful spiritual nature died. The question we must ask ourselves is this: Do we believe what the Bible says, that as born again believers, our sinful nature has been put to death and removed from us? Do we believe this Biblical truth to the point that we act on it? When faced with an opportunity to sin, do we believe this truth to the point that we resist sin by knowing that we have been delivered from sin's power over us because we have died to sin?

Both Circumcision and Baptism Portray the Old Nature is Gone

In his letter to the Colossians, the apostle Paul confirms the Biblical truth that our sinful nature was removed when we were born again. Here, Paul uses the picture of circumcision to describe what happened to our sinful nature when we were saved. "In Him you were also circumcised with a circumcision made without hands, in the *removal* of the sinful nature, by the circumcision of Christ (Colossians 2:11)." We can say with absolute certainty that when someone is circumcised, their foreskin is definitely removed! It is not left attached in just an idle or dormant manner to continually cause infection and disease. Therefore, in this passage of Scripture (Colossians 2:11), Paul declares our sinful nature has been removed in Christ. Paul then shifts in the very next verse (Colossians 2:12) from the Old Covenant seal of righteousness (circumcision) to the New Covenant seal of righteousness (baptism) to further demonstrate that our old sinful nature was removed. Paul logically states that since our old sinful nature died and was removed (verse 11), it was then disposed of by burial: "Having been buried with Him in baptism and raised with Him through your faith in the power of God, who raised Him from the dead (verse 12)." Thus, by linking Old Covenant circumcision with New Covenant baptism, Paul leaves no doubt that the death and removal of the sinful nature (as symbolized by circumcision) is also portrayed by the burial stage of water baptism. Again, we can say with absolute certainty, that when someone dies and is buried, their dead body is definitely removed! In this way, water baptism confirms (just as circumcision also did) that our sinful nature not only died, but once and for all time was definitely *removed* from us when we were born again. We no longer have two natures! We now only have Christ's Spirit indwelling us!

New Wine is Poured into New (Not Old) Wineskins

Thus both the Old Covenant and New Covenant portray what happened to our sinful nature when we were born again of the Spirit. Our sinful nature died with Christ's death and God has completely *removed* it from our being. The old sinful nature is not hiding somewhere in our body just waiting to resurrect its satanic power of sin within us. God does not mix what is holy with what is unholy. God would never pour His Holy Spirit into an unholy vessel containing a sinful nature. Jesus said, "And no one pours new wine into old wineskins. If he does, the wine will burst the skins, and both the wine and the wineskins will be ruined. No, he pours new wine into new wineskins (Mark 2:22)." The reason God is able to pour His Holy Spirit (His new wine) into our hearts is because He made us a new creation - a new wineskin in Christ - and we no longer have an old sinful nature within us. "Therefore, if anyone is in Christ, he is a new creation; the old has gone, the new has come! (2 Corinthians 5:17)."

GOD'S PEOPLE ARE DESTROYED
FOR LACK OF KNOWLEDGE

There are only two kinds of people who would insist that they have a sinful nature. The first person is an unbeliever who really does have a sinful nature because he has never been born again of the Holy Spirit. Even if that person falsely claims to be a Christian, he is still captive to the power of sin because he still has a sinful nature (John 8:34; 2 Timothy 3:2). The second person is a born again Christian who does not believe that God ever removed his sinful nature from him when he was saved. Since he refuses to believe God's Word, he still thinks he is captive to sin even though Christ died to set him free from sin. The word of the cross can only free a Christian from sin if they believe and *act* on it. Jesus said, "If you continue in My word, then you are truly disciples of Mine; and you will know the truth, and the truth will set you free (John 8:32). It is very evident in this particular Scriptural passage that Jesus was specifically referring here to being freed from slavery to sin (see John 8:34).

Therefore, the unbeliever is a wretched and miserable person because he has a sinful nature and *is* in bondage to sin - even if he is religious (Romans 7:14 & 24), whereas the *unbelieving* Christian is a wretched and miserable person because he erroneously thinks he still has a sinful nature and is in bondage to sin. As God said, "My people are destroyed for lack of knowledge (Hosea 4:6)." This mistaken thinking stems from spiritual ignorance concerning the power of Christ's crucifixion and resurrection. Jesus said, "Is this not the reason you are mistaken, that you do not understand the Scriptures or the power of God (Mark 12:24)?" Note: A born again Christian, who believes he has a sinful nature and who is governed by his unrenewed mind instead of the Holy Spirit, can display sinful, lawless behavior that is habitually inconsistent with godly Christian conduct. Although this person may rightfully be called hypocritical because his sinful, carnal behavior is completely at odds with his professed faith, it does not mean he has a sinful nature. Instead, it means his soul-life *(his attitudes, affections and actions)* is not submitted to Christ's authority. Therefore, the life of Christ cannot be formed in this person until he repents and believes and acts on what Jesus Christ has accomplished on the cross.

FAULTY THEOLOGY PROVIDES A COVER FOR SIN

Unfortunately, the false belief that Christians still have a sinful nature also provides a convenient, religious excuse and cover for those Christians who want to keep sinning. In this regard, they should heed the apostle Peter's warning, "Live as free men, but do not use your freedom as a cover-up for evil; live as servants of God (1 Peter 2:16)." Anyone who teaches that Christians have two conflicting inner natures of good and evil, or that God never actually removed our sinful nature through Christ's death, is impeding the church from entering into Christ's fullness and God's eternal purpose. Once again, some teach this falsehood out of spiritual ignorance but others deliberately teach it because they themselves are willfully practicing sin. In their case, Jesus' warning is appropriate, "Woe to you... for you have taken away the key of knowledge; you yourselves did not enter, and you hindered those who were entering (Luke 11:52)."

A HOUSE DIVIDED AGAINST ITSELF CANNOT STAND

When God completed His divine heart transplant through Christ's death on the cross, He did not leave us with two hearts or two natures. If God had left a sinful nature within us, we would be divided in heart and mind. We would be constantly conflicted with two opposing natures and never be able to stand up to Satan's attacks and accusations. Jesus said, "If a house is divided against itself, that house will not be able to stand

(Mark 3:25)." If we still had a sinful nature, the devil would always have a spiritual foothold of sin within us to defeat us. This would have been an incomplete and pitiful salvation that would only be effective to defeat sin and the devil in heaven - not on earth where we need the victory most! But thank God that Christ's death on the cross has given us complete victory over sin! By the cross, Jesus Christ triumphed over the devil. Jesus delivered us not only from the penalty of sin; He also delivered us from the power of sin by destroying and removing our sinful nature. Whoever still has a sinful nature is a child of the devil. That is why our sinful nature had to be removed so that the Holy Spirit could inhabit us and make us saints (holy ones) and sons and daughters of God.

CHRIST HAS FREED US FROM SIN'S CAPTIVITY

The Biblical truth is that Jesus Christ has freed us from sin's power by His death on the cross so that we do not need to practice sin. However, many Christians still believe they have a sinful nature and, therefore, continue to live in sin. Of this situation, the apostle Paul declared, "Shall we continue in sin so that grace may increase? May it never be! How shall we who died to sin still live in it! Or do you not know that all of us who have been baptized *(immersed)* into Christ Jesus have been baptized *(immersed)* into His death (Romans 6:1-3)?" In other words, "Do you not know that you have died to sin, and sin does not have to be master over you anymore?"

Jesus is the first born of God's new creation, His church. Jesus did not have a sinful nature. He was born with a human body and He had a human soul (his personality, will and emotions). However, since Jesus was born of a virgin and God was His Father and indwelt Him, He did not inherit Adam's sinful spiritual nature like we did. This is why He was able to obey God and live a sinless life. Now that we have also been born of God, we no longer have a sinful nature and Christ now dwells in us. Therefore, as the body of Christ, we too are capable of obeying God and not practicing sin by faith in the Son of God who died for us and now lives in us. This is true liberating theology – because *this is the gospel!*

CHRIST DOES NOT SHARE HIS BODY WITH A SINFUL NATURE

To sum up, the Bible is clear that when we were born again, our sinful nature died. The Bible is equally clear that our sinful nature not only died, it was completely removed from us. Our unholy sinful nature is dead and gone! How can we possibly be betrothed as a pure holy virgin to our bridegroom, Jesus Christ (2 Corinthians 11:2), if we still have an adulterous, evil, sinful nature lurking somewhere within our body, which lusts to commit spiritual prostitution and perversion? If we preach and teach anything less than the complete *removal* of our sinful nature by the power of Christ's crucifixion, we are guilty of not proclaiming the true gospel of Jesus Christ and treating as unclean the holy blood of Christ (Hebrews 10:26-31). The gospel truth is Christ's Spirit alone lives within us. Christ does not share His body, His church, which is the temple of the Holy Spirit, with the malignant presence and power of sin. Therefore, we preach and teach the gospel that we are now a holy, new creation in Christ with God's divine nature (2 Corinthians 5:17; Ephesians 4:24; Colossians 1:27; 1 Peter 1:4).

GOD'S PRICELESS GIFT IS TOTAL SALVATION THROUGH CHRIST'S ATONEMENT

Many Christians do not realize the full significance and redemptive power of God's gift of eternal salvation. The gift of salvation is priceless; it was paid for us by the blood of Christ, the Lamb of God. God has given us the gift of total salvation and complete release from sin – not only forgiveness for all our sinful deeds by His Son's death but also deliverance from all the power of sin by including our sinful nature in His Son's death. However, if we reject this precious gift of Christ's life, which God has entrusted within us as a heavenly treasure, by holding to the false belief that we still have a sinful nature in us and then using this as an excuse to practice sin, God will reject us. "From everyone who has been given much, much will be required; and from the one who has been entrusted with much, much more will be required... so take care how you listen *(hear and obey);* for whoever has, to him more shall be given; and whoever does not have, even what he thinks he has shall be taken away from him (Luke 12:48; 8:18)." Only those Christians who receive this word of the cross by faith and wholeheartedly obey it will experience freedom from sin and be able to faithfully serve God as His bondservants (Romans 6:22). Therefore, we pray that God would open the eyes of every believer's heart to see what Jesus Christ has fully accomplished for us on the cross. This is the gospel the apostle Paul preached and this was his testimony: "I have been crucified with Christ and I no longer live but Christ lives in me; and the life that I now live in the body, I live by faith in the Son of God who loved me and gave Himself up for me (Galatians 2:20)."

The Purpose and Meaning of Romans Seven

C hapter Seven of the Book of Romans may be the most misunderstood chapter in the entire New Testament and with the gravest consequences to the Christian faith. Many Christians mistakenly think Romans Chapter Seven highlights the conflict of the two opposing spiritual natures (the old and new) that they believe co-exist within every Christian. However, this is not Biblically correct. In Romans Chapter Six, the apostle Paul taught that God crucified our sinful nature with Christ and removed it from us (Romans 6:6; see also Colossians 2:11). Therefore, if you are born of the Spirit, you now have only one spiritual nature – Christ's holy nature, dwelling in you. The reason why you may keep sinning is not because you still have a sinful nature; it is because your mind still needs to be renewed and your soul transformed by the truth of what Jesus Christ accomplished for you on the cross. The normal Christian experience should be that you sin less and less as you apply this essential truth to your life more and more. God's purpose and provision through Christ's death is that sin would no longer have dominion over you (Romans 6:7 & 14). However, many Christians do not know (believe and act on) the truth that they have died with Christ and that their old sinful nature is dead and gone; therefore, they are overcome by besetting sins and still personally identify with the experience of the "wretched man" in Romans Chapter Seven. Since they are defeated by sin, they mistakenly and tragically conclude that they still have a sinful nature. However, the truth is that God never intended for His people to be overcome by sin; that is why He removed our sinful nature when we were saved.

Note: In Romans Chapter Seven, Paul dramatically uses "the first person" to emphasize the anguish and futility of trying to keep God's Law before you were born again and you still had a sinful nature that was hostile toward God. When reading Romans Chapter Seven, it is important to remember that Paul wrote this epistle in the Greek language, a precise and expressive language which often strategically uses the *present* tense to dramatically describe a *past* action and experience. Therefore, in Chapter Seven, Paul made effective use of this *historical present* tense, as it is called in the Greek language, to vividly describe the futility and misery of a person who wants to serve God but finds himself continually frustrated and sabotaged by his rebellious sinful nature. In writing this chapter, Paul drew from his own past personal experience as a devout Pharisee before he became a born again Christian.

The Purpose of the Law

With this in mind, let us now look at Romans Chapter Seven. The apostle Paul specifically addresses this chapter to his fellow Jews who are following Yeshua ha'Mashiah (Jesus Christ) and know God's Law, but they do not know that in Christ they have died to the Law (Romans 7:1). What is the Law, and what is its divine purpose? The Law, also known as the Mosaic Law or "the Commandments," is a complete system of divine law given by God through Moses to the Hebrews. The Law, which includes the Ten Commandments, is found in its entirety in four books of the Bible (Exodus, Leviticus, Numbers and Deuteronomy). The Law was given to govern man's moral conduct by declaring God's commandments concerning right and wrong. The Law is an exacting standard of statues, which expresses man's duty toward God and man's duty toward his fellow man. Every Jew who was under the Law was expected to keep the whole Law. You were not allowed to pick and choose what part of the Law you wanted to obey and what part of the Law you did not care to obey. This is plainly stated by the apostle James, "For whoever shall keep the whole Law, and yet stumbles in one point, he is guilty of all. For He who said, 'Do not commit adultery,' also said, 'Do not murder.' Now if you do not commit adultery, but you do murder, you have become a transgressor of the Law (James 2:10-11)." Therefore, anyone who is under the Law and breaks just one part of the Law is guilty of breaking the whole Law. "All who rely on observing the Law are under a curse, for it is written, 'Cursed is everyone who does not continue to do *everything* written in the Book of the Law.' Clearly no one is justified before God by keeping the Law (Galatians 3:10-11).'"

No One Can be Justified by the Law

Why can't anyone be justified before God by obeying the Law? Sin uses the Law to strengthen its dominion over anyone who tries to keep the Law. The Bible says, "The power of sin is the Law (1 Corinthians 15:56)." This seeming paradox is a spiritual rule. The more you know God's Law and try to keep His Law, the more you will become aware of the power of your sinful nature (if you are an unbeliever), which will frustrate your every attempt to live by God's Law. In fact, you will never find out how inherently sinful you really are until you try to be holy! As the Bible says, "The Law came so transgression could increase (Romans 5:20)." In this sense, "the Scripture has shut up everyone under sin (Galatians 3:22)." This was certainly Paul's own past experience when he was a dedicated Pharisee who was zealous to keep the Law (but still an unbeliever in Christ). "For when we were in our sinful nature, the passions of sin which were aroused by the Law were at work in our members to bear fruit for death (Romans 7:5). This can also be the experience of a born again Christian who is trying to live a holy life for Christ, but yet still thinks he has a sinful nature.

To sum up our three points concerning the Law: 1) The Law was given to the Jews (not the Gentiles); 2) The Jews had to obey the whole Law, not just selected parts of the Law; and 3) Every Jew under the Law was guilty of breaking the Law. "Therefore, no one will be declared righteous in His sight by keeping the Law; rather, through the Law we become conscious of sin… for all have sinned and fall short of the glory of God (Romans 3:20, 23)." This brings us to our next point. If everyone under the Law is guilty of breaking the Law, then why did God give the Law?

THE LAW IS A TUTOR TO LEAD US TO CHRIST

The Bible says the Law was given for our good to lead us to faith in Christ. This is clearly stated by the apostle Paul. "Therefore the Law has become our tutor to lead us to Christ, so that we may be justified by faith (Galatians 3:24)." The Bible says "The Law is holy, and the Commandment is holy and righteous and good. Therefore, did that which is good become a cause of death for me? May it never be! Rather it was sin, in order that it might be shown to be sin by effecting my death through that which is good (Romans 7:12-13)." The Law, which is God's holy standard or plumbline, places exacting demands on us to reveal that we are lawbreakers and show us that, in our own moral strength, we cannot overcome sin. Paul describes this tutoring "pre-Christian" experience in the first person since he himself had already gone through it. "I would not have come to know sin except through the Law… so that through the Commandment, sin would become utterly sinful... the Law is spiritual, but I have a sinful nature, sold into bondage to sin... for I know that nothing good dwells in me; that is, in my sinful nature, for the willing is present in me, but the doing of good is not (Romans 7:7, 13-24, 18)." God knows who I am; He now wants me to know who I am. God already knows that I am a sinner before I am saved; the Law was given so that I would also know I am a sinner. Before prescribing the cure for us, which is Christ, God must first diagnose our condition, which is indwelling sin. Thus the Law exposes our sin, and the outcome of sin is spiritual death. "I was once alive apart from the Law; but when the Commandment came, sin became alive and I died; and this Commandment, which was to result in life, proved to result in death for me; for sin, taking an opportunity through the Commandment, deceived me and through it killed me (Romans 7:9-10)."

The Law Exposes Man's Sinfulness

Therefore, the purpose of the Law was to reveal our utter sinfulness and spiritual death so that we might cry out to God for His salvation in Christ. Thus, in Romans 7:14-24, Paul is describing a fellow Jew who is trying very hard to keep God's Law. However, this frustrating and miserable experience could also apply to a Christian who is trying to be morally good and live according to the Bible's moral law, but who does not know that his old sinful nature is dead and gone. A Jew is erroneously told the solution is to study the Law because "the more he knows the Law, the more he will be able to keep the Law." In the same way, a Christian is erroneously told the solution is to read the Bible more because "the more he knows the Bible; the more he will be able to live according to the Bible." However, this is not the way God works. As we said before, you will never find out how really entrenched you are in the habit of sinning until you really try to overcome sin. The more a Jew knows the Law, the more he becomes aware of his sins. The same principle also applies to a Christian. In fact, Jesus said our righteousness under the New Covenant must exceed the righteousness of the Pharisees under the Old Covenant (Matthew 5:20). Thus, in the Sermon on the Mount, Jesus gives a more exacting and demanding standard of holiness that is required to enter the kingdom of heaven (see Matthew Chapters 5-7).

GREATER LIGHT PRODUCES GREATER ACCOUNTABILITY

Consequently, the more a Christian knows God's Word, the more he realizes God's standard of holiness is higher than he thought. He knew God would judge his deeds (2 Corinthians 5:10; 1 Peter 1:17) but he now realizes God will judge even his words (Matthew 12:36-37). The more he becomes aware of God's standard of holiness, the more he becomes conscious of his own besetting sins and sin's power over his life. But then he hears another sermon on trying harder to be a good Christian (with the "help" of the Holy Spirit sometimes added in). This erroneous teaching encourages him to decide that he can overcome sin if he just doubles his efforts and goes to church more, reads the Bible more, prays more, gives more, and is involved in ministry more. Yet, once again, the spiritual principle of "greater light produces greater accountability" puts him in a vice grip. And it is meant to do this. For as Paul declared," I would not have come to know sin except through the Law; for I would not have known about coveting if the Law had not said, 'You shall not covet.' But sin, taking opportunity through the commandment, produced in me coveting of every kind; for apart from the Law sin is dead (Romans 7:7-8)."

Thus the more a religious non-Christian or a spiritually ignorant born-again Christian knows God's Word, the more the crushing reality becomes apparent: God's standard of holiness is not merely difficult, it is impossible to fulfill outside of faith in Christ. In despair, he now realizes God will judge not only his words but his very thoughts (Romans 12:16; 1 Corinthians 4:5; Hebrews 4:12). If he is really zealous, he will try to redouble his efforts and try to be even more self-disciplined. But as he redoubles his efforts, he finds himself on a treadmill that is going faster and faster. Yet he is afraid to step off this treadmill and find rest because he thinks he will backslide if he does (and sometimes he does, in an effort to find relief).

Christ Has Delivered Us From Our Sinful Nature

This is the awful dilemma that many sincere Christians find themselves in when they are trying very hard to live a moral life. If you were to ask them if Jesus' yoke was easy and His burden was light, they would inwardly groan from the weight of the yoke under which they labor. At this point (which can take one year or forty, depending on the person's moral self-confidence) many Christians reach a crisis of faith, which leads them to several possible outcomes. Some Christians get angry at God for seemingly giving them a standard of holiness they cannot possibly achieve and they fall away from the faith. Or, they may think they have failed both God and themselves and drift away from the faith because what they think is Christianity, as they experienced it, only brought them impossible stress, condemnation and exhaustion. Or, even worse, they may decide to continue going to church but stop trying to be holy. They may comfort themselves with the thought that everyone else in church is in the same condition as they are – very imperfect yet forgiven. They then settle for much less than God intended - either a life dominated by chronically practicing sin or becoming more religious and ministry-minded but never coming into a knowledge of the truth (2 Timothy 3:7).

And yet others, when the Law has accomplished its divine purpose and exposed their utter sinfulness, may come to the same spiritual place Paul came to. In this case, when you have come to the end of your own abilities and resources and your own righteousness, you will cry out to God, "What a wretched sinful man I am! Who can deliver me from my sinful nature?" Now this is the right response. You no longer ask "what" can deliver you but "who" can deliver you. Having already gone through this experience, Paul's sure answer is, "Thanks be to God through Jesus Christ our Lord! (Romans 7:25)." The truth is that Jesus Christ has already delivered you from your sinful nature and freed you from the tyranny of sin. However, if you do not know this divine truth by faith, then you cannot experience this spiritual freedom and rest, which Christ purchased for you by His death. As Paul wrote to Christians in Romans Chapter Six, "Don't you know that your sinful nature has died with Christ? For he who has died has been freed from the power of sin."

In Christ, We Died to Sin and the Law

In Romans Chapter Seven, Paul explains that not only have we died to sin, but we also died to the Law. "Don't you know, brethren, that the Law has jurisdiction over a person only as long as he lives (Romans 7:1)?" Thus Romans Chapter Six deals with our freedom from sin while Chapter Seven deals with our freedom from the Law. For the Jew this means freedom from trying to keep the Law of Moses; for the Gentile this means freedom from the condemnation incurred by trying to keep (and failing to keep) the moral law. In Romans Chapter Six, Paul taught that when we were saved, we died to sin (Romans 6:2, 7, 11). Now, in Romans Seven, he teaches that when we were saved, we also died to the Law. How did we die to the Law? The same way we died to sin. When Christ died on the cross, the Bible says that we also died with Him so that we would be freed from the Law.

Paul declares, "You also died to the Law through the body of Christ, so that you might be joined to another, to Him who was raised from the dead, in order that we might bear fruit for God (Romans 7:4)." We could never be freed from the power of sin and the condemnation of failing to keep God's Law until we died. Therefore, God spiritually included us in Christ's death so that when He died, we died with Him. "What the Law was powerless to do because of man's sinful nature, God did by sending His Son (Romans 8:20)." For those who long to bear fruit for God and bring glory to His Name, this is indeed good news.

We Are No Longer Under Law But Under Grace

But why was it necessary for us to die not only to sin but also to the Law? Since we no longer have a sinful nature, why can't we now obey God's Law? The answer is that we cannot obey the holy requirements of the Law even after God removed our sinful nature; only Christ can fulfill the Law. We are incapable in our natural moral strength of keeping the Law. As long as we believe that we are under the Law, sin will still have dominion over us. This is why we died to the Law so that we might be joined to Christ who then fulfills the Law by living through us. This leads us to our next point concerning the Law. The only way to escape the domination and condemnation of the Law and sin is to come under grace. Therefore, when you are in Christ, you are no longer under the Law; you are under grace. "For the Law was given through Moses; grace and truth came through Jesus Christ (John 1:17)." This is what Paul clearly taught in Romans Chapter Six. "Sin shall not be master over you: for you are not under Law, but under grace (Romans 6:14)."

What does "grace" mean? The Law means I must do something to obtain God's righteousness; grace means God does something to impute

His righteousness to me. Therefore, righteousness based on the Law depends on my work; righteousness based on grace depends on God's work. This is the difference between the Law and grace. Grace and the Law are mutually exclusive. You cannot be under grace and be under the Law at the same time. If you are under grace, then you are not under the Law. Whether you are a Jew or a Gentile, once you trust Christ for your salvation, He becomes your righteousness. "Christ is the end of the Law for righteousness to everyone who believes (Romans 10:5)." This is why the apostle Paul stated, "By His doing, you are in Christ Jesus, who has become for us wisdom from God, and righteousness and sanctification and redemption (1 Corinthians 1:30)." Once you are in Christ, your righteousness no longer depends on your ability to keep the Law. "But now we have been released from the Law, having died to that to which we were bound, so that we serve in newness of Spirit and not in oldness of letter (Romans 7:6)." Serving in the newness of Spirit means we are no longer under the "law of works" but we are now under the "law of faith (Romans 3:27)." When the eyes of your heart are opened to see this in Christ, this is real freedom!

Do Not be Subject Again
to a Yoke of Slavery

Therefore, Paul's purpose in writing Romans Chapter Seven was to persuade his fellow Jews that when they received Jesus as the Messiah, they died to the Law so that they might be joined to Christ and bear the spiritual fruit of God's righteousness. Paul uses his own past experience as a Pharisee to describe a person who is zealous to obey God's Law but whose sinful nature frustrates him and makes him unable to do so. However, this could also be the experience of any Christian who is zealous to serve God but does not know that God removed his sinful nature through the cross of Christ. The truth is no born again Christian, whether Jew or Gentile, has a sinful nature and no Christian, whether Jew or Gentile, is under the Law! "When you were dead in your sins and in the uncircumcision of your sinful nature, God made you alive with Christ. He forgave us all our sins, having *canceled the written code,* with its regulations, that was against us and that stood opposed to us; He took it away, nailing it to the cross. And having disarmed the powers and authorities, He made a public spectacle of them, triumphing over them by the cross (Colossians 2:13-14)." What a triumph! What a victory! Thanks be to God!

Paul here declares that the Law, with its written code of regulations, was cancelled and removed from us by Christ's death on the cross (Note: In Colossians 2:11, Paul also declared our sinful nature was removed from us by Christ). Thus by Christ's death on the cross, we have been set free from both the dominion of sin and the dominion of the Law. "Through Him everyone who believes is freed from all things, from which you could not be freed through the Law of Moses (Acts 13:39)." For a Jew, the Law of Moses was like an unscalable, towering mountain that you had to try to climb each day to be right before God even though you knew from past experience that you would continually fail and fall. This is why the apostle Peter called the Law of Moses "a yoke which neither our fathers nor we have been able to bear (Acts 15:10)." This is why the ministry of the Law under the Old Covenant is called the "ministry of death and condemnation;" whereas, in contrast, the ministry of the Spirit of life under the New Covenant is called the "ministry of righteousness (2 Corinthians 3:7-9)." To be freed from the crushing burden of the Law was to be free indeed. Paul prized this spiritual freedom from the Law of Moses so highly that he declared, "It was for freedom that Christ has set us free. Stand firm, then, and do not be burdened again by a yoke of slavery (Galatians 5:1)." This is also why Paul warned others that they must never allow themselves to come under the Law, not even a part of the Law. "You have been severed from Christ, you who are seeking to be justified by the Law; you have fallen from grace (Galatians 5:4)."

CHRIST IS THE FULFILLMENT OF THE LAW

Paul also confirmed the divine truth that we are freed from the Law in his letter to the Ephesians. "For He Himself is our peace, who made both groups into one and broke down the dividing wall, *by abolishing in His flesh the enmity, which is the Law of Commandments* contained in ordinances, so that in Himself He might make the two into one new man, thus establishing peace, and might reconcile both in one body to God through the cross, by it having put to death the enmity (Ephesians 2:14-16)." Paul here explained that Christ, through His death on the cross, has done away with the Law of Moses, which was the great dividing barrier between the Jews and Gentiles, and has now made it possible for Jews and Gentiles, through faith in Christ, to be reconciled to both God and each other as members of Christ's body.

However, it is important to point out that the requirement of obeying the Law to be righteous is only taken away for those whom God has made righteous through faith in Christ. Christ is the end of the Law for the believer as a means of achieving righteousness. "Knowing that a man is not justified by observing the Law, but by faith in Jesus Christ (Galatians 2:16)." For a Christian, Christ is the end of the Law because He is the fulfillment of the Law. Jesus said, "Do not think that I have come to abolish the Law or the prophets; I have not come to abolish them but to fulfill them (Matthew 5:17)." However, for those who are still unbelieving sinners, the Law is neither abolished nor fulfilled. This different relationship of the Law to the righteous and the unrighteous is made clear by Paul when he wrote, "The Law is not made for a righteous person, but for the lawless and insubordinate, for the ungodly and for sinners, for the unholy and profane (1 Timothy 1:8-10)." This is why Jesus said, "For truly I say to you, until heaven and earth pass away, not the smallest letter of stroke shall pass from the Law until all is accomplished (Matthew 5:18/see also Luke 16:17)." The Law is still necessary to convict the unrighteous of their sin.

WHEN WE ARE LED BY THE SPIRIT, WE FULFILL THE LAW

Paul further clarified this when he said, "If you are led by the Spirit, you are not under the Law (Galatians 5:18)." To be led by the Spirit we must not only be born of the Spirit; we must be genuinely governed by the Spirit. Paul also said, "For as many as are led by the Spirit of God, they are the sons of God (Romans 8:14)." From these two verses we can conclude that the sons of God, who have been born of the Spirit (whether Jew or Gentile), are not under the Law because they are now under grace and led by the Spirit. "But now that faith has come, we are no longer under a tutor (Galatians 3:25)." Therefore, "God has made us adequate as servants of a New Covenant, not of the letter but of the Spirit; for the letter kills, but the Spirit gives life (2 Corinthians 3:6)." Since we are no longer under the Law, does this mean we are then to be lawless? Of course not! As Paul declares, "What then? Shall we sin because we are not under Law but under grace? May it never be! (Romans 6:15)." The Bible says we are under grace "so that the righteous requirement of the Law might be fulfilled in us who do not walk according to the flesh *(the sinful nature)* but according to the Spirit (Romans 8:4)." Once again, this means we must be ruled by the Spirit, which is now possible through faith in Christ's completed work on the cross. "Do we then nullify the Law through faith? May it never be! On the contrary, we establish the Law (Romans 3:31)."

Love is the Fulfillment of the Law

How is the righteous requirement of the Law fulfilled in us when we walk by the Spirit? Jesus declared the righteous requirement of the entire Law can be summed up by the following commandment: "You shall love the Lord your God with all your heart and all your soul and with all your mind *(and)* you shall love your neighbor as yourself (Matthew 22:37-39)." The apostle Paul proclaimed this same truth when he taught, "The whole Law is fulfilled in a single word, in the statement, 'You shall love your neighbor as yourself (Galatians 3:14)'" and "Owe nothing to anyone except to love one another; for he who loves his neighbor has fulfilled the Law... love does no wrong to a neighbor; therefore, love is the fulfillment of the Law (Romans 13:8-10)." The apostle James called this the royal law. "If, however, you are fulfilling the royal law according to the Scripture, 'You shall love your neighbor as yourself,' you are doing well (James 2:8)." Thus the standard of righteousness, which is revealed by the Law of Moses in the Old Covenant, and the standard of righteousness, which is revealed by the gospel of Christ in the New Covenant, are one and the same and can be summed up in one word – *love* - to love God and love man. Therefore, the difference between the Old Covenant and the New Covenant is not in God's righteous standard but in His divine means to achieve this righteousness.

What the Old Covenant Law was unable to accomplish because of man's sinful nature, God accomplished in the New Covenant through His Son's death. When Christ died on the cross, God performed a divine heart transplant and exchanged our terminally sin-sick heart with His Son's divine heart. By the cross of Christ, we have been forever freed from the power of sin. "And through Him everyone who believes is freed from all things, from which you could not be freed through the Law of Moses (Acts 13:39)." We no longer have a sinful nature, which would render us powerless to obey

God. By the cross of Christ, our old nature is forever gone and we are now a new creation in Christ. The Bible says our old nature died with Christ; was buried with Christ; and our new nature has been raised with Christ. This is the Christian faith. Because we now have Christ's holy nature, we are able to obey God, overcome sin and live the royal law of love. "For the law of the Spirit of life in Christ Jesus has set you free from the law of sin and death (Romans 8:2)." The apostle James calls this law of the Spirit "the perfect law of liberty (James 1:25)." The apostle Paul simply calls it the "law of Christ" since Christ, who lives in us, enables us to fulfill God's Law (1 Corinthians 9:21; Galatians 6:2).

THE NEW COVENANT IS GOD'S DIVINE HEART TRANSPLANT

This divine heart transplant is the fulfillment of the Old Covenant prophecies, the promise of the New Covenant, the purpose of Christ's Atonement and the power of Christ's gospel (Colossians 1:27). This divine heart transplant was promised by the Old Testament prophet Ezekiel, "I will give you a new heart and put a new spirit within you; and I will remove the heart of stone from your flesh. I will put My Spirit within you and cause you to walk in My statutes and you will be careful to observe My ordinances (Ezekiel 36:26-27)." It was also promised by the prophet Jeremiah, "Behold, the days are coming, declares the Lord, when I will make a New Covenant... I will put My Law within them and on their heart I will write it; and I will be their God and they shall be My people (Jeremiah 31:31-33)." This is why the New Covenant is called a "better covenant, which has been enacted on better promises (Hebrews 8:6)." Because we have received the New Covenant promise of God's divine heart transplant, we can now walk in the Spirit by faith in Jesus Christ and what He has accomplished for us on the cross.

What can we then conclude from Romans Chapter Seven? Paul wrote this passage to his fellow Jews who "have a zeal for God but not in accordance with knowledge. For not knowing about God's righteousness and seeking to establish their own, they did not subject themselves to the righteousness of God (Romans 10:2-3)." Tragically, this is also the normal experience for many Christians who do not know that their old sinful nature died, through the body of Christ, to both sin and the Law. Since they do not know the truth that God has removed their sinful nature through Christ's death, they remain a slave to sin in their personal experience. Since they do not know they died to the Law, they impotently try to obey God's Law by their natural moral strength. Like the Jews who do not know what Christ has accomplished for them through the cross, they are trying to establish their own righteousness instead of submitting themselves to Christ's righteousness. Paul wrote of this, "I do not nullify the grace of God, for if righteousness came through the Law, then Christ died needlessly (Galatians 2:21)."

WE ARE FREED FROM SIN AND THE LAW TO SERVE GOD IN THE SPIRIT

God does not want His people to be lawless and habitually overcome by sin. Neither does He want them to pursue a man-made morality and form of godliness apart from faith in Christ's crucifixion and sovereignty. Those who teach that the miserable soul enslaved to sin in Romans Chapter Seven is a portrait of the normal Christian life should repent from this misunderstanding of the Scriptures and begin to lead God's people into the truth. Otherwise, they will incur God's judgment for keeping His people captive to sin and lawlessness. The apostle Paul declared the way of deliverance in Romans 7:25 to anyone who finds himself caught in this wretched state when he proclaimed that Jesus Christ has freed us from our sinful nature (this body of death). When you are at the end of yourself and ready to be delivered from the power of sin, God will reveal the divine heart transplant that He has provided you through His Son's death on the cross. In Christ, we have been freed from sin and the Law so that we might serve God in the Spirit. This powerful and liberating truth was Paul's testimony, "I have been crucified with Christ and I no longer live, but Christ lives in me and the life that I now live in this body, I live by faith in the Son of God (Galatians 2:20)."

APPENDIX C:

Questions and Answers

Q1.   Why did God allow His Son, Jesus Christ, to be crucified?

Q2.   What is the gospel of Christ crucified?

Q3.   Why do you emphasize Christ crucified instead of Christ risen?

Q4.   Why does your teaching have the recurrent theme of Christ's crucifixion?

Q5.   When the apostle Paul reviews the facts (1 Corinthians 15:3) upon which the gospel is based, why does he list "Christ died for our sins" but not "we died with Christ?"

Q6.   What does the Bible mean by "we have been crucified with Christ?"

Q7.   Why not just proclaim Jesus Christ instead of focusing on Christ crucified?

Q8.   Where does the Bible say our sinful nature is dead after we receive Christ?

Q9.   Why do some Christians think our sinful nature has died but not been removed from us?

Q10. Aren't we just "reformed sinners" after we are saved?

Q11. If my sinful nature is dead and removed, then why do I keep on sinning?

Q12. Are you teaching that we will never sin again?

Q13. Isn't this just the same basic teaching we heard when we were water baptized?

Q14. Why is the message of the cross so important to the church?

Q15. How do we know the removal of the "body of flesh" in Colossians 2:11 refers to our sinful nature?

Q16. In Galatians 2:20, the apostle Paul says it is not I but Christ who dwells in me. But then in Romans 7:17, Paul says it is not I but sin which dwells in me. How do we reconcile these two contradictory statements?

Q17. Don't Christians just have two natures, like a white dog and a black dog fighting within them, and whichever one they feed the most gets stronger?

Q18. I do not find the term "the divine exchange" in the Bible. What is this?

Q19. Isn't faith in Jesus all that I need?

Q20. But doesn't the message of the cross add to the gospel? Didn't Jesus just ask people to just believe in Him?

Q21. If our old man of sin (our sinful nature) has died and been removed, then why does the apostle Paul tell us to put off the old man and put on the new man?

Q22.　Do I need to believe I died with Christ in order to be His disciple?

Q23.　I want to believe I died to sin. However, I can't seem to get past just mentally understanding this concept and I still can't stop practicing sin. What can I do?

Q24.　What did the apostle Paul mean when he said he wanted to be conformed to Christ's death (Philippians 3:10) when he already had said he was crucified with Christ (Galatians 2:20)?

Q25.　Is the apostle Paul's gospel different than the other apostles' gospel?

Q26.　What did Jesus mean when He said we must "bear our own cross?"

Q27.　What did Jesus mean when He said we must "lose our soul-life?"

Q28.　I thought I was already holy in God's eyes because of Jesus' Atonement. Then why should practicing holiness be important to me?

Q29.　What does the "Spirit-filled life" mean and how do I live it?

Q30.　How can the church fulfill God's eternal purpose?

Q1.　Why did God allow His Son, Jesus Christ, to be crucified?

　　A1.　God has a Father's heart. Every good earthly father lovingly wants to have fellowship with his children. Every good earthly father hopes that, after his constant love and sacrifice, the end result will be a relationship of real affection and trust with his children. Every good father hopes that his children will thankfully acknowledge him and recognize his selfless love by responding with a love of their own. This is the desire of every good earthly father, and even more so, the desire of our heavenly Father! And so God created man to have a divine family and to have spiritual fellowship, but man chose to break that fellowship through disobedience and rebellion. Yet God knew that man would rebel against Him and be lost in spiritual darkness and death. In His eternal foresight, God planned for this event. Thus God, in His Father's love, procured our redemption from spiritual separation through Christ's obedience (even to death on the cross). Jesus Christ was crucified for this purpose: to redeem God's children back to Himself and restore our fellowship and communion with Him. "This is eternal life, that they may know You, the only true God, and Jesus Christ whom You have sent (John 17:3)."

To fulfill the desire of His Father's heart, Jesus Christ died on the cross to provide for our complete redemption and reconciliation to God. "For if, when we were God's enemies, we were reconciled to Him through the death of His Son, how much more, having been reconciled, we shall be saved by His life (Romans 5:10)." Therefore, Christ not only died to provide us forgiveness for our sins; He died to provide us freedom from our sinful nature. For when Christ died on the cross, God performed a divine heart transplant. God exchanged our terminally sin-sick heart with Christ's divine heart so that we would no longer be slaves to sin but would be sons and daughters of God. "When the fullness of the time came, God sent forth His Son, born of a woman, born under the Law, so that He might redeem those who were under the Law, that they may receive adoption as sons. Because you are sons, God has sent forth the Spirit of His Son into our hearts, crying, 'Abba! Father! (Galatians 4:4-6).'" This is the divine transformation that occurred within us when we received Jesus Christ as our Lord and Savior and were born again of the Spirit. Whereas once we had been naturally born into sin and were the captive children of the devil; now, by Christ's death on the cross, we have been born again of God's Spirit so we might be His holy sons and daughters. Thus Christ's death on the cross was planned by God before time began and is the most momentous event in human history and the eternal triumph of God's love.

Jesus Christ's willingness to be crucified for fallen mankind was a witness to the heavenly host of the Father's righteousness and selfless love. When just one person comes into a relationship with God because of Christ's death on the cross and then values the Person of God so much that he lays aside his very life – "selling all for the Pearl of Great Price" – when just one person "sees" God to the extent that they respond by turning away from all forms of evil and they begin to practice doing the will of God, this brings glory to God. It reveals to all the heavenly creation who God is, because all the heavenly host know the magnetic power and pull of sin. When just one person sees and knows God enough to choose God instead of choosing sin – that reveals the power and majesty of God. "No one who continues to sin has either seen Him or known Him (1 John 3:6)."

Therefore, Jesus Christ died for this purpose: to bring God His just due of glory and honor and majesty – that mankind, so born of the earth, could be reborn into the heavenly realm and "see" God and, therefore, know God the Father and fellowship with Him. Jesus said, "The glory which You have given Me I have given them, that they may be one, just as We are one; I in them and You in Me, that they may be perfected in unity, so that the world may know that You sent Me, and loved them, even as You have loved Me (John 17:22-23)."

Q2.   What is the gospel of Christ crucified?

A2.   The gospel of Jesus Christ and His crucifixion is the cornerstone of the house of God, His church (1 Corinthians 1:18, 23; 2:2; 3:11). The gospel of Christ crucified can be summed up as follows: Christ died for us and included us in His death so that He might sovereignly live in us (Romans 5:8; 6:6; Galatians 2:20).

Here is a fuller explanation of this glorious gospel: Jesus Christ was crucified as the sacrificial Lamb of God to redeem us from slavery to sin. By His death, Jesus Christ purchased for us forgiveness from the penalty of our sins as well as deliverance from the power of sin. When Christ was crucified, we were crucified with Him. Therefore, our old man of sin (our sinful nature) died with Christ and Christ now lives in us through His Holy Spirit. Thus, by the power of His crucifixion, Jesus Christ exchanged our sinful nature with His holy nature. We might consider this a divine heart transplant by which God replaced our terminally sin-sick heart with His Son's divine heart and saved us from the power of sin and certain doom. The power of Christ's crucifixion is, therefore, the foundation of our entire relationship with God - our justification and salvation, our spiritual life and growth, our sanctification and transformation, and ultimately our glorification and co-regency with Christ. This is why God the Father ordained the practice of water baptism for all new disciples because baptism outwardly expresses our spiritual union with Jesus Christ and His death, burial and resurrection. Water baptism should continually remind the church how the power of Christ's death on the cross has spiritually transformed us by removing our sinful nature and making us a holy new creation in Christ.

Some Christians might think this is the ABCs of the gospel. Yes, it is the ABCs, but it is also the XYZs. Our faith must begin and end with the power of Christ's crucifixion. The trouble is that many of us have bypassed the cross of Christ and are trying to grow in Christ by our own will-power and natural strength. This is Galatianism. Having started our Christian life in the Spirit, we are now trying to perfect ourselves in the soul (Galatians 3:3). This is a wrong and dangerous path. The Bible says Jesus Christ is not only the author of our faith; He is also the finisher or perfecter of our faith (Hebrews 12:2). When we live by the power of our soul instead of by the power of the Spirit, we are living in unbelief and actually strengthening our will to be independent of God. If we persist in not having faith in the power of Christ's Atonement, our unbelief becomes disobedience to God's Word, lawlessness to the Holy Spirit and a gateway to demonic deception even though it may outwardly appear that we are behaving in a righteous "Christian" manner.

However, when we know we have been crucified with Christ, we will realize that we no longer live but Christ is our life. In other words, we will know our old sinful nature is dead and removed and, in its place, the Holy Spirit now indwells us. When we know we have died with Christ, we will see the futility and evil of depending on our natural personality and ability to try to live the Christian life and do Christ's work. From that time on, we will want to no longer depend on our natural ability to serve Christ but instead we will want look by faith to Jesus Christ, the Son of God, to sovereignly live His life through us as our Lord and King.

Q3.   Why do you emphasize Christ crucified instead of Christ risen?

A3.   A similar question might be asked why the apostle Paul focused his foundational teaching on Christ crucified rather than Christ risen? Paul and his fellow apostles were determined to proclaim nothing else except Jesus Christ and Him crucified (1 Corinthians 1:23; 2:2). Of course, the whole gospel that Paul and the other apostles preached included both the crucifixion and resurrection of Jesus Christ. Therefore, it's not a question of the relative importance of Christ's crucifixion and resurrection but of their divine order. The importance of the resurrection of Jesus Christ cannot be overstated. As the apostle Paul declared, "If Christ has not risen, then our faith is worthless and our preaching is futile (1 Corinthians 15:14-17)." However, there is a divine principle: Death must come before resurrection life (Romans 6:5; 1 Corinthians 15:42).

Therefore to enter into the power of Christ's resurrection, we must first enter into the power of Christ's crucifixion. This divine fact is clearly portrayed through the practice of water baptism. Water baptism outwardly demonstrates the spiritual regeneration that inwardly occurred within us when we were saved. In water baptism, our old man (or sinful nature) is symbolically immersed or buried in a watery "grave," after which we are raised or resurrected from this "grave" as a new man in Christ. Water baptism, therefore, illustrates the Biblical truth that our sinful nature had to die and be removed before Jesus Christ could sovereignly live in us. This is what it means to be born again of the Spirit.

Until we see by divine revelation that God has dealt a death-blow (our co-crucifixion with Christ) to our sinful nature, we can mistakenly think we possess (even if we acknowledge we are weak) something of spiritual virtue within ourselves, which makes us morally able to serve Christ. However, God wants us to know that the central purpose of the cross was to make sure our sinful nature died with Christ. When we see God's verdict for our sinful nature was a death sentence (execution not reformation), we will cease to have any confidence in our natural ability to reproduce Christ's life. As we abide in the power of Christ's crucifixion, we will then experience the power of His resurrection. This is the true Christian life as God ordained it and the apostle Paul described it in Galatians 2:20, "I have been crucified with Christ and I no longer live but Christ lives in me; and the life which I live in the body I live by faith in the Son of God who loved me and gave Himself up for me."

Q4.   Why does your teaching have the recurrent theme of Christ's crucifixion?

A4.   Most Christians agree that the ultimate goal of the gospel is to produce a church that is holy and devoted to Christ and through which Christ can wholly express Himself (2 Corinthians 11:2-3; 13:5; Ephesians 1:23; 2:2; 3:10-11; 5:25-27; Colossians 1:22. 27). Yet there are many different opinions among Christians on the way to achieve this goal. We are convinced that believing and acting on what Jesus accomplished on the cross is the only way to fully realize God's eternal purpose. Jesus Himself said, "I am the way (John 14:6)," and that the power of His crucifixion would spiritually draw the elect to Himself (John 12:32). We are also convinced that only the cross of Christ can provide total victory over sin, the world and the devil.

Therefore, we believe the gospel of Christ crucified is the only sure foundation for the birth, growth and vitality of the church. Like the apostle Paul, we are determined to proclaim nothing else except Jesus Christ and Him crucified (1 Corinthians 2:2). We believe teaching on all other Christian subjects such as church or body life, evangelism, ministry, marriage, parenting, relationships, spiritual fruit, spiritual gifts, praise and worship and spiritual warfare must always be grounded and centered in this truth – the victory of the cross of Christ. The cross is the fixed center of true Christianity. All other Christian teachings are like spokes of the wheel, which radiate out from the hub - the cross of Christ. For example, if the spokes of a wheel are not properly aligned with the hub, the wheel itself can become distorted and eventually warped. In the same way, if Christian teachings are not properly aligned with *(interpreted from)* the central doctrinal truth of the cross of Christ, this "off-alignment" will produce a distorted and warped version of Christianity. The cross is the very basis of our relationship with Jesus Christ and His holy work in us. We may be saved, but unless our spiritual eyes are opened to believe and act on what Christ has accomplished through His death on the cross, we will not be able to consistently walk in holiness and know and express Christ in fullness.

Without the power of the cross in our lives, Christianity becomes a Biblical behavioral standard or cultural model to try to follow by our best efforts rather than believing that Jesus Christ can live His life in us. This might be called churchianity rather than Christianity. Teaching about Christianity without focusing on the cross of Christ would be like teaching how the solar system works and omitting the power of the sun. Such a world would be lifeless! That is why the apostle Paul always emphasized the power of Christ's crucifixion when establishing the first century church. Consequently, all of Paul's subsequent teaching on church life and ministry was based on the assumption that the Christians in his field of work already knew their inclusion in the cross of Christ was the foundation of the New Covenant. Whenever Paul discovered that any of the churches that he had planted had strayed from this message of Christ crucified, he would always remind them of this vital truth of the cross (see Romans 6:1-11; 1 Corinthians 1:17-18, 23; 2:2; 3:16; 6:19; 2 Corinthians 13:5; Galatians 2:20-21; 3:1-5).

Q5.   When the apostle Paul reviews the facts (1 Corinthians 15:3) upon which the gospel is based, why does he list "Christ died for our sins" but not "we died with Christ?"

   A5.   "We died with Christ" is a divine event that occurred simultaneously when "Christ died for us." Therefore, this provision of Christ's Atonement is included in the gospel which declares Christ died for us. This is the full divine meaning of what happened when Jesus Christ was crucified. Jesus died to free us from the penalty of our sins; He also died to free us from the power of sin. God accomplished this latter provision of Christ's Atonement by spiritually including us in Christ's death on the cross. God intended that this truth be taught to new believers immediately upon their salvation by means of water baptism. Whenever someone was saved in the first century church, they were normally water baptized that same day. This is God's way for all new disciples to be immediately instructed and for the whole church to be continually reminded that their old sin-driven nature is dead, buried and removed and they are now a new spiritual person in Christ, capable of being Spirit-led and overcoming sin.

It is not necessary to understand the full implications of "you died with Christ" to be saved. However, once you are saved, it is essential to believe this vital truth of the gospel. Otherwise, you will not be able to come into your full inheritance in Christ because knowing that you have died with Christ is the door that leads to sanctification and truly knowing Christ and walking in His power.

Q6.   What does the Bible mean by "we have been crucified with Christ?"

A6.   It is essential that we understand what this Biblical truth means. Otherwise our spiritual growth in Christ will be stunted and may even die. Since there are common misconceptions about what the apostle Paul meant by this statement (see Romans 6:6; Galatians 2:20 and 6:14), we will first examine these misunderstandings.

First of all, Paul did not mean that we must now emotionally identify with Christ's torturous death on the cross to be holy. He didn't mean we must vicariously experience Christ's death by visualizing and empathizing with the physical pain and spiritual darkness of His crucifixion before we can appreciate our salvation. This is a man-made idea that is soulish and therefore ineffectual. It cannot substitute for true understanding of the transforming power of the cross of Christ within us.

Paul also did not mean that we must now crucify ourselves to be holy. Many Christians mistakenly practice some form of counterfeit crucifixion because they have never been accurately taught what Jesus Christ accomplished for them on the cross (by removing their sinful nature and replacing it with His nature). They find themselves continually tripped up by sin and regret their spiritual weakness and their failure to lead a holy life. As a result, they become preoccupied with the power of sin and their inability to conquer it. They naturally think that if only they were stronger, they could finally overcome sin. Therefore, they redouble their "religious" efforts. But this only makes them more "religious" and does not deliver them from the power and deception of sin. Other Christians try to put to death their sinful nature (even though Christ has already done that) through self-denial and self-sacrifice. However, this focus on self-discipline is self-motivated and self-empowered. It is impossible for self to kill self. Self can only reinforce and strengthen self, which leads to pride and further alienation from God.

Our willpower or self-determination will never be strong enough to overcome Satan and the deceitful power of sin. These efforts at controlling and dealing with the "sin question" pale in the light of the cross of Christ. They are self-deceiving and self-defeating. They are not what the Bible means to be crucified with Christ. The idea that we must crucify ourselves through self-discipline and self-denial originates from man and not God and is self-destructive. There are many subtle variations of this kind of counterfeit crucifixion. For example, many Christians think that when they suffer affliction, they are "bearing their own cross." Although God certainly uses adversity to achieve His eternal purpose in us, this is not what Jesus meant when He said we must bear our own cross. Unfortunately without sound Biblical teaching on this subject, we can simply develop a soulish capacity to stoically endure adversity, rather than coming into a divine revelation of what it means to be crucified with Christ.

Besides these well-intended but misguided efforts, one of the more deceptive ways that Christians try to crucify their flesh is by suffering in difficult interpersonal relationships. Many Christians mistakenly think they are crucifying their flesh by yielding, accommodating, deferring and submitting to others in trying situations. For example, they may work for a demanding and dysfunctional boss or find themselves in an extremely difficult marriage. Or, they may be members of a local Christian community and think they are crucifying their flesh by always submitting to the church/community leadership and deferring to others in the community. However, many people are born with what is called a natural "emotional intelligence" or develop the kind of emotional intelligence needed to successfully accommodate and work with others, including those who may be difficult or demanding.

Our self-development of these interpersonal relational skills (even if gained from trying experiences) may have some practical merit and benefit, but it is just another form of soul-power that has nothing to do with truly being crucified with Christ. Nor does our suffering in difficult relationships necessarily produce authentic sanctification in Christ which is essential to knowing God. As we said before, this does not mean that God does not use difficult circumstances and relationships to achieve His eternal purpose in us. However, all our futile attempts at self-crucifixion (whether as individuals or as a group) only strengthen our self-identity leading to further spiritual deception. Instead of really being crucified with Christ, we are merely feeding our secret religious pride. We may appear to be "bearing our cross," but we are actually projecting a fleshly imitation that may fool others but not God. The unrenewed mind of a saved person can be just as self-satisfied and secretly proud of his moral dedication, Christian service and sacrifice, and identification with his Christian community as the unsaved person is proud of his moral dedication, humanitarian service, and identification with his social community. The Adam way of thinking *(the unrenewed mind of a Christian which has not been transformed by the Word of God)* can be extremely deceptive and find ways, even so-called "Christian" ways, to avoid depending on Christ and His completed work on the cross for righteousness. Every form of counterfeit crucifixion that is practiced by professing Christians springs from the unconverted mind, which is not submitted to Christ's sovereignty and righteousness.

Finally, when Paul taught that we have been crucified with Christ, he did not mean that we can continue to practice sin because Christ's crucifixion was substitutionary on our behalf. Many Christians mistakenly believe that since Christ's death on the cross atoned for their sins, they can now keep sinning as much as they want and Christ will forgive them. Paul addressed this doctrinal error when he said, "Should we continue in sin so that grace may increase? God forbid! (Romans 6:1-2)" If we use 1 John 1:9 as an excuse for practicing sin each day, we are actually practicing lawlessness instead of obedience to Christ. We are insulting God's grace and causing Christ's death to have no effect in our lives. This most certainly is *not* why the Son of God died on the cross for us. Of course this is not what the Bible means to be "crucified with Christ."

Other Christians have sincerely tried to stop sinning but found it impossible to live up to the Bible's standard of holiness. The Bible commands us to "be holy yourselves also in all your behavior; because it is written, 'You shall be holy for I am holy (1 Peter 1:15-16).'" And Jesus taught, "Be perfect, therefore, as your heavenly Father is perfect (Matthew 5:48)." Because many Christians do not understand how they can live a holy life, they have become discouraged and have lost hope. They have resigned themselves into thinking that the Bible's standard of holiness is a noble but distant goal that they might try slowly working toward. They mistakenly presume that God "understands" why they are practicing sin and that He does not expect them to be holy, when nothing could be further from the truth. Tragically, they have been beaten down by sin and become apathetic toward the sins that beset and compromise them. As a result, they are experiencing Christian lives that are constantly defeated and distressed by the power of sin and they eventually give up seeking to be holy.

Now that we have briefly reviewed what the Biblical statement "we have been crucified with Christ" *does not* mean, let look at what it *does* mean. "We have been crucified with Christ" simply means our Adam nature (our inherited sin nature) died with Christ when He was crucified. The real crucifixion of our sinful nature could only be done by God Himself. Since bondage to sin came by our birth, deliverance from sin had to come by our death (Romans 6:7). Since we couldn't spiritually kill ourselves to escape sin's captivity, God in His wisdom and power delivered us from slavery to our sinful nature by including us in His Son's death (Romans 6:3-5). Thus God's plan of redemption wasn't to sanctify or improve our sinful nature but to kill it and remove it (Romans 6:6; Colossians 2:11). Therefore, when Christ died, we died with Him (Romans 6:3-8; 2 Corinthians 5:14; Colossians 3:3). When Christ died on the cross, He took our sinful nature upon Himself (Isaiah 53:5-12; Galatians 3:13; 2 Corinthians 5:21). Through His Son's crucifixion, God destroyed that spiritual "sin factory" within us that continually produced sinful attitudes and actions. Therefore, we now work out our salvation and overcome sin solely by faith in Jesus Christ and what He accomplished for us on the cross. Christ is not only the author of our faith; He is the finisher of our faith. This is God's wisdom and power in the cross of Christ. This is true freedom from "the flesh" that Christ purchased for us by His death.

We would make one final point on this divine truth. God did not reserve this Biblical experience of overcoming sin for a special class of super Christians. When Paul said, "I have been crucified with Christ and I no longer live but Christ lives in me," he was declaring what God intended to be the normal Christian life. This is why God ordained the act of water baptism to clearly demonstrate this foundational truth to all new believers and to regularly remind the church of the power of the cross of Christ to bring us into glorious freedom of Christ's resurrection life.

Q7. Why not just proclaim Jesus Christ instead of focusing on Christ crucified?

A7. We definitely believe in boldly and clearly proclaiming Jesus Christ. The apostle Paul proclaimed that the mystery of the gospel is Christ in us - Christ our riches, Christ our life, and Christ our all (Colossians 1:27; 3:4; 3:11). However, Paul also proclaimed the cross is the only way we can know Christ and fully experience His life in us. The crucifixion of Jesus Christ is the sole foundation of our salvation (our spiritual birth in Christ), our sanctification (our spiritual growth in Christ) and our overcoming sin and the devil (our spiritual triumph in Christ). This is why Paul declared, "We preach Christ crucified (1 Corinthians 1:23)" and "I am determined to know nothing among you except Jesus Christ and Him crucified (1 Corinthians 2:2)." Paul, more than anyone, understood the only way to truly know that the resurrected Christ lives in you is to truly know that you have died in Christ. This was his personal testimony, "I have been crucified with Christ and I no longer live but Christ lives in me (Galatians 2:20)." The message of the cross is the power of the gospel (1 Corinthians 1:17-18).

This is the gospel that Paul personally received from Jesus Christ (Galatians 1:11-12) and this is the gospel we preach and teach.

Jesus said, "If I am lifted up from the earth" *(by this, He meant His crucifixion),* "I will draw all men to Myself (John 12:32-33)." By this, Jesus meant that all who are destined for salvation would be drawn to Him by the power of His crucifixion. This is the Biblical truth: We cannot know God except through His Son Jesus Christ and we cannot know Christ except through His cross. The goal of the gospel is "Christ living in us" and the way of the gospel is "the cross of Christ." Our life in God through Christ must not only begin by faith, it must be sustained by faith in Christ's completed work on the cross and this same faith must endure to the end.

Sharing Christ without sharing the power of His cross (for deliverance from both the penalty and the power of sin) is an incomplete gospel. Proclaiming a crossless Christianity will not produce the fruit of Christ's sanctification or a true knowledge of Jesus Christ. Omitting the power of the cross *to not only save but to also sanctify the elect* from the gospel of Christ is not just a harmless oversight, for without sanctification no one can see the Lord (Hebrews 12:14). To sum up, we cannot know Jesus Christ and the power of His resurrection unless we abide in the power of His death. This is why Paul testified, "I want to know Christ and the power of His resurrection... being conformed to His death (Philippians 3:10)." This is why we proclaim and explain Christ crucified to all "so that they may know the mystery of God, namely Christ, in whom are hidden all the treasures of wisdom and knowledge (Colossians 2:2-3)."

Q8.   Where does the Bible say our sinful nature is dead after we receive Christ?

A8.   There are a dozen Scripture verses that state we died with Christ. The New Testament Greek word used in many of these verses is *apothnesko*, which means expired or died and conveys a sense of finality - of being very dead. For example, in Romans 6:7-8, the apostle Paul declared, "Because anyone who has *died* has been freed from sin... we have *died* with Christ (see also Colossian 3:3)." Based on the New Testament Greek, this is clearly not just a figurative or symbolic or even merely a positional death. Our sinful nature, which was central to who we were and at the very core of our self-identity, actually died when we received Christ. A key verse explaining what died within us is found in Romans 6:6, "Our old man has been crucified with Christ in order that our sinful nature *(our body of sin)* might be done away with." Our old man of sin *(otherwise known as our sinful nature)* died and was removed from us when we received Christ. The fact that our sinful nature died and was removed is confirmed by Colossians 2:11: "And in Him you were also circumcised with a circumcision made without hands, in the removal of the sinful nature (the body of flesh) by the circumcision of Christ."

The Bible says we have died with Christ (Romans 6:8; 2 Corinthians 5:14; Colossians 2:20; 3:3), we were buried with Christ (Romans 6:4; Colossians 2:12) and we were raised with Christ (Ephesians 2:6; Colossians 2:12; 3:1). Consider this divine fact: resurrection means to be raised from the dead. Just as Christ was raised from the dead, we were raised from the dead with Him. Therefore, we had to die and be buried before we could be raised from the dead. Water baptism outwardly demonstrates this divine truth by burying the old man of sin (our sinful nature) in a watery "grave." But when we died with Christ, who died and was then buried? Was it our physical body? No. We know our physical body did not die when we received Christ. Was it our soul? No. We know our soul (our natural personality) did not die when we received Christ. Yet, the Bible clearly states that we died with Christ when we received Christ. Then who died? According to the Bible, our sinful spiritual nature died. The question we must ask ourselves is this: Do we believe what the Bible says, that as born again believers, our sinful nature is dead and has been removed from us? Do we believe this Biblical truth to the point that we act on it? When faced with an opportunity to sin, do we believe this truth to the point that we resist that sin because we know we have been delivered from that sin's power over us?

Q9.   Why do some Christians think our sinful nature has died but not been removed from us?

A9.   This theory is not Biblically correct and is likely based on the repeated failure of many Christians to overcome sin. Therefore, some teachers have wrongly concluded (from their personal experience) that although our sin nature died with Christ, it must have never been actually removed from us. They then also mistakenly think that the old man of sin (their sinful nature) can be reactivated like a dormant volcano whenever a Christian sins. This in turn has led to the wrong belief that Christians will always experience the inner conflict of two opposing natures (their new nature and their sinful nature). We believe that this mistaken thinking stems from unbelief and ignorance of the power of Christ's crucifixion. Jesus said, "Is this not the reason you are mistaken, that you do not understand the Scriptures or the power of God (Mark 12:24)?" Unfortunately, this erroneous belief that we still have an old sin nature also provides a convenient religious excuse for those Christians who want to keep sinning. In this regard, we should heed the apostle Peter's warning, "Live as free men, but do not use your freedom as a cover-up for evil; live as servants of God (1 Peter 2:16)."

Sometimes those who think that their old sinful nature is still resident within them focus their argument on the interpretation of one Greek word, *katargeo*, as it appears in the following verse in the Book of Romans: "Knowing this, that our old self was crucified with Him, in order that our body of sin might be *done away with*, so that we would no longer be slaves to sin (Romans 6:6/emphasis added)." In this verse, the New American Standard Bible translates the Greek word *katargeo* by the phrase, "done away with." We believe this is an appropriate translation within this Scriptural context since our sin nature has died and was buried (done away with) by our baptism (immersion) into

Christ. "We have been buried with Him through baptism *(immersion)* into death (Romans 6:4)." The King James Version translates *katargeo* in this verse as "destroyed," which also fits this Scriptural context. Those who mistakenly believe our sin nature still resides within us think the word *katargeo* should be translated as "idle" or "unemployed." In other words, they think the sin nature is just sitting "idle" in a Christian and that a Christian can unwittingly "reemploy" or "reactivate" their sin nature whenever they sin.

However, this is neither Scriptural nor logical. We believe a careful review of the 27 times that *katargeo* is used in the New Testament reveals that "done away with" or "destroyed" is the proper translation of *katargeo* in Romans 6:6. In fact, *katargeo* could even be more accurately and clearly translated as *"removed"* within the context of this verse. This is exactly how *katargeo* is translated in 2 Corinthians 3:14 to describe how the Old Covenant veil that blinds Jews to seeing Jesus as their Messiah is *removed* whenever someone turned to Christ. This spiritual veil certainly was not just rendered idle or unemployed! It was forever taken away! With this in view, the Old Covenant prophet Ezekiel foretold of the divine heart transplant that God would perform in the New Covenant: "Moreover, I will give you a new heart and put a new spirit within you; and I will *remove* the heart of stone from your flesh and give you a heart of flesh (Ezekiel 36:26; see also Jeremiah 31:31-33)." The Bible here does not need any subjective interpretation; it is very straightforward. God, through His prophet Ezekiel, declared our heart of stone (our sinful nature) would be *removed* by the New Covenant (which was put into operation by Christ's death on the cross)!

The apostle Paul confirms this Biblical truth that our sinful nature was *removed* in his letter to the Colossians. Here, Paul uses the picture of circumcision to describe what happened to our old man when we were saved. "In Him you were also circumcised with a circumcision made without hands, in the *removal* of the sinful nature, by the circumcision of Christ (Colossians 2:11)." We can say with absolute certainty when someone is circumcised their foreskin is definitely *removed*. It is not left attached in an idle or dormant manner to continually cause infection and disease.

Therefore, in this passage of Scripture (Colossians 2:11), Paul declares our sinful nature has been *removed*. Paul then shifts in the very next verse (Colossians 2:12) from using the Old Covenant seal of righteousness (circumcision) to using the New Covenant seal of righteousness (baptism) to further prove that the old sinful nature was *removed*. Paul logically states that since our old sinful nature died and was removed (verse 11), it was then disposed of by burial: "Having been buried with Him in baptism and raised with Him through your faith in the power of God, who raised Him from the dead (verse 12)." Thus, by linking Old Covenant circumcision with New Covenant baptism, Paul leaves no doubt that the death and *removal* of the sinful nature, as symbolized by foreskin circumcision, is also portrayed by the burial stage of water baptism. Again, we can say with absolute certainty, that when someone dies and is buried, their body has definitely been *removed* from the household of the living. In this way, water baptism confirms (just as circumcision also did) that our old sinful nature not only died but was certainly *removed*.

To sum up, both the Old Covenant and New Covenant portray what happened to our sinful nature when we were born again of the Spirit. Our sinful nature died and God completely *removed* it from our being. The old sinful nature is not hiding somewhere within us just waiting to resurrect its satanic power of sin over us. God does not mix what is holy with what is unholy. God would never pour His Holy Spirit into an unholy vessel such as the old man of sin (the sinful nature). Jesus said, "No one pours new wine into old wineskins. If he does, the wine will burst the skins, and both the wine and the wineskins will be ruined. No, he pours new wine into new wineskins (Mark 2:22)." The reason God was able to pour His Holy Spirit (His new wine) into our spiritual being is because he has made us a new creation, a new wine skin in Christ (2 Corinthians 5:17).

Our unholy sinful nature is dead and *removed* from us for all eternity! How can we possibly be betrothed as a pure holy virgin to our bridegroom, Jesus Christ (2 Corinthians 11:2), if we still have an evil sinful nature residing within our body that lusts to commit spiritual adultery? Therefore, if we preach and teach anything less than the complete *removal* of our sin nature by the power of Christ's crucifixion, we are treating as unclean the holy blood of Christ and insulting God's Spirit of grace (Hebrews 10:26-31). Anyone who teaches that Christians have two conflicting inner natures of good and evil, or that God never actually removed our sinful nature through Christ's death, is impeding the church from entering into Christ's fullness and God's eternal purpose. Some teach this falsehood out of spiritual ignorance but others deliberately teach it because they themselves are willfully practicing sin. In their case, Jesus' warning is appropriate, "Woe to you... For you have taken away the key of knowledge; you yourselves did not enter, and you hindered those who were entering (Luke 11:52)."

Q10. Aren't we just "reformed sinners" after we are saved?

A10. Many Christians call themselves (or at least inwardly think of themselves as) "sinners" or "reformed sinners." However, this is not Biblically true. After you are saved, it is crucial for your spiritual growth in Christ that your identity be based solely on the Word of God and not on man's opinion or the devil's lie. Faith is seeing God as He is and seeing ourselves the way God sees us. The Bible says that, once we are saved, we are new creations in Christ (2 Corinthians 5:17) and we are holy and beloved of God (Colossians 3:12). But the Bible also says that before God could make us a new creation, He had to first deal with the old creation. Therefore, by the power of His Son's crucifixion, God dealt not only with its fruit (our sinful actions); God removed its very root (our sinful nature). By Christ's death, we have been reconciled to God and we are no longer sinners and enemies of God (Romans 5:8-10; 2 Corinthians 5:18-20; Ephesians 2:12-19). Although we may occasionally carelessly sin, we should no longer be practicing sin because we are no longer sinners by nature. We are saints who have

God's divine nature within us (2 Peter 1:4). This is a divinely important distinction.

Some Christians cite the apostle Paul's testimony that he was the worst sinner of all as evidence that we are all just reformed sinners. But let us carefully examine Paul's overall testimony. Paul said, "It is a trustworthy statement, deserving full acceptance, that Jesus Christ came into the world to save sinners, among whom I am foremost of all (1 Timothy 1:15)." Just before this statement, Paul used the past tense to describe himself as a sinner. "Even though I was once a blasphemer and a persecutor and a violent man, I was shown mercy because I acted in ignorance and unbelief (1 Timothy 1:13)." Before he was saved, Paul had been responsible for organizing the imprisonment and murder of Christians. Therefore, in this letter to Timothy, Paul used his own personal testimony of salvation as an example of God's amazing grace toward sinners. However, we cannot and should not draw any theological conclusion or formulate any Christian doctrine based on the fact that Paul starts his personal testimony in the past tense and then switches to the present tense. At other times in his letters to the churches, Paul also switched from past to present tense to dramatically illustrate an example or personally demonstrate a case in point.

It is important to remember that Paul wrote his letters to the churches and his co-workers in the Greek language, a precise and expressive language which often strategically uses the *present* tense to describe a *past* action and experience. Here, in his letter to Timothy, Paul made effective use of this *historical present* tense, as it is called in the Greek language, to dramatically illustrate God's mercy toward sinners. Therefore, Paul's use of tense in one particular verse should definitely not be used as the deciding factor in determining Christian doctrine. Instead, the context of the individual verse and the overall body of Scriptural evidence should be carefully examined.

A comprehensive review of all of Paul's letters in the New Testament makes it very clear that Paul believed once you were born again you now have a totally new spiritual identity in Christ – you are no longer a sinner, you are now a saint! The New Testament Greek word for saints is *hagios,* which means holy ones. In his letters to the churches, Paul used the word "saints" over three dozen times to address those who are called as Christ's disciples. It is interesting to note that although Christ's disciples are called "Christians" only three times in the entire New Testament; they are called "saints" sixty times. In fact, Paul did not even use the term "disciples" in any of his letters to the churches; he always called Christ's followers "saints." In his letters to the churches, Paul never once calls Christ's devoted followers "sinners." For example, Paul never wrote, "To the reformed sinners who are at Ephesus." Instead Paul wrote, "To the saints who are at Ephesus." In fact, in his letter to the Romans, Paul clearly stated that before we were saved by Christ, we were ungodly "sinners" and enemies of God (Romans 5:8, 10). Paul's judgment that the term "sinner" refers to someone who is unrighteous in the eyes of God is perfectly consistent with the whole Bible. A review of both the Old and New Testaments reveals the term "sinner" is almost exclusively used to designate either unbelievers or backslidden believers (see Psalm 1:1; 51:13; Proverbs 23:17; Ecclesiastes 9:2; Romans 5:8; Galatians 2:15, 17; 1 Timothy 1:9; 1 Peter 4:18; Hebrews 12:13).

Paul, more than any of the apostles, was keenly aware of the dynamic spiritual transformation that occurred in a person's heart when they received Christ as their Lord and Savior and were born again of the Holy Spirit. This is the gospel that Christ personally revealed to Paul (Galatians 1:11-12). When we were physically born, we were born sinners because we spiritually inherited Adam's sinful nature (Romans 5:19). However, God used the crucifixion of His only Son to perform a divine heart transplant. When Jesus Christ died, God replaced our terminally sinsick heart with His Son's divine heart (Romans 6:3-11; Galatians 2:20). Therefore, we are no longer sinners by nature because our sinful nature has been removed from us (Romans 6:6; Colossians 2:11). Instead, we now have Christ's holy nature indwelling us (2 Corinthians 13:5; Colossians 1:27). Since our sinful nature is dead and gone, we have been freed from the power of sin (Romans 6:7). The Bible says that by Adam's disobedience, the many were made sinners, and by Christ's obedience the many will be made righteous (Romans 5:19). Therefore, by the power of Christ's death on the cross, God the Father has made us righteous saints (holy ones) and members of Christ's body and His heavenly family.

Jesus Christ died to make us saints! Why would we want to call ourselves "sinners" and negate what He accomplished on the cross? From a Biblical perspective, the term "reformed sinner" actually means someone who is an unbeliever (one who has not been born again and still has a sinful nature) but who is applying his willpower to reform his behavior. Unfortunately, there are many unsaved individuals who fit this description that are populating our churches today. The term "reformed sinner" reveals a fundamental misunderstanding and spiritual ignorance of Christ's completed work on the cross. God is not in the business of reforming sinners. God knew sinners were beyond reformation (Jeremiah 17:9; Romans 3:23). God's verdict for sinners is never reformation; it is always execution. Since we were born sinners, we could only be freed from sin through our death (Romans 6:7). Therefore, when Jesus Christ died on the cross, God included us in His Son's death so that our sinful nature would be crucified (executed) and buried (removed) in Him (Romans 6:3-6; Colossians 2:11-12). This is the spiritual lesson of water baptism. The truth is that we were sinners saved by grace, but we are now sons of God sustained by grace because God has put the Spirit of His Son into our hearts (Galatians 4:6). By the power of Christ's crucifixion, God has spiritually translated us from sinners into saints!

The Bible says there will be no sinners in the congregation of the righteous (Psalm 1:5). As the blind man healed by Jesus said, "We know that God does not hear sinners but if anyone fears God and does His will, He hears him (John 9:31)." What is the difference between a righteous saint and an unbelieving sinner? A saint is holy by nature. A saint has been freed from the power of sin. A saint is living under God's sovereignty and authority. A sinner is unholy by nature. A sinner is captive to sin. A sinner is living under the sovereignty and authority of his own soul; not under God's Kingship and rule. Therefore, a sinner cannot do anything but sin, whereas a saint can choose not to sin. Before we were saved, we sinned because we were sinners by nature. Our sinful nature was like a powerful "sin factory" within us, which day and night could only produce sinful attitudes and actions. But God, through Christ's death, has completely destroyed and removed that sin factory from us.

After we have been saved, there are three reasons why Christians might continue to habitually practice sin, which is different than unintentionally or occasionally sinning: 1) They do not know (believe and act on) the divine truth that they are dead to sin and freed from the power of sin, or 2) They have forgotten the truth that they are dead to sin, or 3) They do not want to come under God's Sovereignty and they want to continue to willfully and disobediently prac- tice sin. In this last case, since they are willfully practicing sin, it is appropriate to call these backslidden Christians "sinners" and not saints. Since they willfully continue to practice sin, they have proven themselves to be "sinners" and not saints (see Galatians 2:17). "Of them, the proverbs are true: 'A dog returns to its vomit' and 'A sow that is washed goes back to wallowing in the mud (2 Peter 2:22).'" The apostle James wrote of Christians who have returned to willfully practicing sin, "My brothers, if one of you should wander from the truth and someone should bring him back, remember this: Whoever turns a *sinner* from the error of his way will save him from death and cover a multitude of sins (James 5:19)."

God has removed our sinful nature and replaced it with His Son's holy nature. The devil would like nothing better than to trick the saints into thinking of themselves as sinners with a sinful nature. After succumbing to sin many times, many Christians begin to erroneously believe this "boogie man of sin" still lives in them and will eventually overpower them anyway. Then whenever the devil tempts them to sin, they put up very little resistance since they mistakenly think it's natural, normal and inevitable for them to succumb to sin since they still have a sinful nature. This is the devil's strategy to prevent Christians from ever entering into the overcoming spiritual life, which Christ sacrificially purchased for us by His death on the cross. This has grave consequences since overcoming sin is not optional for a Christian. Jesus Christ warned that only those Christians who overcome sin would share in His spiritual inheritance and have their names written in His Book of Life and rule with Him in the age to come (Revelation 2:26; 3:5; 21:7).

This is why Christians need to renew their minds by the truth of God's Word (Romans 12:2; Ephesians 4:23). When we believe and act on the truth (not just mentally assent) to what Jesus Christ accomplished through His death to transform us from sinners into saints, we will no longer call ourselves sinners. From that moment on, we will believe and confess that we are saints of God through Jesus Christ. Christ died to free us completely free us from sin. He died to not only set us free from the penalty of sin; He also died to set us free from the power of sin. By His death, Jesus Christ has given us a new spiritual birthright and identity - we are no longer the devil's sinners; we are now God's saints. This is our spiritual inheritance in Christ. But if we do not know (believe and act on) the power of Christ's crucifixion, we will not experience the overcoming Christian life and freedom from the power of sin. This is why Paul said, "I pray that the eyes of your heart may be enlightened, so that you will know what is the hope of His calling, what are the riches of the glory of His inheritance in the saints (Ephesians 1:18)."

Q11.   If my sinful nature is dead and removed, then why do I keep on sinning?

A11.   This is a very common question for sincere Christians. The truth is that Jesus Christ has freed us from sin's power over us by His death on the cross so that we do not need to practice sin. However, most Christians still live in sin and thereby fulfill the words that the apostle Paul wrote, "Shall we continue in sin so that grace may increase? May it never be! (Romans 6:1-2)" Even though Christians may be beset with entangling sins, God's Word is still true. "If we are faithless, He remains faithful (2 Timothy 2:13)." How then can we stop practicing besetting and compromising sins? The Bible gives us the clear answer, "Anyone who has died has been (past tense) freed from the power of sin (Romans 6:7)." Therefore, if we do not know (believe and act on) the truth that we have died with Christ, we cannot overcome sin. For example, if we do not know (believe and act on) the truth that Christ died for the forgiveness of our sins, how can we possibly experience freedom from guilt and condemnation? In the same way, if we do not know (believe and act on) the truth that our sinful nature has died with Christ, how can we possibly experience freedom from the power of sin? As God said, "My people are destroyed for lack of knowledge (Hosea 4:6)."

We need to remember that spiritual knowledge is not the same as mental knowledge. A key New Testament Greek word for "knowledge" is *gnosis*, which means knowledge based on personal experience. This is the Greek word used by the apostle Paul in Philippians 3:10: "I want to *know* Christ." This spiritual knowledge is the divine truth, which the Spirit of God has revealed to your spirit, so that it becomes so real in your personal experience that you act on it and depend on it. This is also the Greek word which Paul used when he declared, "For we *know* that our old self was crucified with Him so that our body of sin (our sinful nature) might be done away with, so that we would no longer be slaves to sin (Romans 6:6)." Our mind needs to be spiritually renewed by the Word of God (Romans 12:2; Ephesians 4:23). Our sinful nature is dead, but our unrenewed mind will still continue in the habit of worldly thinking until it is transformed by God's Spirit of truth. This is like the sound of a ringing church bell. Long after the bell has stopped ringing, the sound of its repeated ringing can still echo in your mind. Although you mentally know the bell has stopped, you can still experience the after-effects of its ringing. This is why we must stand firm by faith in the divine fact that our sinful nature has died with Christ and we have been freed from sin. As we continue to persevere in faith over time, the Holy Spirit will confirm and establish this spiritual truth within our soul (in our thoughts and emotions). The unrenewed, ungodly thinking of our dead and removed sinful nature will then fade away.

It is also important to remember that no matter how mature we are in Christ, if we begin to look inward instead of at Christ, we will fail to overcome sin and the devil. This is because faith requires that we "fix our eyes on Jesus" not on ourselves. It is only by remaining united with Him (by faith in the truth) that we can walk steadily and successfully in the Spirit. We shouldn't become overly self-conscious or introspective! That is the devil's trick to get us "cut off" from the source of our life and power – Jesus Christ! If we look to anything or anyone besides Christ and His completed work, we will give Satan an opportunity to deceive and accuse us of being very much alive to sin. Therefore, we must resist believing anything, especially Satan's distortion of the truth, which contradicts God's Word that we have died in Christ (Romans 6:3-11). Of course, when we do sin, we repent and ask Christ's forgiveness for our sins. However, there is a difference between carelessly and occasionally committing a sin and willfully and continually practicing sin. By Christ's death, we have been freed from the power of sin, including all entangling sins. If we stand firm by faith in this powerful truth of the cross of Christ, over time and through testing, our experience will conform to the Word of God. Our lives will then be transformed into the image of Christ. This truth brings great hope to every sincere believer who finds himself caught in entangling sins and deeply desires to stop sinning.

Therefore, the whole gospel of God can be summed up this way: Christ died for us and included us in His death so that He might sovereignly live in us. If we wholeheartedly obey this gospel to the point of acting on the truth, we will overcome sin and be Christ's effective witnesses in the midst of this sin-filled world.

Q12.   Are you teaching that we will never sin again?

A12.   Of course not! The Bible declares there is only one person on earth who ever lived a sinless life – the Lamb of God, Jesus Christ (Hebrews 4:15; 9:14; 1 Peter 1:18-19). "For it was fitting for us to have such a high priest, holy, innocent, undefiled, separated from sinners and exalted above the heavens (Hebrews 7:26)." The Bible says Jesus Christ has sanctified us (made us holy) by His sacrificial death as the Lamb of God (Hebrews 10:10). This is the divine exchange of the cross by which Christ replaced our sinful nature with His holy nature when we were born again. Following our initial salvation and sanctification in Christ, we must now by faith in Christ work out our salvation in progressive sanctification. The Bible says, "Work out your salvation in fear and trembling; for it is God who is at work in you, both to will and to work for His good pleasure (Philippians 2:12-13)." Therefore, in one sense, we are made perfectly holy because Christ the Holy One now lives in us. But, in another sense, we are becoming more holy as Christ's life becomes more fully formed in us. "By one sacrifice Christ has made perfect forever those who *are being sanctified* (Hebrews 10:14)."

Therefore, even as our faith in Jesus Christ grows in maturity, we will still occasionally sin and always need Christ's forgiveness for our sins. With this in mind, the apostle John wrote, "If we say we have no sin, we are deceiving ourselves and the truth is not in us. If we confess our sins, He is faithful and righteous to forgive us our sins and to cleanse us from all unrighteousness. If we say we have not sinned, we make Him a liar and His word is not in us (1 John 1:8-10)."

However, there is a great difference between overcoming sin and being overcome by sin. This is the powerful difference that Christ's crucifixion makes in all those who believe and act on what our Lord accomplished for us by the cross. Although we may still occasionally sin as we learn to walk in the power of Christ's overcoming life, this is far cry from continually being defeated and practicing besetting and compromising sins. The Biblical truth is that because we have died with Christ and our sinful nature has been removed from us, we have been decisively freed from the power of sin. "Because when anyone has died, they have been freed from sin (Romans 6:7)." Many professing Christians believe it is unrealistic to think that they can stop practicing sin. However, God Himself expects us (and even commands us) to stop practicing sin (see 1 Corinthians 15:32; 1 Thessalonians 4:7-8; Hebrews 10:26). And if God Himself expects us to stop practicing sin, would He not have also provided the way for us to stop sinning? And this what He has surely done through His Son's death on the cross.

With this in view, the apostle John wrote, "No one who abides in Him keeps on sinning. No one who continues to sin has either seen Him or known Him... no one who is born of God practices sin, because His seed abides in him; and he cannot sin, because he is born of God (1 John 3:6, 9)." Thank God for the entirety of Jesus Christ's completed work on the cross and our deliverance from the power of sin! Because of Christ's completed work on the cross, every Christian has been completely freed from entangling and tormenting sins. Because of the power of Christ's crucifixion, every Christian can overcome their natural temperament and carnal desires, which stem from their unrenewed minds. This is why the apostle Paul declared, "What shall we say then? Are we to continue in sin so that grace may increase? Absolutely not! We died to sin; how can we live in it any longer (Romans 6:1-2)." Paul then goes on to say that if you continue to sin, it is because you do not yet truly know you have died with Christ and have been freed from sin (Romans 6:3-11).

At this point, we need to note the difference between the Christian who "overcomes" sin by trusting in his own morality and willpower and the Christian who overcomes sin solely by trusting what Jesus Christ has accomplished by His death on the cross (when Christ died, He included us in His death so He might sovereignly live in us). The Christian who "overcomes" sin by his own ability does so by his naturally-endowed determination and/or his naturally-developed discipline. This type of naturally-controlled moral behavior may sometimes even appear outwardly "more together" than the life of a Christian who is just beginning to trust solely in Jesus Christ to transform his attitudes and actions (this does not mean that real faith does not also have its own actions but, in this case, the actions spring from our faith in the cross of Christ and not faith in our natural strength).

In the Day of Judgment, God who knows the secret motives and attitudes of men's hearts, will appraise each Christian's deeds. Those deeds that were birthed from the power of the Holy Spirit will be rewarded by God and treated as gold, silver and precious stones. Those deeds that were generated by our own soul strength will be deemed worthless to God. They will be treated as wood, hay and straw and burned up. Whenever Christians practice man-made morality they are actually disobeying Christ's authority and abusing Christ's crucifixion. We should all repent from the sin of practicing carnal morality, the root of which is unbelief in Jesus Christ and His completed work on the cross. This man-made "morality" apart from Christ's Sovereignty is actually hostile to the gospel message because it is a counterfeit of true Christianity, which is based on faith alone. The Bible says, "Whatever is not from faith is sin (Romans 14:23)."

In summary, the Bible does not say we will never sin again after we are saved. However, the Bible does say that we do not *have* to ever sin again after we are saved. Now that we have died with Christ and been freed from sin (Romans

6:7), we have a choice whether to sin or not. Before our redemption by Christ, we were slaves to sin and had no choice. But we no longer have an excuse to sin (now that we no longer have a sinful nature and Christ lives in us). No temptation is so great that we cannot overcome it by faith in the cross of Christ and no sin is so great that we are forced to commit it. The Bible goes on to say that if we willfully persist in practicing sin, we cannot claim to know Christ. Our Lord Jesus also emphasized this fundamental truth when He said to those who professed to know Him as their Lord but who willfully practiced sin, "I never knew you; depart from me, you who practice lawlessness (Matthew 7:23)." Jesus would say to anyone who teaches that Christians can never stop practicing sin, "You are mistaken because you do not know the Scriptures or the power of God (Mark 12:24)."

Q13. Isn't this just the same basic teaching we heard when we were water baptized?

A13. Yes, if you were correctly taught on the spiritual meaning of water baptism. Water baptism is a public commitment of our decision to follow Christ as our Lord and Savior. Therefore, water baptism is the outward expression of the divine transformation which inwardly occurred within us when we were saved. The basis for our teaching on water baptism should be Romans Chapter Six. It is here that the apostle Paul teaches what spiritually transpired when we were born again. The Greek word to baptize is *baptizo*, which means to immerse or to "dip under fluid." When we receive Christ into our heart as our Lord and Savior, we are spiritually immersed and united into Christ's death and resurrection (Romans 6:3-5). "We have been buried with Him through baptism *(immersion)* into death (Romans 6:4)." Therefore, when we are water baptized, we are first immersed into a "watery grave." This burial demonstrates that our old sinful nature has died in Christ (Romans 6:6). Burial also demonstrates that God has removed that dead man of sin (our sinful nature) from us (see also Colossians 2:11). Next, we are raised out of our watery grave. This demonstrates that we now have a new resurrection life in Jesus Christ who lives in us and we are no longer slaves to sin (Romans 6:4-7). Therefore, water baptism is the outward demonstration that we are now "dead to sin but alive to God in Christ Jesus (Romans 6:11)."

Since water baptism is for new believers, we can mistakenly think teaching on water baptism is only elementary and not for older Christians. However, the fact that "we have died in Christ and Christ now lives in us (Galatians 2:20)" is the central truth of the gospel and the New Covenant. God has expressly commanded that we observe the water baptism of new believers to continually remind the church of this crucial truth. God knows it is impossible for us to live the overcoming Christian life, grow strong into spiritual maturity, bear healthy spiritual fruit, wage effective spiritual warfare and serve Christ wholeheartedly unless we are firmly established in this vital truth that our sin nature was removed from us at spiritual birth and that we were then freed from the power of sin. This is what Jesus accomplished when he triumphed over the devil and disarmed him by the cross (Colossians 2:15). Therefore, the gospel of Christ crucified is not just basic teaching for beginners in the faith; it is also deeper life teaching, since we can experience no deeper spiritual life apart from walking by faith in the true knowledge of Jesus Christ and the power of His cross.

Q14.   Why is the message of the cross so important to the church?

A14.   The church is central to God's purpose and the cross is central to the church. God's divine plan is to reveal His Son Jesus Christ through the church. Christ put God's plan into effect by coming to earth to die on the cross. Apart from the cross, there simply would be no church since the church was birthed from Christ's death. By Christ's death on the cross, we have been rescued from Satan's dominion and brought into God's kingdom. By Christ's death on the cross, we have been forgiven for our sinful attitudes and actions. By Christ's death on the cross, we have been forever freed from our sinful nature, which has been crucified with Christ and been removed from us. By Christ's death on the cross, we have been delivered once and for all time from the power of sin.

By Christ's death on the cross, we have Christ's Spirit indwelling us. By Christ's death on the cross, we now have the mind of Christ. By Christ' death on the cross, we have become God's new creation, Christ's body, His church. By Christ's death on the cross, we become willingly enslaved to God. By Christ's death on the cross, we can overcome the sin of the world and walk in the holiness and love of God. By Christ's death on the cross, we can lose our soul-life for Christ's sake and the gospel's sake. By Christ's death on the cross, we can suffer with Christ so that we might reign with Him. By Christ's death on the cross, we triumph over Satan. Once the church sees and believes what Christ has fully accomplished by His death on the cross for her, she will be able to fully experience and express Christ's life and His kingdom purpose here on earth. The church will then be ready to be Christ's glorious bride and co-regent in the age to come.

Everyone who has the Holy Spirit living in them makes up the church. If Christ lives in you, you are a member of His church, His body. The spiritual health of Christ's body is made up of the health of all its members. Therefore, when one member is weak, the whole body is weak. If one member is overcome by sin, the whole body suffers. The power of Christ's death is the only basis for the body of Christ's resurrection life and power. Therefore, we cannot teach on church life or body life without teaching on the divine meaning and practical application of the power of Christ's crucifixion.

Apart from the cross of Christ, the church can do nothing of any spiritual value. Apart from the cross of Christ, the church's morality is at best worthless; at worst it is hypocrisy, lawlessness and rebellion against God. Apart from the cross of Christ, the church is filled with selfish ambition and every evil thing. Apart from the cross of Christ, the church does more harm than good. To put it plainly, apart from the cross of Christ, the church cannot and will not fulfill God's eternal purpose.

The only way the church will walk in the power of Christ's life is if she knows how to abide (stay rooted by faith) in the power of Christ's death. This is why we proclaim the gospel of Christ crucified to enable the church to have unbroken fellowship with Christ (1 John 1:3-7); equip the church for ministry in the fullness of Christ (Ephesians 4:11-13); and prepare the church for the coming tribulation and the return of Christ (Matthew 24:9-31).

Q15. How do we know the removal of the "body of flesh" in Colossians 2:11 refers to our sinful nature?

A15. The New Testament Greek word for flesh is *sarx*. One of the contributing factors to Christians' misunderstanding on how God has dealt with their old sinful nature is the translation of the Greek word *sarx*, which appears 140 times in the New Testament. The King James Version (KJV) translated *sarx* simply as "flesh." Most versions of the Bible since then have followed the KJV's lead and also translated *sarx* as "flesh." However, the word "flesh" is not only archaic and rarely used; it is vague, ambiguous and has multiple meanings.

The New Testament Greek word for *sarx* actually has four possible meanings depending on the Scriptural context. The first possible meaning of *sarx* is "flesh" or "skin," the thin, soft living membrane that covers the body. However, this particular definition for the word "flesh" is only appropriately used in one tenth of all the Scriptures that contain the Greek word *sarx*. One of the few cases in which *sarx* is fittingly translated as flesh (or skin) is the following verse: *(sarx) flesh* and blood cannot inherit the kingdom of God (1 Corinthians 15:51)."

The second possible meaning of *sarx* is the physical or natural body. This is the meaning of *sarx* in the following verse: "For this reason a man shall leave his father and mother and be joined to his wife, and the two shall become one *(sarx) body* (Ephesians 5:23)." The third possible meaning of *sarx* is the human or natural soul when it is *not* submitted to Christ's authority. This can also be described as the natural man (with his will and inherent abilities) or the natural mind, which is also called the unrenewed, carnal mind. This is the meaning of *sarx* when Paul said, "Having begun by the Spirit, are you now being perfected by your *(sarx) natural ability?* (Galatians 3:3)." One version of the Bible aptly translates this verse, "Are you now trying to attain your goal by *human effort?*"

The fourth possible meaning of *sarx* is the sinful nature. This is man's fallen spiritual nature (before he is born again of the Spirit) which he inherited from his spiritual ancestor Adam. This sinful nature, which the Bible also refers to as the old man or the old self, is hostile and rebellious to God. Since this is man's inward nature before he is born again of the Spirit, it controls man's attitudes and actions and compels man to sin. The sinful nature is like a "sin factory" inside unregenerate man that continuously produces sinful thoughts and behavior that are alien and hostile to

God. This is the meaning of *sarx* when Paul wrote, "For what the law was powerless to do in that it was weakened by the *(sarx) sinful nature* (Romans 8:3)." In this context, *sarx* means more than just the body or soul; it means man's sinful nature or spiritual sin factory within him. Paul continues, "However, you are not controlled by the *(sarx) sinful nature* but by the Spirit, if indeed the Spirit of God lives in you (Romans 8:9)." In other words, you no longer have Adam's spiritual nature but Christ's spiritual nature, if the Spirit of God lives in you.

With these four definitions of the Greek word *sarx* in mind, let's now return to Colossians 2:11. After examining the Scriptural context of this verse, we must conclude that the "body of flesh," which Christ removed through spiritual circumcision, could not have been our physical body nor could it have been our human soul. Therefore, it is both Scriptural and logical to state that Jesus Christ removed our *sinful nature* through spiritual circumcision when we were born again of the Spirit.

We believe there is a reason why most modern Bible translations continue to use the archaic and ambiguous word "flesh" instead of translating *sarx* in a more accurate and understandable manner depending upon the Scriptural context. Most Christians, even most contemporary Bible scholars, lack divine clarity on the Biblical truth that when we were born again, our sinful nature was crucified with Christ and *totally* removed from us (Romans 6:6). Consequently, almost all translations of the Bible continue to use the confusing term "flesh," which obscures the powerful and liberating truth that God decisively removed our sinful nature from us by Christ's crucifixion.

Even the New International Version (NIV), which attempted to more specifically translate *sarx*, has compounded the problem by using a "shotgun" approach. By translating the Greek word *sarx* as "sinful nature" in nearly all instances, the NIV occasionally hits the target (see Romans 8:3 & 9; Colossians 2:11); but, more often than not, it misses the target. For example in Romans 8:12-13, the NIV translates *sarx* as sinful nature. However, this mistranslation has given the mistaken impression to many Christians that a born again believer still has a sinful nature. The word *sarx* in this Scripture passage should have been translated as the carnal mind. The passage would then properly read as follows: "Therefore, brothers, we have an obligation - but it is not to the *carnal mind*, to live according to the *carnal mind*. For if you are living according to the *carnal mind*, you will die; but if by the Spirit you put to death the misdeeds of the body, you will live (Romans 8:12-13)."

In closing, we thank God there can be no doubt that when Paul used the picture of circumcision; he meant to graphically and decisively show that God completely *removed* our *sinful nature* when we were born again. Just as the foreskin is definitely cut off and *removed* by physical circumcision, our sinful nature is definitely crucified and *removed* from us by Christ's spiritual circumcision of our heart through the operation of the cross. It is also worth noting that God's *removal* of our sinful nature in the New Covenant is the fulfillment of Ezekiel's Old Testament prophecy, "I will give you a new heart and put a new spirit within you; and I will *remove the heart of stone* from your flesh. I will put My Spirit within you and cause you to walk in My statutes, and you will be careful to observe My ordinances (Ezekiel 36:26)."

Q16.   In Galatians 2:20, the apostle Paul says it is not I but Christ who dwells in me. But then in Romans 7:17, Paul says it is not I but sin which dwells in me. How do we reconcile these two contradictory statements?

A16.   In Galatians 2:20, Paul is expressing how he presently lives and how every believer should live free from sin if they know their sinful nature has died and been removed by Christ's death on the cross. In Romans 7:17, Paul is expressing how an *unbeliever* who wants to serve God is driven to frustration, futility and failure in his attempts to obey God because he is still a slave to sin and his sinful nature. Paul writes this passage in the first person since this was an experience he himself had passed through. Therefore, these two contrasting statements (Galatians 2:20 and Romans 7:17) illustrate the great divide between a *believer* who is freed from sin and an *unbeliever* who is enslaved to sin. However, Romans 7:17 can also express what a believer feels if he does not know his sinful nature is dead and, therefore, mistakenly thinks he is still enslaved to sin. In this case, these two contrasting statements (Galatians 2:20 and Romans 7:17) illustrate the dramatic difference between a believer who *knows* he has died to sin and a believer who *does not know* he has died to sin.

In Galatians 2:20, it is clear Paul knows sin no longer dwells in him because his sinful nature has been crucified with Christ (see also Romans 6:6). In Romans 7:17, Paul uses the present tense to describe the awful predicament of someone who zealously wants to obey God but is still enslaved to sin. For example, Paul states this is the case of Jews who "are zealous for God but their zeal is not based on knowledge (Romans 10:2)." Note: When reading Romans Chapter Seven, it is important to remember that Paul wrote the Epistle to the Romans in the Greek language, a precise and expressive language which often strategically uses the *present* tense to dramatically describe a *past* action and experience. In Chapter Seven, Paul made effective use of this *historical present* tense, as it is called in the Greek language, to vividly describe the futility and misery of a person who wants to serve God but finds himself continually frustrated and sabotaged by his rebellious sinful nature because he is not born again. In writing this chapter, Paul drew from his own past personal experience as a devout Pharisee before He became a born again Christian.

It would be a serious mistake to think Romans 7:14-24 is how the apostle Paul viewed himself *after* he was born of the Spirit in light of God's personal revelation to him ("God was pleased to reveal His Son in me so that I may preach Him (Galatians 1:15-16)." It would be inconceivable for Paul, who was a bondslave to God and so fully indwelt by Jesus Christ, to declare he was a slave to sin (v. 14) because evil indwelt him (v. 21). If this were the case, Paul would have suffered a form of religious schizophrenia. If this were Paul's spiritual condition, it would deny the power of Jesus Christ's work in him. It would also directly contradict his own previous statement in Romans 6:6 where he clearly declared our old man was crucified with Christ and our sinful nature (this body of sin) has been removed. Paul further adds that since our sinful nature is dead; we have been freed from slavery to sin (verses 7, 14, 18, 22). In Colossians 2:11, Paul also declares Christ has removed our sinful nature (this body of flesh). Finally at the end of Romans Chapter Seven, Paul solves the dilemma of this confused and conflicted person by answering the question of who delivers us from our sinful nature (this body of sin) with the triumphant response, "Thanks be to God through Jesus Christ our Lord (Romans 7:25)!" This also described Paul's personal experience and testimony.

When we are born again of the Spirit, God removes our sinful nature and replaces it with His Son's holy nature. This is the present spiritual reality and identity of every true believer in Christ and why Paul could confidently proclaim, "I have been crucified with Christ and I no longer live but Christ lives in me (Galatians 2:20)."

Q17. Don't Christians just have two natures, like a white dog and a black dog fighting within them, and whichever one they feed the most gets stronger?

A17. Many Christians erroneously believe that after they are saved they have a new spiritual nature, which is righteous and holy, and an old sinful nature, which is depraved and evil, living within them. They believe the life of a born again Christian depends on the outcome of the war between these two natures within them. They compare this internal conflict to having a white dog and a black dog living within them who are always fighting each other for supremacy. They mistakenly think that as long as they keep the black dog under control and the white dog properly fed, they will have victory and peace.

The main reason this thinking is not correct is because it is not Scriptural. There are many Bible verses that clearly indicate that a born again Christian's sinful nature is dead and removed. If we are in Christ, there is no black dog of sin living in us. There is only Christ living in us. This thinking also reveals an ignorance and misunderstanding about God's eternal purpose. The Bible declares that man is born a sinner and needs Christ the Savior to deliver him from sin, death and eternal hell. We could never become good enough to be saved and, once saved, we could never become good enough to be holy in God's eyes. That's why Jesus Christ had to die on the cross for us in the first place. By the crucifixion of Jesus Christ, God dealt with the guilt of our sinful actions once and for all time by providing His forgiveness of sins. At the same time, God also dealt with our sinful nature once and for all time by crucifying it on the cross with His Son (Romans 6:6; Colossians 2:11). Once we are born again, Jesus Christ dwells in us (1 Corinthians 13:5; Galatians 2:20; Colossians 1:27).

Since our sinful nature died (which compelled us to sin) was removed from us when we were born again, we have been freed from the power of sin. However, this does not mean our minds were instantly transformed to never sin again. After we are saved, we need to stand firm by faith in the word of the cross so that our minds will be renewed by the Spirit of truth. This is what the Bible calls the process of sanctification by which our souls are transformed to express the image of Christ. There is a great difference between the old sinful nature and the unrenewed mind. Our old sinful nature was like a continuously operating "sin factory" that had to be destroyed by Christ's death on the cross before we could be set free from sin. The unrenewed mind, on the other hand, is simply our unconverted mindset, which the Holy Spirit within us can convert and transform now that we no longer have a sinful nature. Since our sinful nature has been removed and replaced with Christ's holy nature, we now have the spiritual capability by faith in Christ's completed work on the cross to stop practicing sin and to practice righteousness instead.

To sum up, we are Christ's body and Christ's home (the temple of the Holy Spirit). Jesus said a "house divided against itself will not stand (Matthew 12:25)." Jesus would never share His house and body with a "devil dog" (the sinful nature) whose intent is to divide and destroy. Thank God, by the cross of Christ, that so-called "black dog" (our sinful nature), which was controlled and ruled by Satan, and whose sole aim was to deceive and devour us, has been completely and utterly destroyed and removed from us!

Q18. I do not find the term "the divine exchange" in the Bible. What is this?

A18. The term "trinity" also does not appear in the Bible but the doctrine of the trinity of God is established, confirmed and supported by many Scriptures throughout the Bible. The term *"trinity"* is used to explain the eternal triune (three-in-one) relationship between God the Father, God the Son, and God the Holy Spirit. In the same manner, the term the "divine exchange" can be used to explain how God the Father, by His Son's death, exchanged our sinful nature with Christ's holy nature so that His Holy Spirit could indwell us. It also can be used to explain how we live the Christian life - not by trying to live like Christ but by trusting Christ to live His life in us. Thus the Christian life is not a changed life; it is an exchanged life. God knew man's sinful nature was completely corrupt and beyond reform. Therefore, His divine plan was not to "improve" our sinful nature. Instead, He "executed" our sinful nature with Christ on the cross and exchanged it with His Son's nature. This "divine exchange" describes the inward spiritual transformation that occurred when we were "born again."

There are many Scriptures that support the Biblical principle of the "divine exchange." One Bible verse that sums up the divine exchange is 2 Corinthians 5:21: "God made Christ who had no sin to be sin for us, so that we might become the righteousness of God." Thus, by His death, Christ exchanged His holy nature for our sinful nature and reconciled us to God (Romans 5:10; 1 Corinthians

1:30; Colossians 1:21-22; 1 Peter 2:24; 1 John 5:11-12). Therefore, when we received Jesus as our Lord and were born again by God's Spirit (John 3:3-8); our sinful nature was crucified and removed (Romans 6:6; Colossians 2:11) and we have become a new creation in Christ (2 Corinthians 5:17; Galatians 6:15). By Christ's sacrifice, God translated us from our sinful nature into His divine nature (2 Peter 1:4). The Son of God now lives in us (Romans 8:10; 2 Corinthians 12:9; 13:5; Galatians 1:16; 2:20; Colossians 1:27). Our body is no longer a temple of sin but is now a temple of the Holy Spirit (1 Corinthians 3:16; 6:19). We were born sinners; but now by the power of the cross of Christ, God has transformed us into His saints (holy ones). We were once sons of the devil by nature; but now by the power of Christ's crucifixion, we have become sons of God with His holy nature.

The divine exchange is like receiving a divine heart transplant since God replaced our terminally sin-sick heart with His Son's divine heart. Of course, Jesus had to die for this heart transplant to take place. Since we have been born again of the Spirit and Christ now lives in us, we now have God's *"DNA - Divine Nature from Above."* The Bible also describes this divine surgery in terms of spiritual circumcision: "In Him you were also circumcised with a circumcision made without hands, in the removal of the sinful nature by the circumcision of Christ... When you were dead in your sins and in the uncircumcision of your sinful nature, God made you alive with Christ (Colossians 2:11-13)."

The term the "exchanged life" or what we call the divine exchange may have originated in 1869 with Hudson Taylor, pioneer missionary to China, who wrote, "The Lord Jesus tells me I am a branch. I am part of Him and I have just to believe and act upon it. I have seen it long enough in the Bible but I believe it now as a living reality. In a word, 'whereas once I was blind, now I see.' I am dead and buried with Christ - aye, and risen too and ascended; and now Christ lives in me. I now believe I am dead to sin. God reckons me so and tells me to reckon myself so. Oh, the joy of seeing this truth: I pray that the eyes of your understanding may be enlightened, that you may know and enjoy the riches freely given us in Christ." Note: from the chapter entitled *The Exchanged Life* in *Hudson Taylor's Spiritual Secret* by his son, Howard Taylor.

The apostle Paul may have best summed up the divine exchange with his statement, "I have been crucified with Christ and I no longer live but Christ lives in me; and the life that I now live in the body, I live by faith in the Son of God (Galatians 2:20)."

Q19.   Isn't faith in Jesus all that I need?

A19.   Yes, if your faith is based on the real Jesus and the real gospel. To more fully answer your question, let's review what the Bible says about faith. Six centuries before Christ's birth, God gave the prophet Habakkuk divine revelation that "the righteous will live by faith (Habakkuk 2:4)." This Scripture expresses the theme of God's relationship with man. Habakkuk's prophecy is fulfilled in the New Covenant where it provides the basis for the gospel: "I am not ashamed of the gospel, because it is the power of God for the salvation of everyone who believes… for in the gospel a righteousness from God is revealed, a righteousness that is by faith from first to last, just as it is written: *The righteous will live by faith* (Romans 1:16-17; see also Galatians 3:11; Hebrews 10:38).'" The Greek word for faith is *pistis*, which in its various forms (faith, believe, belief, faithful, etc.) is used 600 times in the New Testament. It is clear that faith is the underlying theme of the New Covenant and the very foundation of the gospel.

The Biblical definition of faith is found in the Book of Hebrews, which says, "Faith is the assurance of things hoped for, the conviction of things not seen (Hebrews 11:1/The New American Standard Bible). Another translation says "Faith is being sure of what we hope for and certain of what we do not see (The New International Version). And yet another translation says "Faith is the substance of things hoped for, the evidence of things not seen (The King James Version)." From a Biblical perspective, faith enables us to see God and see things the way God sees them. The Bible says that Moses "endured by seeing Him who is unseen (Hebrews 11:27)." And the apostle Paul wrote, "So we fix our eyes not on what is seen, but what is unseen. For what is seen is temporary, but what is unseen is eternal (2 Corinthians 4:18)." Biblical faith is not faith in faith for faith's sake or a philosophy of "whatever you believe, you can achieve." Biblical faith is not some kind of "mind over matter" pop psychology or visualization technique. That kind of counterfeit faith is based on man's psychic/soul power and is actually hostile to the Spirit of God.

Biblical faith is based solely on the Word *(the Logos)* of God revealed to us. The Bible says Jesus Christ is the Word *(the Logos)* of God (John 1:1). Therefore, Biblical faith is based on God's revelation of His Son to us. All true faith comes from seeing the Lord Jesus Christ - who He is and what He has done on the cross. When Jesus asked, "Who do you say I am?" Simon Peter answered, "You are the Christ, the Son of the living God." Then Jesus replied, "Blessed are you, Simon Barjona, because flesh and blood did not reveal this to you, but my Father who is in heaven. I also say to you that you are Peter, and upon this rock I will build the church and the gates of Hades will not overcome it (Matthew 16:17-18)." Thus God's revelation of Jesus Christ to us is the bedrock of our faith, the foundation of the gospel and the cornerstone of the church.

Therefore, in order for our faith to be true Biblical faith it must correspond to the revealed Word of God. For example, after Jesus Christ rose from the dead, God gave the disciple Thomas divine revelation to see Christ as He really is. In response, Thomas exclaimed to Jesus, "My Lord and my God (John 20:28)!" Based on their Judaic heritage and knowledge of the Old Testament prophets, the disciples knew that when the Messiah (Christ) came, he would be God in the flesh (Isaiah 9:6; Psalm 45:6-7; John 1:1, 14, 18; Romans 9:5; Titus 2:13; Hebrews 1:8; 1 John 5:20).

Therefore, when the disciples recognized and confessed Jesus as the long-awaited Messiah, they acknowledged He was God. Do you also confess that Jesus Christ is your Lord and God? If your answer is "Yes, certainly!" then you have saving faith. On the other hand, if anyone thinks that Jesus is not God but is only a great prophet or teacher or a divinely created being such as an angel, then that person does not have saving faith. In the same way, anyone who confesses Jesus is their Savior, without making Him their Lord, is also not saved. The Bible says, "If you confess with your mouth *Jesus is Lord,* and believe in your heart that God raised Him from the dead, you will be saved (Romans 10:9; see also Acts 2:36)." Thus saving faith in Jesus means we are following the real Jesus in the right way according to the Word of God.

What about sanctifying faith? For our salvation is not complete without works of sanctification, which confirm the validity of our faith (James 2:26). And without sanctification, no one will see the Lord (Hebrews 12:14). On the cross, Jesus Christ died to forgive us from the penalty of our sins (Romans 5:8; Ephesians 1:7). This is a vital provision of Christ's Atonement, but God also knew we needed to overcome Satan and the power of sin in this world. Therefore, Jesus Christ also died on the cross to free us from the power of our sinful nature. When Christ died, we died with Him (Romans 6:8). When we were born again, God removed our sinful nature and replaced it with His Son's holy nature (Romans 6:6; Galatians 2:20). Because our old nature of sin is dead and gone, we have been freed from the power of sin (Romans 6:7). This is a central feature of

Christ's Atonement but if we do not believe it and act on it, this vital provision of Christ's death will not be effective in our life.

Neither our initial salvation nor ongoing sanctification (the outworking of our salvation) is based on our merit or effort. Otherwise, our boast would be in ourselves instead of in the cross of Jesus Christ (Galatians 6:14). There is nothing we can receive from God (whether our salvation or sanctification) by relying on our natural ability (Galatians 3:2-5). God is only pleased and works on our behalf when we demonstrate faith in Jesus Christ and His completed work on the cross.

Therefore, we are not only saved by faith in Jesus Christ and His completed work on the cross (Christ died for us so we might be forgiven from sin's penalty); we are also sanctified by faith in Jesus Christ and His completed work on the cross (we died with Christ so we might be delivered from sin's power). Once again, we must follow the real Jesus in the right way or we will not have sanctifying faith, which results in eternal life. "But now having been freed from sin and enslaved to God, you derive your benefit, resulting in sanctification, and the outcome, eternal life (Romans 6:22)."

To sum up, Biblical faith must be based on the specific and accurate *truth* of the Word of God. Jesus said, "God is Spirit, and those who worship Him must worship in spirit and *truth* (John 4:24)." This is not just faith in a general belief about God. In these dark and perilous days, deceiving spirits are misleading many with a counterfeit faith and a counterfeit gospel (1 Timothy 4:1; Matthew 24:11). This is why we contend earnestly for the true faith and proclaim the whole gospel of Christ that was entrusted to us (1 Corinthians 3:1. Jude 3). If the Jesus Christ you believe in is truly your Lord and God, you are saved. On the other hand, if He is not truly your Lord and God, you are not following the real Jesus and you are not saved. In the same way, if the gospel of Christ you believe in does not deliver you from besetting sins so that you can walk in the power of the Spirit, you are not following the real gospel. When you have real faith in the real gospel, you will know Jesus Christ, the Son of God, and He will set you free from slavery to sin so you might walk in His new, sanctified life and have intimate fellowship with Him (John 8:31-36; John 14:21-23; Romans 6:4-7; 1 John 1:3-7).

Q20. But doesn't the message of the cross add to the gospel? Didn't Jesus just ask people to just believe in Him?

A20. It's true that Jesus told people to just believe in Him (John 6:29). However, Jesus also went on say, "He who does not take up his cross and follow after Me is not worthy of Me. He who has found his life will lose it, and he who has lost his life for My sake will find it (Matthew 10:38-39)." Jesus also said, "If anyone wishes to come after Me, he must deny himself and take up his cross and follow Me. For whoever wishes to save his life will lose it but whoever loses his life for My sake and the gospel's will save it (Mark 9:34)." And Jesus further said, "Whoever does not carry his own cross and come after Me cannot be My disciple...no one can be

My disciple if he does not give up everything he has (Luke 14:27, 33).

In these passages, Jesus explained what it meant to believe in Him. Are we suffering alienation and, if need be, persecution for the gospel by carrying our own cross and identifying with Jesus' death each day? Are we forsaking the worries and pleasures and riches of this life for His sake? Are we denying ourselves the pursuit of self-fulfillment for the sake of the gospel? Are we yielding our personal preferences and natural desires to Christ's Sovereignty? Are we giving up worldly ambitions, associations and activities to lose our soul-life for the sake of Christ? This is the Scriptural evidence that we believe in Jesus. The Bible says that when we lay down our soul-life for Christ's sake, we show that we are Christ's disciples and are expressing true love for the body of Christ (John 13:35; 15:12-13; 1 John 3:16). Is this the Christianity we are practicing each day by faith in Christ's completed work on the cross? If our life does not demonstrate this distinguishing mark of discipleship and love, there is no Scriptural proof that our faith is authentic and that we are truly Christians.

The gospel is the message of Jesus Christ and the transforming power of His death on the cross. Jesus Christ died once for all eternity to completely redeem us from sin. Therefore, Christ's death on the cross redeemed us from both the penalty of our sinful deeds and the power of our sinful nature. Knowing this truth, the apostles did not preach the gospel of Christ as two phases of the Atonement or two stages of salvation (initial salvation and then future sanctification). They taught the gospel – the word of the cross - as one seamless truth: Christ died for us and included us in His death so that He might sovereignly live in us.

If we believe in the true gospel and our faith is real, then our sanctification and obedience to Christ will confirm our faith (James 2:26). This is what the apostle Paul called "the obedience of the faith (Romans 1:5; 16:26)." The evidence of true faith in Christ is an increasingly holy life (Romans 6:22), from which grows all the fruit of the Holy Spirit (Galatians 5:22-23). No one can say they know the Lord if they do not practice sanctification or holiness (Hebrews 12:14; 1 John 2:4; 3:6). This is what it means to really believe in the gospel of Jesus Christ.

Q21.   If our sinful nature (the old man of sin) has died and been removed, then why does the apostle Paul tell us to put off the old man and put on the new man?

A21.   We can better understand Paul's statement if we look at the whole context of these Scriptures. In Ephesians 4:22-24, Paul exhorted the church at Ephesus to renew their minds and *put off* the old man and *put on* the new man. Paul also exhorted the church at Colossae the same way, except in their case, he used the past tense: "You have *put off* the old man (and) you have *put on* the new man (Colossians 3:9-10)." The Greek word for "put on" is *enduo,* which means "to be clothed with." This is the same Greek word that Paul used in Romans 13:14 when he said *"Put on* the Lord Jesus Christ." Here, Paul exhorts Christians to *be clothed* with Christ. Yet Paul also said Christians have *already been clothed* with Christ: "For all of you who were baptized into Christ *have clothed* yourselves in Christ (Galatians 3:27)."

So how do we reconcile these Scriptures? The truth is that God put us in Christ when we were born again (1 Corinthians 1:30), but now we must substantiate or personalize this truth in our life and conduct by faith. This is what Paul meant when he said, "work out your salvation with fear and trembling for it is God who is at work in you, both to will and to work for His good pleasure (Philippians 2:12-13)." In other words, we must "take hold of" or "put on" *by faith* what God *through Christ* has already accomplished on the cross. Then God *through the Holy Spirit* will substantiate it and work it out in our life. If we do not "put on" by faith *what Christ has accomplished on our behalf by His sacrificial death* we cannot and will not experience the benefit of Christ's Atonement. The apostle Paul exhorted, "*Take hold* of the eternal life to which you were called (1 Timothy 6:12)." This spiritual principle to "put on," to "lay hold of," and to "take hold of" by faith applies not only to our salvation; it applies to our sanctification and eternal inheritance. Paul declared, "I press on so that I may *lay hold of* that for which also I was *laid hold of* by Christ Jesus (Philippians 3:12)."

The Bible says, "Our *old man* was crucified with Christ (Romans 6:6)" and "If anyone is in Christ, he is a *new man* (2 Corinthians 5:17)." This is the truth of the gospel of Christ crucified. Our responsibility is to now obey and act on God's Word by faith. Therefore, since we *know* with certainty that our old man has died and we are now a new man in Christ and that sin no longer dwells in us, we can *put off* the old man's clothing (the old way of thinking and acting) and *put on* the new man's clothing (the new way of thinking and acting). This is what the Bible calls being transformed by the renewing of your mind (Romans 12:2; Ephesians 4:23). In this way, we walk by faith in the righteous clothing of God's new creation – fashioned by Christ in us, the hope of glory (Colossians 1:27; Galatians 4:19).

Q22.　Do I need to believe I died with Christ in order to be His disciple?

A22.　Before followers of Christ were called Christians (Acts 11:26), they were called disciples. The Greek word for disciple is *mathetes,* which means pupil or learner. Within the New Testament context, a disciple is one who follows and embraces the life, views and practices of Jesus Christ. What did Jesus say His disciples must do in order to follow Him? Jesus said that to follow Him we must deny ourselves, give up everything, and carry our own cross daily (Matthew 10:38-39; Mark 8:34-35; Luke 9:23-24). He also declared that if we do not practice these things, we cannot be His disciple (Luke 14:27 & 33).

Therefore, we certainly need to believe *Christ died for us* to become a Christian (Christ's disciple). However, we then need to believe *we died with Christ* in order to satisfy the conditions that Jesus said were required to follow Him as His disciple (deny ourselves, give up everything, and carry our own cross daily). This is why God ordained water baptism ("burial under water") to immediately impress upon all new disciples that, when they were born of the Spirit, they died with Christ and their sinful nature was removed from them. If we do not believe we have already died with Christ, then all we can do is try to deny ourselves and carry our own cross by the best of our ability. Not only is this is a mission impossible; it is not Scriptural. As the apostle Paul declared, "Having begun by the Spirit, are you now trying to perfect yourselves by human effort (Galatians 3:3)?"

There is only one person who could ever live a genuine holy life of true self-sacrifice and undivided devotion to God and that is Jesus Christ. And in that great fact is found the divine answer to our dilemma. The only way we can live an authentic life of Christian discipleship is to know and act on the truth that we have died with Christ and that God has exchanged our sinful nature with Christ's holy nature. Then we can live as Christ's disciples by faith in the Son of God who lives in us (Galatians 2:20).

Q23.   I want to believe I died to sin. However, I cannot seem to get past just mentally understanding this concept and I still can't stop practicing sin. What can I do?

A23.   True faith is acting on divine revelation of God's Word. In the original Greek translation of the New Testament, there are two different words used for the "Word" of God. One is *logos*; the other is *rhema*. Although they are sometimes used interchangeably, they have two distinct meanings. *Logos* means the eternal counsel or mind of God. *Logos* could also be described as the divine blueprint of God's eternal purpose. For example, the apostle John used the word *logos* in introducing his gospel of Christ, "In the beginning was the Word *(Logos),* and the Word *(Logos)* was with God, and the Word *(Logos)* was God... and the Word *(Logos)* became flesh (John 1:1, 17)."

The *Logos* or total counsel of God is made available to us through both the written Word of God – the Bible, and the living Word of God – Jesus Christ. But the whole *Logos* of God is too vast and too comprehensive for us to grasp in its entirety. Therefore, *rhema* is the way the Holy Spirit divinely reveals a portion of His heavenly, eternal, total *Logos* in our human experience. *Rhema* specifically means a word that is spoken in time and space. Jesus said, "Man shall not live by bread alone, but on every word *(rhema)* that proceeds out of the mouth of God (Matthew 4:4)." This is the *rhema* of God that is revealed by the breath of God, which is the Holy Spirit.

In other words, through the spoken word *(rhema)* of God, the *Logos* (the mind) of God becomes real and produces faith in us. This is what the apostle Paul meant when he said, "Faith comes by hearing, and hearing by the word *(rhema)* of God (Romans 10:17)." From the context of this passage (Romans 10:8-17), we can conclude that when someone hears and acts on the word *(rhema)* of God that Christ died for them (Romans 5:8), they will experience deliverance from the penalty of sin. In the same way, when someone hears and acts on the word *(rhema)* of God that they died with Christ (Romans 6:8), they will experience deliverance from the power of sin. "Because anyone who has died has been freed from sin (Romans 6:7)."

Therefore, you cannot "reckon" yourself dead to sin (Romans 6:11) unless you "know" your sinful nature has died (Romans 6:6). And you cannot know you have died with Christ unless you have had divine revelation from the Holy Spirit. The Greek word for "reckon" is *logizomai,* which means to "credit to the account" as in bookkeeping or accounting. Accounting is the precise reckoning of facts. There is no uncertainty in mathematics. Two plus two equals four in every language of the world. To reckon yourself dead to sin means you can count with certainty on the divine fact that your sinful nature has been crucified with Christ. Mere mental assent will not give you this kind of absolute conviction; only divine revelation from the Holy Spirit can. Therefore, it is essential that you personally receive divine revelation (the *rhema* of God) concerning the divine fact that you have died with Christ and your sinful nature is dead and gone. Humbly ask God to open your spiritual eyes and reveal this crucial truth of His Word to you. Remember our faith is based on what Jesus has already accomplished for us on the cross. Your sinful nature has already died and been removed (Romans 6:6-8; Colossians 3:3). You do not need to ask God to help your sinful nature die. God has already included you in Christ's death. When Jesus died, you died with Him (1 Corinthians 5:14). This is a divine fact. Therefore, when you pray, thank God for what Jesus has already done for you. Thank God that you have already died with Christ.

Perhaps you are under the mistaken impression that you can live the Christian life by applying more self-discipline and trying harder to be moral and good. However, you cannot walk in this "divine exchange" of the cross except by faith in the truth of God's Word. All forms of self-effort will fail. Here is a Biblical illustration from the Old Testament that might help: In Exodus, the children of Israel were saved from Egypt (a picture of the world) and the Pharaoh (a picture of Satan). This is just like us when we were born again and saved from the world and the devil. Then, just as the children of Israel began to be tested in the "wilderness of sin," we begin to learn many lessons that are meant to purify our faith. It is in this "wilderness" that we find out for ourselves what kind of faith we have (God already knows). Eventually, God brings us to the edge of the "Promised Land," and gives us a *rhema* word that we are capable of going into this Land and possessing it. Unfortunately, the majority of people, like the unbelieving children of Israel, will not believe what God has told them is true. They will only believe what their eyes and ears reveal to them. They might say, "No way. There are too many giants over there and I am too small and weak. I better stay where I am." They did not have faith to enter into their inheritance because they depended on themselves instead of God, and they did not believe what God told them.

But there were two people who did believe the *rhema* word, which God had given to the whole congregation of Israel – Joshua and Caleb. They wanted to go into the Promised Land the first time that God told them to go in but nobody would go with them, so they had to wait until that whole generation that had come out of Egypt died in the wilderness. Then God raised up a new generation who would believe His *rhema* word to take the Land that God said was already theirs. Now here is the important thing to note - when they went in, from the moment they put their feet into the Jordan, they had to do it by faith because any self-effort on their part always resulted in disaster. When they walked around Jericho seven times, it was at God's *rhema* command. They did it by faith and had success. But every time they got it in their minds to do something on their own initiative or in their own timing or by their own plans, they met with failure. God was training them that the only way to take the Land was by obeying what God had initiated and told them to do. This lesson went on for years. Sometimes they learned it well and had great success. Other times, they forgot what God had told them and experienced terrible failure.

Here is the lesson for us, especially if you are finding it hard to enter into the "Promised Land," which God has already given you: every failure that God is allowing you to experience is meant to teach you that you can only enter into this "Promised Land" and make it your own *by faith*. Now faith is always faith in something. Faith is not an entity that stands alone. Real Christian faith is faith in what God has accomplished and what God has said. Faith stands and falls on this precept. So, every time that you try to enter in by self-discipline, self-effort, or your own initiative, but not by faith, you will fail. But every time that you venture even a baby toe into the Jordan by faith, God will give you success. This is the "law" of reward and consequences.

This long process (longer for some than others) is supposed to teach you that the only way to enter into the "Promised Land" that God has already purchased for you is *by faith and faith alone.* This is how you enter into your inheritance in Christ, and this is how you keep it. Here are four things you can do that will help you on your way:

1. First, immerse yourself in the Word of God continually. God's Word is pregnant with power to transform you and give you spiritual insight beyond human understanding. If you are born again, God has already given you the mind of Christ (1 Corinthians 2:16). Immersing yourself in God's Word will enable His Son's attitudes and thoughts to become yours. Coming into the experience of the exchanged life can be described this way: When a person believes and receives Christ, it is as if God has planted a "seed of truth" in the good ground of their heart (Luke 8:15). Once God has planted it, do not "dig up" this seed every day to "look at it" to see if it has sprouted. Leave God's seed of truth in the ground, trusting that this seed of truth, which God planted in you, has the power to spring forth into life. Make sure you water this seed of truth every day by contemplating the Word of God (especially Scriptures pertaining to this central, foundational gospel truth). Psalm 19:7 says, "The law of the Lord is perfect, *converting* the soul." Next, continually affirm to God (and yourself) verbally that you are *already* dead to sin and alive to God (Romans 6:11). The Bible says, "I believed, therefore I spoke (2 Corinthians 4:13)." You might say a prayer like this: "God, I thank you that I am dead to sin

and alive to God." Actively exercising your faith this way (and of course, really meaning it, since it is based on true divine facts), is a way of building up your faith in the truth. Eventually, that seed of truth, which God planted in you, will burst out into new life. God will make it happen because He is the One who causes the growth (1 Corinthians 3:7). Jesus is the *author* and the *finisher* of your faith (Hebrews 12:2) and He will accomplish this miracle of life in you.

2. Second, seek God in prayer constantly for His divine revelation. This is a prayer that delights the heart of God because it is aligned perfectly with His will. Jesus said, "Ask and it will be given to you; seek, and you will find; knock, and it will be opened to you. For everyone who asks receives, and he who seeks finds, and to him who knocks it will be opened (Matthew 7:7-8)." If your heart's desire is to know Him, He will gladly give you the kingdom (Luke 12:32).

3. Third, wait. God is in charge of your growth in the kingdom and His timing is perfect. Sit at the Lord's feet listening to His word like Mary (Luke 10:39), and trust that He will give you the insight you need at the right time, for He is the author and finisher of your faith.

4. Fourth, surround yourself with people who have real faith. Do you know any? There may be relatively few where you live. Jesus said, "For where two or three are gathered together in My name, there I am in their midst (Matthew 18:20)." If all you can find is one or two

others, that is enough. The Bible says, "As iron sharpens iron, so a man sharpens the countenance of his friend (Proverbs 27:17)." It would be better to have one or two quality friends of faith than have hundreds who are living to fulfill their soul-lives religiously and have no true interest in knowing and obeying Jesus. Remember that Jesus said, "Not everyone who says to Me, 'Lord, Lord,' will enter the kingdom of heaven, but he who does the will of My Father who is in heaven will enter. Many will say to Me on that day, 'Lord, Lord, did we not prophesy in Your name, and in Your name cast out demons, and in Your name perform many miracles?' And then I will declare to them, 'I never knew you; depart from Me, you who practice lawlessness (Matthew 7:21-23).'" You cannot be yoked together with "unbelieving believers" and be constantly influenced by them and then expect to enter into your inheritance with Christ. Why? Because Satan has blinded the minds of the unbelieving and as long as you are under their influence, teaching and carnal insight, you will not only lose sight of your inheritance in Christ, you may never realize it is there in the first place. Your ears will be filled with teachings that "tickle them" (2 Timothy 4:3), and you will be caught up with religious worldliness, which is really lawlessness. When Paul told Timothy to flee temptation, he wasn't only talking about immorality. He was also talking about turning away from fellowship with "unbelieving believers" who have "a form of godliness, although they have denied its power (2 Timothy 3:5)." The Bible says, "Have nothing to do with them." As the apostle

Paul said, "What fellowship can light have with darkness (2 Corinthians 6:14)?"

5. Finally, until you are willing to lose everything for Christ, He will not let you find Him. He does not reveal Himself to anyone who is insincere. The Bible says, "Blessed are the pure in heart, for they will see God (Matthew 5:8)" and "the intimate communion of the Lord is reserved for those who fear Him (Psalm 25:14)." If you have the heart of "the Bride" in you, you will increasingly find His fellowship irresistible, compelling and well worth giving up everything you own, everything you are and everything you might have had just to catch even a glimpse of the train of His robe as it fills the temple! (Isaiah 6:1). This is why everyone who sees the Lord in heaven cries, "Holy, Holy, Holy," because He is beauty personified! As King David testified, "One thing I have desired of the Lord, that I shall seek: That I may dwell in the house of the Lord all the days of my life, to behold the beauty of the Lord and to inquire in His temple (Psalm 27:4)."

Q24. What did the apostle Paul mean when he said he wanted to be conformed to Christ's death (Philippians 3:10) when he already had said he was crucified with Christ (Galatians 2:20)?

A24. These two statements by Paul express the difference between our salvation and our sanctification. At the time of our salvation, we died with Christ (Romans 6:8) and our sinful nature was crucified with Christ (Romans 6:6). This is a divine fact that all new Christians should immediately be taught when they are water baptized. There is nothing we can humanly do to crucify our sinful nature. Jesus Christ is God's only Holy One (John 6:69); therefore, His death is the only Holy Death. That is why God spiritually included us in Christ's death. What God requires of us now is to believe in His Son and what He has accomplished for us when He included us in His death.

It is a common mistake for Christians to receive Christ by faith (salvation) but then try to spiritually grow in Christ (sanctification) by the best of their ability. This is an impossible mission doomed to defeat because we cannot save ourselves and we cannot sanctify ourselves; we can only present ourselves to God for sanctification. The way we grow in Christ is the same way we received Christ - by faith! We don't just identify with Christ's death only on the day we are water baptized. Instead, we must continually identify by faith with Christ's death by "taking up our cross" – that implementation of death – everyday to lose our soul life for Christ's sake (Luke 9:23-24). When we were born again of the Spirit, God spiritually included us in Christ's death so that when Christ died, we died with Him and our sinful nature was removed from us (Romans 6:6). As we abide (remain united by faith) in Jesus Christ and what He accomplished on the cross through the power of His crucifixion, the power of His resurrection life will effectively work through us and produce "sanctification without which no one will see the Lord (Hebrews 12:14).".

Just as there is only one Holy Death, there is only one Holy Life - Christ's life. God has miraculously included us in

His Son's Holy Death and His Son's Holy Life. "For if we have been united with Him in the likeness of His death, certainly we shall also be in the likeness of His resurrection (Romans 6:5)." Our joyful obligation is to always abide (remain united by faith) in Jesus Christ and His death and resurrection (Romans 8:12-13). The authentic Christian life is one of expression not suppression. We do not try to live the Christian life by practicing willpower and suppressing sinful desires. Instead, we continually fix our eyes on Jesus Christ, the author and finisher of our faith and each day present ourselves to Him. As we abide by faith in the power of His crucifixion (the divine truth that when Christ died, we also died), *God will cause* the power of His Son's resurrection life to be formed in us. Over time and by faith, God will - by the power of Christ's death and resurrection in us - transform and convert our soul (our will, mind and personality) to reflect and express the image of Christ. When we lose our soul life for Christ, we will find our soul in Christ. We will exchange our attitudes, affections and abilities for Christ's attitudes, affections and abilities.

To sum up, our sinful nature has already been crucified with Christ (Romans 6:6); and as we now abide in Him, our soul will be conformed into the image of Christ's death (Philippians 3:10) so that we might express the image of Christ's life (Romans 8:29). For without death, there can be no resurrection life. This is what Jesus meant when He said, "Unless a kernel of wheat falls to the ground and dies, it remains only a single seed; but if it dies, it bears much fruit (John 12:24)." Paul knew this and, wanting to be conformed to Christ's death, he knew that he would then be filled with Christ's life so that he could help bring many other brethren into their divine inheritance of salvation and sanctification in Christ.

Q25. Is the apostle Paul's gospel different than the other apostles' gospel?

A25. Paul's gospel is not different than the other apostles' gospel, but it more clearly reveals and explains the full meaning of the good news of the cross. Paul described the basic gospel that he preached as follows: "Now I make known to you, brethren, the gospel which I preached to you, which also you received, in which also you stand, by which you also are saved, if you hold fast the word which I preached to you, unless you believed in vain. For I delivered to you as of first importance what I also received, that *Christ died for our sins* according to the Scriptures, and that He was buried, and that He was raised up on the third day according to the Scriptures (1 Corinthians 15:1-4)." This basic gospel message can be summed up as the good news that *Christ died for our sins,* which is the same gospel that Peter and the other apostles preached.

However, Paul also personally received divine revelation from Jesus Christ that gave him greater insight into the fuller meaning and provision of Christ's death on the cross. In this regard, Paul wrote, "I would have you know, brethren, that the gospel which was preached by me is not according to man. For I neither received it from man, nor was I taught it, but I received it through a revelation of Jesus Christ (Galatians 1:11-13)." What is this fuller gospel message that Jesus commissioned Paul to preach? It is the gospel that Jesus Christ not only bore our sins on the cross with Him; He also bore our sin nature on the cross with Him (2 Corinthians 5:21). In particular, Paul revealed that God used the death of His only Son to put to death our sinful nature and remove it from us. "Do you not know that all of us who have been immersed into Christ Jesus have been immersed into His death? Therefore, we have been buried with Him through immersion into death... for we know that our old man was crucified with Him, in order that our body of sin *(our sinful nature)* might be done away with, so that we would no longer be slaves to sin; for he who has died has been freed from sin (Romans 6:3-4, 6-7; see also Colossians 2:11-12)." Consequently, Paul preached not only that *Christ died for us* (Romans 5:8); he also preached that *we died with Christ* (Romans 6:8)!

Paul's gospel reveals the divine truth that God removed our sinful nature through His Son's death on the cross so that His resurrected Son would now indwell us. Paul testified, "God... was pleased to reveal His Son in me so that I might preach Him (Galatians 1:15-16)." And Paul wrote to fellow believers, "Do you not realize that Jesus Christ is in you? (2 Corinthians 13:5; see also Colossians 1:27)." This was the gospel that Paul preached and this was his personal testimony: "I have been crucified with Christ and I no longer live but Christ lives in me; and the life that I now live in the body, I live by faith in the Son of God who loved me and gave Himself up for me (Galatians 2:20)." Paul's gospel unfolds the glorious truth of the cross that Christ not only died for our sins; we also died with Him in order that He might now sovereignly live through us.

Paul's gospel also revealed the divine truth that the church is the body of Christ. Once again, this truth is a further unfolding of the mystery of the cross of Christ. Just before His death, Jesus told His disciples, "The hour has come for the Son of Man to be glorified. Truly, truly, I say to you, that unless a grain of wheat falls into the earth and dies, it remains alone; but if it dies, it bears much fruit (John 12:23-24)." Jesus spoke here of His impending death on the cross from which the church would be birthed. Paul taught, "We have been buried with Him through baptism into death, so that as Christ was raised from the death through the glory of the Father, so we too might walk in newness of life. For if we have become united with Him in the likeness of His death, certainly we shall also be in the likeness of His resurrection. (Romans 6:4-5)." In other words, Christ's death on the cross provided the divine means for us to be born again of the Spirit. For when we were born again, God spiritually immersed us in Christ's death and resurrection. Therefore when Christ died, our sinful nature died with Him and when Christ was raised from the dead, we were also raised from the dead to live in Christ and He in us. And since Christ lives in each of us, together we make up His body here on earth (1 Corinthians 12:12).

The revelation that the church is the living body of Christ may not seem new to us today but in the first century church, Paul was the first apostle to proclaim this divine truth and explain it. When Paul shared this gospel that he had received from Jesus Christ with Peter and the other apostles, they concurred with it and gave him their blessing to preach his gospel to the Gentiles (Galatians 2:1-9). Indeed, in his own epistle to the churches, Peter stated that he believed Paul's gospel teaching was the wisdom of God (2 Peter 3:15-16).

Clearly, the gospel Paul preached gives us greater revelation and essential understanding on what Jesus Christ has accomplished for us on the cross. For Jesus not only died to free us from the penalty of our sins; He also died to free us from the power of our sin nature so that we might be indwelt by His Spirit and be His body, His church, here on earth. As a chained prisoner in Roman judicial custody, Paul himself described his apostolic commission to King Agrippa. Paul testified that Jesus personally appeared to him in a vision and told him, "I am sending you to open their eyes so they *(the Gentiles)* may turn from darkness to light and from the dominion of Satan to God, so that they may receive forgiveness of sins and an inheritance among those who are sanctified by faith in Me. So, King Agrippa, I was not disobedient to this heavenly vision (Acts 26:17-19)." Therefore, Paul's divine mission was not only to bring God's elect into *justification by faith* but to also bring them into *sanctification by faith*, without which no one can know the Lord and receive their inheritance in Christ.

In closing, the basic gospel can be summarized as *"Christ died for us,"* whereas Paul's gospel message expands on this and can be summarized as *"Christ died for us and included us in His death so that He might sovereignly live through us, His body and church."* This is the same gospel that we preach.

Q26.   What did Jesus mean when He said we must "bear our own cross?"

A26.   Jesus Christ bore our sins on His cross but He also said we must bear our own cross. "Whoever does not carry his own cross and follow Me, cannot be My disciple (Luke 14:27)." What does this mean? As we present ourselves to God daily (Romans 12:1), the Holy Spirit begins to reveal that our Lord's cross, which was the implement of His death, must now to become the implement of our own death. Therefore the cross is not just His; it must by faith become ours. This is how we "work out our salvation" and prove we are His disciples (Philippians 2:12). But what is it that now dies? If we allow it, it is the unrenewed mind and self-governing and unconverted soul that dies to its own sovereignty and embraces submission at the feet of Jesus. "Every knee will bow, in heaven and on earth and under the earth, and every tongue will confess that Jesus Christ is Lord (Philippians 2:10-11)."

Some Christians mistakenly believe that they still have a sinful nature indwelling them. They believe that through their own self-discipline, this sinful nature can be "put to death." This is not only prideful and untrue; it is vanity and impossible. God knew that we could not crucify ourselves or put our sinful nature to death. Therefore, He accomplished the death of our sinful nature for all of us who are saved through the body of His Son (2 Corinthians

5:14). A dramatic spiritual breakthrough occurs in our life when God reveals to us that He dealt a death-blow to our sinful nature when we were born again. We will then understand that we do not have to crucify the sinful nature because it has *already been* crucified with Christ (Romans 6:6; Galatians 2:20; Colossians 3:3).

God not only crucified our sinful nature with Christ on the cross, He removed it when we received the risen Christ into our hearts (Colossians 2:11-12). This is the divinely powerful work that only God could accomplish. By faith in God's Word, we can now count ourselves dead to sin and alive to God in Christ Jesus (Romans 6:11). When we understand that our sinful nature has died with Christ and was buried (removed) with Christ (Romans 6:3-6), we will recognize the futility of trying to put to death a sinful nature that is no longer within us! We will not try to overcome sin by our willpower and self-discipline, but by faith in what Christ accomplished on the cross (Galatians 3:3). In Christ, we do not practice self-crucifixion; we identify with the work of His cross by faith and make it our own.

When we were born again, our spirit and Christ's Spirit were joined together in union (Romans 7:4; 1 Corinthians 6:17). However, our soul (our individual personality - our will, intellect and emotions) was not instantly transformed into Christ's image nor did it automatically come under Christ's Sovereignty. Since Christ's death on the cross has already dealt with our sinful nature, we do not have to put it to death every day over and over again. However, we now have the obligation and privilege as Christ's disciples to carry our own cross and "put to death" our old sinful way of thinking (the unrenewed mind or unconverted soul). This is what it means to "carry our own cross." God knew that our willpower would never be strong enough to overcome the world, the flesh, the devil and the overwhelming power of sin. This is why the precious Lamb of God had to die in our place for us. We could not deliver ourselves from sin's power! In the same way, we cannot deliver ourselves from the unconverted soul-life, which is lawlessly in the habit of practicing self-sovereignty. This death to our unconverted soul-life can only be a divine work of the Spirit, as we present ourselves to God by faith in His Word (Romans 1:17; 12:2).

Although most Bible translations confusingly use the term "flesh" for both the sinful nature and the unconverted soul (the unrenewed mind), there is a crucial difference. Our unrenewed mind is not like the sinful nature, which was a powerful entity - a "sin factory" within us that continuously produced sinful attitudes and actions and, therefore, had to be destroyed by Christ's death on the cross. Now that we no longer have a sinful nature, our unrenewed mind can be transformed and submitted to Christ's sovereignty by believing the Word of God. We are now able *by faith* to put to death (and rid ourselves of) the carnal mindset of our unconverted soul and put on the mind of Christ (1 Corinthians 2:26). By faith in Christ's completed work on the cross, we are able to exchange our carnal attitudes and affections for Christ's attitudes and affections.

This is what the apostle Paul called "taking every thought captive to the obedience of Christ (2 Corinthians 10:5)." Paul taught, "If you are living according to the flesh *(the unconverted soul-life)*, you will die; but if by the Spirit, you are putting to death the misdeeds of the body, you will live… and do not be conformed to this world, but be transformed by the renewing of your mind, so that you may prove what is the will of God… now all those who belong to Christ Jesus have put to death on the cross the flesh *(the unconverted soul-life)* with its passions and desires (Romans 8:13; 12:2; Galatians 5:24)." If we love Christ Jesus and the body of Christ, this is how we carry our cross and this is how we lay down our soul-life for the sake of our fellow brothers and sisters (1 John 3:16).

There *is* a cost to following Jesus Christ! The Bible calls it "sanctification." This is what Jesus meant when He said the cost of discipleship was "carrying our own cross." He said, "If anyone wishes to come after Me, he must deny himself and take up his cross daily and follow Me. For whoever wishes to save his soul-life will lose it, but whoever loses his soul-life for My sake, he is the one who will save it (Luke 9:23-24)." When we take up this cross of discipleship, the process of sanctification begins. This is our cooperation *by faith* with the daily inworking of Christ's death in our unconverted soul-life. This is the essential basis and prerequisite for us to have intimate fellowship with Christ and His sufferings. Then, we can know Him and live in the power of His resurrection (Philippians 3:10). If we want to follow Jesus Christ in discipleship and carry our own cross, we must be prepared to suffer in our soul-life.

Our flesh (the Greek word is *sarx*, which in this Scriptural context means body and soul) will suffer the grief and pain of the loss of self-sovereignty and self-identity as we yield our soul-life to Christ in sanctification. "Since Christ has suffered in the flesh, arm yourselves also with the same purpose, because he who has suffered in the flesh *(body and soul)* has ceased from sin so as to live no longer for the lusts of men but for the will of God (1 Peter 4:1-2)."

When we bear our cross daily, God uses the inward revelation of His Word and the external pressure of His trials to "put to death" our carnal attitudes and affections and conform our soul-life to Christ's image. This is what the apostle Paul called "being conformed to His death (Philippians 3:10)." It is important to remember that this inworking of Christ's suffering and death in our soul-life is only possible because Jesus Christ has already obtained the victory over sin by His sacrificial death on the cross. As a result of His death on the cross, our sins have been forgiven and our sinful nature has been removed from us. However, Jesus Christ not only died in our place; He now wants to sovereignly live in our place (Galatians 2:20). If we believe the truth that we no longer have a sinful nature and that we are now a holy new person in Christ (Christ now lives in us), this truth will set us free!

God created the human soul. Therefore, He does not want to destroy it nor does He want us to vainly try to suppress it or eradicate it. God wants to *restore* our soul to its original, eternal purpose. The work of the cross will not annihilate our soul; we will still possess our soul and its faculties, just as we still possess our physical body with its faculties. But when the mark of the cross is imprinted on our soul, we will no longer independently assert ourselves. Instead, we will be transformed as yielded, obedient and useful vessels for God's use (2 Timothy 2:21). And like Jesus Himself was submitted to the Father, we will be able to say, "I can do nothing on my own initiative (John 5:19 & 30)."

As we learn to carry our cross daily, we will increasingly experience and express the power of Jesus Christ's resurrection life. Paul testified, "We always carry about in our body the death of Jesus, so that the life of Jesus may also be revealed in our body (2 Corinthians 4:10)." Therefore, the way of the cross is the *only* way of fruitfulness in Christ! Jesus said, "Truly, truly, I say to you, unless a grain of wheat fall into the earth and dies, it remains alone; but if it dies, it bears much fruit. He who loves his soul-life loses it, and he who hates his soul-life in this world will keep it to life eternal (John 12:24-25)." To those who know it, the way of the cross is a precious path that leads us into a more and more intimate relationship with Jesus Christ. We learn the truth in Christ and He sets us free from sin's stranglehold on our minds (John 8:32-36). As our mind becomes increasingly harmonized with the truth, Jesus reveals to us the beautiful, divine mystery and communion of knowing Him intimately.

If you are a serious follower (disciple) of Jesus Christ, then the meaning of Christ's death on the cross and what it means for you to carry your *own* cross is vitally important for you to understand. The Book of Romans, for example, contains far more than the basic salvation message; it reveals the full meaning and application of Christ's death on the cross (see Romans Chapter 5-8). This full meaning of the cross of Christ is a central, foundational doctrine of Christianity and understanding its significance is crucial to not only your salvation but your sanctification. Knowing and acting on the truth of the cross has eternal consequences because without sanctification no one will receive their spiritual inheritance in Christ (Acts 26:18) and without sanctification no one will see and know the Lord Jesus Christ (Hebrews 12:14). Yet, tragically, most professing Christians are woefully ignorant of what it means to carry their own cross.

This is why it is essential that every true believer in Christ diligently seek God for divine revelation on what His Son fully accomplished on the cross and what it really means to carry your own cross. Jesus said, "Anyone who does not take his cross and follow Me is not worthy of Me. Whoever finds his soul-life will lose it, and whoever loses his soul-life for My sake will find it (Matthew 10:38-39)." This is the truth that must be understood. This is the truth that must be lived if we are to fulfill our divine destiny for which Christ died.

Q27. What did Jesus mean when He said we must "lose our soul-life?"

A27. Jesus said, "If anyone wishes to come after Me, he must deny himself, and take up his cross daily and follow Me. For whoever wishes to save his soul-life *(psyche)* will lose it, but whoever loses his soul-life *(psyche)* for My sake, he is the one who will find it (Luke 9:23-24)." Our soul is our individual personality and consists of our will, intellect and emotions. The English word, *psychology*, is derived from the Greek word *psych* and means the study of the soul or self. God made each of us with a unique soul and individual personality. The issue, however, is one of ownership. Will you remain captive and governed by your unrenewed, natural temperament or will your natural temperament and inclinations be governed by the Holy Spirit? True Christianity is not natural; it is spiritual. Jesus did not die on the cross so that His people would remain governed by their natural instincts and desires and just do whatever comes naturally to them. Jesus said, "That which is born of the flesh is flesh, and that which is born of the Spirit is spirit... it is the Spirit who gives life; the flesh has no spiritual value (John 3:6; 6:63)."

Just as we were born again of the Spirit, we must now live by the Spirit and not according to our natural temperament. "So I say, live by the Spirit and you will not carry out the desire of the flesh *(the unconverted and unsubmitted soul)*. For the flesh *(unsubmitted soul)* sets its desire against the Spirit, and the Spirit against the flesh *(unsubmitted soul)*; for these are in conflict with one another (Galatians 5:16-17; see also 6:7-8)." If you remain controlled by your natural temperament and desires and you are not governed by the Holy Spirit, you will be of no use to God and His kingdom. However, if your soul-life *(your attitudes and affections)* is submitted to Christ's Sovereignty, then God can transform your soul *(your individual personality)* by His Holy Spirit so that you become His sanctified and useful vessel. As the Holy Spirit increasingly governs your soul, any carnal character traits such as arrogance, anger, lust, laziness, lying, gossiping and fearfulness will increasingly disappear. As your soul-life becomes progressively transformed and conformed into Christ's image, you will increasingly experience more intimate fellowship with God the Father and His Son.

Jesus said, "Greater love has no one than this, that one lay down his soul-life *(psyche)* for his friends (John 15:13). We know that we should give up our physical life for Christ's sake; however, in this passage Jesus is saying that we must also lay down our soul-life *(psyche)* on a daily basis if we want to love the brethren. We must exchange our soul-life (our natural affections, attitudes and abilities) for Christ's affections, attitudes and abilities (Matthew 16:23-25; Colossians 3:1-3). When we practice laying down our soul-life out of love for Jesus Christ in this manner, we demonstrate by our actions that we truly love the body of Christ. The Bible says, "This is how we know what love is: Jesus Christ laid down His life *(psyche/soul-life)* for us and we ought to lay down our lives *(psychikos/soulish-lives)* for our brothers (1 John 3:16)."

It is absolutely essential that you know your sinful nature has died with Christ and been removed in Christ (Romans 6:6; Colossians 2:11) before you try to lay down your soul-life. Why? Because it is impossible to lay down your soul-life without faith, and your faith must be based on Biblical truth to be real and effective. When you know (believe and act on) the divine truth that your sinful nature has been crucified with Christ and is dead and gone, you will be freed from protecting and promoting your natural (soulish) self-identity and pursuing your natural desire for soulish self-fulfillment and self-ambition (Galatians 6:14). Then the power of Christ's death can work in your soul-life *(psyche)* so that the power of His resurrection life *(zoe)* might be revealed through you to others (2 Corinthians 4:12).

A picture of this spiritual principle may be found in the parable of the light and the lampstand (Luke 11:33-36). Jesus Christ is the light that illumines the lamp – our spirit (John 1:9; 8:12: Proverbs 20:27). Our soul (our natural personality) is like the lampshade. If we do not allow the Holy Spirit to govern our soul-life, our unsubmitted and unbroken natural personality will obscure the light of Christ from clearly shining through us. Jesus said a light hidden under a basket cannot be seen. This is similar to a smoke-blackened lampshade and illustrates what happens when a born again Christian still has an unconverted, untransformed and lawless soul-life. However, a light with a clear lampshade (a person who has their soul governed and transformed by God) shines brightly and Christ can be clearly seen in them. Once we know (believe and act on) the divine truth that we have already died with Christ, God can cleanse and purify our soul by conforming us to His Son's image.

The Bible calls this process "sanctification." "Now may the God of peace *sanctify* you entirely; and may your *spirit, soul and body* be preserved complete, without blame at the coming of our Lord Jesus Christ (1 Thessalonians 5:23)." The

Bible says, "Pursue *sanctification* without which no one will see the Lord (Hebrews 12:14)." The more we allow God to purify and cleanse our soul *(our lampshade)* of spots and blemishes *(carnal attitudes and affections)* (Ephesians 5:27), the more the light of Christ within our spirit can be transparently seen through our individual personality. "If therefore your whole body is full of light, with no dark part in it, it will be wholly illumined, as when the lamp illumines you with its rays (Luke 11:36)." The consummation of this sanctification process in the body of Christ can be seen in the Book of Revelation. "And I saw the holy city, new Jerusalem, coming down out of heaven from God, made ready as a bride for her husband... and the city has no need of the sun or of the moon to shine on it, for the glory of God has illumined it, and its lamp is the Lamb (Revelation 21:2 & 23)."

Remember, it is God's perfect design that each of us would have a vibrant, God-governed soul. He does *not* want to destroy or annihilate our soul (our natural personality) and He does *not* want us to try to suppress it or change it by our own willpower and self-effort. The Bible says Jesus Christ is the shepherd and guardian of our soul (1 Peter 2:25). Jesus wants to save our soul (James 1:21); heal our soul (Psalm 41:4); purify our soul (1 Peter 1:21); convert our soul (Psalm 19:7); transform our soul (Romans 12:2); and restore our soul (Psalm 23:3).

Jesus Christ died on the cross to deliver us from self-governance and bring rest to our soul. He said, "Come to Me, all who are weary and heavy-laden, and I will give you rest. Take My yoke upon you and learn from Me, for I am gentle and humble in heart, and you will find rest for your souls.

For My yoke is easy and My burden is light (Matthew 11:28-30)." When we put on His yoke of discipleship, laying down our soul-life for His sake, we are free to give up the constant struggle to protect, fulfill and promote our soulish identity, which always leads our soul into a perpetual and grievous state of unrest. We are then capable of experiencing a transformed soul-life and identity found only in Christ, which brings us into God's rest and freedom from sin's domination.

This is the divine exchange made possible by Christ's death on the cross! "For you have died and your life is now hidden in Christ with God (Colossians 3:3)." This is the spiritual rest God promises to all those who believe and act on His word. "Therefore, let us fear if, while a promise remains of entering His rest, any one of you may seem to have come short of it... for the one who has entered His rest has also ceased from his works, as God did from His. Therefore, let us be diligent to enter that rest (Hebrews 4:1, 10-11)."

If we present ourselves daily to Jesus Christ our Lord and King, His Sovereign Spirit will progressively permeate our entire being – starting in our spirit and extending to our soul and body. Jesus said, "The kingdom of heaven is like leaven, which a woman took and hid in three pecks of flour until it was all leavened (Matthew 13:33)." When the Holy Spirit becomes Master of our soul, we will love God with all our *spirit, soul and body* (Deuteronomy 6:5; 10:12) bearing fruit for God (Romans 7:4). And our *spirit, soul and body* will be an entirely useful vessel to our Lord Jesus Christ for the work of His kingdom (2 Timothy 2:21). The work of the cross will have restored and transformed our soul to God's original, eternal purpose – that we might know Him and serve Him – forever and ever!

Q28.   I thought I was already holy in God's eyes because of Jesus' Atonement. Then why should practicing holiness be important to me?

A28.   Above all, God is holy. "I the Lord your God am holy (Leviticus 19:2)." "There is no one holy like the Lord (1 Samuel 2:2)." "God is Light and in Him there is no darkness at all (1 John 1:5)." And because God is holy, He also requires that we be holy if we want to know Him and fellowship with Him. From a Biblical perspective, *holy* means pure – separated from sin and separated to God. The Bible says, "Beloved, let us purify ourselves from everything that contaminates the flesh and spirit, perfecting holiness in the fear of God (2 Corinthians 7:1)." When we were born again, God exchanged our sinful nature with Christ's holy nature (Romans 6:6; Galatians 2:20). Whereas we were once sinners by nature; we are now saints (*holy ones*) and members of God's family because we have Christ's holy nature. "Both He *(Jesus Christ)* who makes men holy and those who are made holy are of the same family. So Jesus is not ashamed to call them brothers (Hebrews 2:11)."

God not only made us holy when we were saved (1 Corinthians 1:2; Ephesians 4:24), He also calls every Christian to live a holy life *after* they are saved (1 Thessalonians 4:7). The Bible says, "God... has saved us and called us to a holy life (2 Timothy 1:9)." For a

Christian, there are no exceptions to God's call. The apostle Peter declared, "Like the Holy One who called you, be holy yourselves also in all your behavior; because it is written, 'You shall be holy for I am Holy (1 Peter 1:15-16).'" The apostle Paul prayed, "May He establish your hearts without blame in holiness before our God and Father Himself at the coming of our Lord Jesus Christ and His saints *(holy ones)*... now may the God of peace Himself *sanctify* you entirely; and may your spirit and soul and body be preserved complete, without blame at the coming of our Lord Jesus Christ (1 Thessalonians 3:13; 5:23)."

The English word "church" is derived from the Greek word *kuriakos*, which means "to belong to the Lord." In the New Testament, however, the word "church" is actually translated from the Greek word *ekklesia*, which means assembly or congregation (Matthew 16:18) and whose root meaning is "called out from." Based on the Greek words *kuriakos* and *ekklesia,* the church consists of all people who belong to the Lord and have been called out from the world. "'Therefore come out from them and be separate,' says the Lord, 'And do not touch what is unclean; and I will receive you. I will be a Father to you and you will be sons and daughters to Me,' says the Lord Almighty (2 Corinthians 6:17-18)." Consequently, we might say that God has set a "double seal" on every son and daughter who belongs to Him. The first seal is His indwelling Holy Spirit, *which confirms our salvation* (Ephesians 1:13). This was made possible through Christ's death on the cross, by which God removed our sinful nature and replaced it with His Son's holy nature. The second seal is the evidence of the indwelling

Holy Spirit manifest in our conduct, *which confirms our faith.* The Bible says, "For just as the body without the spirit is dead, so also faith without works is dead (James 2:26)," and "The firm foundation of God stands, having *this seal*, 'The Lord knows those who are His,' and, 'Everyone who names the name of the Lord is to abstain from wickedness (2 Timothy 2:19).'" Jesus said, 'You shall know them by their fruit." He did not say, "You shall know them by their gifts and ministries." Anyone who does not have this double seal of the Holy Spirit upon them does not belong to God. "For God did not call us to be impure, but to live a holy life. Therefore, he who rejects this instruction does not reject man but God, who gives you His Holy Spirit (1 Thessalonians 4:7-8)."

It is a grievous and tragic mistake to think that because our spirit was made righteous and holy when we were born again, we can now live as though our conduct was of no consequence. "What shall we say then? Are we to continue in sin so that grace may increase? May it never be! How shall we who died to sin still live in it (Romans 6:1-2)?" It is a lie to think that when we are practicing sin, God can only see Christ living in us *because* of His blood that was shed for us. Our sins are only forgiven and wiped clean from God's sight if we confess and repent (turn away) from the darkness of practicing sin and turn to God and walk in His Light. "*If* we walk in the Light as He Himself is in the Light... the blood of Jesus His Son cleanses us from all sin... *if* we confess our sins, He is faithful and righteous to forgive us our sins and to cleanse us from all unrighteousness (1 John 1:7 & 9)."

God's Holy Word commands us to "pursue holiness for without holiness no one will see the Lord (Hebrews 12:14)." God does not command us to practice holiness merely for holiness' sake. He wants us to practice holiness in order that we might see Him and intimately know Him. Our holy obedience to Jesus Christ is God's "love language." Jesus said, "If anyone loves Me, he will obey My teaching. My Father will love him, and we will come to him and make our home with him. He who does not love Me, does not obey My teaching (John 14:23-24)." The apostle John said no one who abides in Christ can continue to practice sin. "No who lives in Him keeps on sinning. No one who continues to sin has either seen Him or known Him (1 John 3:6)." Jesus Christ said anyone who claims to be a Christian but continues to practice sin will not enter the kingdom of heaven (Matthew 7:21-23). Jesus said that any Christian who continues to practice sin will have their name erased from the Book of Life (Revelation 3:4-5). The apostle Paul said we are the temple of the Holy Spirit but if we destroy the temple (by practicing sin) then God will destroy us (1 Corinthians 3:16-17). The Bible says the way into God's city, the new Jerusalem, is by the highway of holiness (Isaiah 35:8). There is no other way that we can enter the gates of the kingdom of heaven. "Now that you have been set free from sin and have become slaves to God, the benefit you reap leads to holiness, and the result is eternal life (Romans 6:22)."

If we understand these Scriptures, they should give us the fear of God to want to stop practicing sin (Proverbs 8:13). But even with such a godly fear, how can we cease from practicing sin and perfect holiness in our lives? A zealous desire to be holy is not enough. Far too many Christians have pursued holiness and tried to perfect themselves by applying their own zeal and strength (Galatians 3:3). This is not true Christianity. Trying to be holy by our own willpower and self-effort nullifies the cross of Christ and will eventually burn out every honest disciple of Christ. This kind of man-made religious "morality" apart from Christ's Sovereignty is a bastard holiness, the offspring of flesh (man's strength) and not born of the Spirit and by faith in the power of the cross of Christ. Everyone who is a true disciple must repent from the sin of practicing carnal religious morality, the root of which is unbelief in Jesus Christ and His completed work on the cross and the fruit of which is inward lawlessness and death. If we persist in practicing this kind of counterfeit morality that masquerades for Christianity, it is not harmless; it is hypocritical and hostile to God.

But here is the dilemma: if we do not preach holiness, we are not preaching the whole counsel of God. On the other hand, if we preach holiness without telling God's people *how* they can practice holiness, we also are not preaching the whole counsel of God. In fact, we inflict "cruel and unusual punishment" on God's people whenever we preach holiness to them but then do not also tell them how Christ's death on the cross has delivered them from the power of sin and enabled them to live a holy life. The apostle Paul rhetorically asked, "Wretched man that I am! Who will set me free from this body of death *(this sinful nature)* (Romans 7:24)?" And Paul then gives us the divine answer: "Thanks be to God through Jesus Christ our Lord! (Romans 7:25)."

Jesus Christ is not only the author of our faith; He is the *perfecter* of our faith (Hebrews 12:2). When we were saved, God made us holy because of our faith in His Son and His Atonement *(Christ died for us/Romans 5:8)*. In the same way, God enables us to now live a holy life by our faith in His Son and His Atonement *(we died with Christ/Romans 6:8)*. The Bible says that Christ not only died for us, we died with Christ! When we were born again of the Holy Spirit, our sinful nature was crucified with Christ. God destroyed and removed our sinful nature, which compelled us to sin (Romans 6:6). Since our sinful nature is dead and gone, we have been freed from the power of sin (Romans 6:7). *How* then do we live a holy life? *By faith* in Christ's completed work on the cross! Just as we know (and act by faith) that our sins have been forgiven, we can know (and act by faith) that our sinful nature is dead and removed. It would have been a pitiful salvation if Christ's death only provided us forgiveness of sins and still left us powerless to overcome sin in this world, where we need it most. But God knew we needed not only deliverance from the penalty of our sins; we also needed deliverance from the power of sin. Therefore, just as we can count ourselves forgiven for our sins because of Christ's death on the cross (Ephesians 1:7); in the same way, we can count ourselves dead to sin but alive to God in Christ Jesus (Romans 6:11).

Consequently, the whole message of the cross of Christ can be summarized as this: Christ died for us and included us in His death so that He might sovereignly live in us. When we abide (stay rooted by faith) in the truth that we are united with Christ in His death and His resurrection, we will bear the fruit of holiness (John 15:1-5). We are incapable in ourselves of being holy; only Jesus Christ, the Holy One who lives in us, can do God's holy work of transformation within us. "For it is God who works in you to will and to act according to His good pleasure (Philippians 2:13)."

God intends that our salvation will lead to sanctification and the practice of holiness so that we might know Him. Our salvation is only the beginning and not the end of God's purpose. At the consummation of this age, our Lord Jesus Christ will "present to Himself a glorious church, having no spot or wrinkle or any such thing; but that she would be holy and blameless (Ephesians 5:27)." Therefore, we were *made* holy when we were born again of the Holy Spirit - a salvation made possible by Christ's death on the cross. The Bible says, "We *have been made holy* through the sacrifice of the body of Jesus Christ once and for all (Hebrews 10:10)." And we are also now *being made* holy through the renewing of our minds by the Holy Spirit - a sanctification also made possible by Christ's death on the cross. "Because by one sacrifice He has perfected for all time those who *are being made holy* (Hebrews 10:14)." After we are saved, we work out our salvation by presenting ourselves each day as a living and holy sacrifice to God so that He might perfect Christ's holiness in us (Romans 12:1-2). "Beloved, now we are children of God, and it has not appeared as yet what we will be. We know that when He appears, we will be like Him, because we will see Him just like He is. And everyone who has this hope fixed on Him purifies himself, just as He is pure (1 John 3:2-3)."

Q29.　What does the "Spirit-filled life" mean and how do I live it?

A29.　The term, "the Spirit-filled life" is based on the Scripture in Ephesians 5:18 where the apostle Paul instructs believers to *"be filled"* with the Spirit. The New Testament Greek word to *"be filled"* is *pleroo*, a continuous action verb, which conveys the sense of "being continuously filled" with the Holy Spirit. Paul's expectation was that all Christians should live the Spirit-filled life. But how can we live a life continuously full of the Holy Spirit? What is the key to this victorious Spirit-filled Christian life?

Each year, a multitude of self-help books are marketed to the Christian community. Each one claims to have the right key to living in spiritual victory. Some claim that the key is doing more of the right things such as reading the Bible, fasting, praying, worshipping or witnessing. Others say that the key is having the right attitudes such as humility, forgiveness or thankfulness. And others claim that the key is being in the right kind of church. If changing our attitudes, actions or the church we attend were the solution for spiritual victory, then our Christian lives should be even more victorious if we found the right church, read the Bible more, prayed more, worshipped more, and witnessed more. Of course, anyone who has been a Christian for a long time and has already tried many, if not all, of these so-called "keys" knows this is certainly not the case. Trying to change our thoughts and behavior or home church (although this may be necessary for other reasons) is not the solution and will never, in themselves, enable us to truly know Jesus Christ and walk in the fullness of His Spirit.

God's answer for spiritual victory is not the changed life but the *exchanged* life. Jesus said that, apart from Him, we can do nothing that has spiritual life or value (John 6:53; 6:63). He also said that, unless we remain united in the Vine, we could bear no fruit. What did He mean by this? Living in the fullness of the Spirit means to trust that Christ has already done in us what we could not do for ourselves. We can only live the Spirit-filled life if we know (believe and act on) the truth of God's divine exchange, which was made possible by Christ's crucifixion. The term "divine exchange" describes what spiritually occurred when Jesus Christ died on the cross for us: when Christ died, He not only bore our sins on the cross, He also bore our sin nature on the cross (1 Corinthians 5:21). Christ's divinely powerful and sacrificial act made it possible for God to exchange our sinful nature with His Son's divine nature at the moment we believed and received Christ as our Lord and Savior (Romans 6:6). Knowing (believing and acting on) this Biblical truth that our sinful nature has been removed and that Christ now lives in us is the true secret to living the Spirit-filled Christian life and living united to the Vine, who is Christ (John 15:1-5; Colossians 1:27). This is the way we can bear real "fruit that lasts (John 15:16)."

Why is it so crucial to understand and believe this before someone can live the Spirit-filled life? Because until we are convinced that we have been crucified with Christ and that God has destroyed and removed our sinful nature when we were born again, we will be walking in misconceptions, ignorance and unbelief concerning the pivotal Biblical fact upon which the whole gospel is based. For example, if we do not know and believe the Biblical fact that Jesus Christ died on the cross so that our sins could be forgiven – if we have never heard this fact or believed it – how can we be saved? "How will they believe in Him whom they have not heard? (Romans 10:14)." In the same way, it is impossible to live the Spirit-filled life without hearing, believing and acting on the spiritual truth that we have (also through Christ's death on the cross) been delivered from living the *self*-controlled life. As believers, we now have the ability by faith to live the *Christ*-controlled life. This was what Paul meant when he said, "I have been crucified with Christ and I no longer live, but Christ lives in me; and the life that I now live in the body, I live by faith in the Son of God who loved me and gave Himself up for me (Galatians 2:20)."

If we do not know or believe this Biblical, life-giving, emancipating fact of the gospel, we will forever remain fruitless and bound to earthly works of the soul, because walking in the Spirit and doing the work of the Spirit can only be done in response (by faith) to a Biblical fact. Simply said, the Spirit-filled life, like salvation, is a response by the sincere believer to have faith in what God has revealed in His word. If we do not know and believe the fact that our sinful nature has died and been removed in Christ, our natural tendency will be to rely on our soul-power (our natural temperament and talent) to live the Christian life. This would not be a life of faith; it would be a life of "trying harder." We would then be relegated to living a *soul-fulfilled* "Christian" life, but mistakenly calling it a *Spirit-filled* life. Of course, this really is not true Christianity. This ignorance and unbelief is not just harmless; it is, in fact, actually hostile to the Holy Spirit, since we would then be fulfilling our unconverted soul-life under the guise of "Christianity" instead of losing our soul-life for Christ's sake.

We must mention one very important point before we continue: to be Spirit-filled means that you must give God sovereignty over your life. This may seem obvious, but it is a point that is often grossly overlooked and neglected. When a person "receives" Christ and becomes a "believer," they must receive Him not only as Savior, but as Lord. What does this mean? It means that you turn over the mastery and control of your own life to the mastery and control of Christ. You then give Him the right to rule and reign over your life continuously. If you do not want Christ's Lordship in your life in this way, then it will be impossible to be Spirit-filled, since these two are inseparably linked.

Why do we even mention this? Because many today are trying to live the Christian life without coming under God's sovereignty, and are governed by their unconverted soul-lives and trying to fulfill their "destiny" rather than coming under the Master's hand. These are those of whom Christ will say, "Not everyone who says to Me, 'Lord, Lord,' will enter the kingdom of heaven, but he who does the will of My Father who is in heaven will enter. Many will say to Me on that day, 'Lord, Lord, did we not prophesy in Your name, and in Your name cast out demons, and in Your name perform many miracles?' And then I will declare to them, 'I never knew you; depart from Me, you who practice lawlessness (Matthew 7:21-23)." Therefore, first and foremost there must be, in your desire to live a Spirit-filled life, a deep and lasting commitment to practicing the sovereignty of Christ. Without it, you will not be able to be genuinely "Spirit-filled."

Many sincere Christians might be momentarily and spontaneously filled with the Holy Spirit when they engage in spiritual activities such as worshiping, reading the Bible, praying, exercising the spiritual gifts, etc. However, these brief periods of being filled with the Spirit are usually experience-based, event-focused and, unfortunately, short-lived. These passing experiences are far different than being firmly grounded and continually practicing the overcoming truth of Christ's Atonement. This is why it is common for many Christians to repeatedly have to seek "spiritual" experiences that might give them periodic "heavenly" inspiration. Many Christians try to recapture those inspiring moments by going to Christian conferences and concerts to hear their favorite Christian speakers and musicians. However, these fleeting experiences cannot yield the dynamic spiritual transformation and lasting fruit that only being continuously filled with the Holy Spirit can produce.

The only way we can be continuously full of the Spirit is to be full of faith in the truth of Jesus Christ (who He is and what He has done on the cross). Being filled with the Spirit does not depend on our transient feelings; it depends on continually practicing faithful obedience to Jesus Christ and His Word. Jesus said the Holy Spirit is the Spirit of truth and anyone who worships God must worship Him in spirit and truth (John 4:24; 14:17). The Bible says if we walk in the light, as God Himself is light, we walk in the truth, but if we walk in the darkness, we do not walk in the truth (1 John 1:6-7; John 3:21). In other words, if we walk by faith in the truth of Jesus Christ and what He has accomplished on the cross, we will be filled with the Spirit (and be filled with light). If we do not walk by faith in this truth, we will not be filled with the Spirit (since we will be walking in darkness). "For I was very glad when brethren came and testified to your truth, that is, how you are walking in the truth. I have no greater joy than this, to hear of my children walking in the truth (3 John 3-4)." Walking in the truth essentially means we are walking in sanctification and not practicing sin (1 John 3:6). Therefore, when we believe and act on the Biblical truth that we have been crucified with Christ and that our sinful nature is dead and gone, Christ's Spirit will continuously fill us and accomplish God's eternal, holy work through us (Romans 6:6; 1 Corinthians 5:17; Galatians 2:20).

In Ephesians Chapter Five, the apostle Paul instructs believers to "be filled with the Spirit (Ephesians 5:18)." Then, in Chapter Six, he instructs them to "put on the full armor of God, that you may be able to stand firm against the schemes of the devil (Ephesians 6:11)." These two spiritual exhortations are Scripturally linked, since we cannot be full of the Spirit unless we put on the full armor of God. Of the six items of divine armor that Paul describes, five are defensive and one is offensive. The first defensive armor on Paul's list is the belt of truth to protect our loins. If we don't know the full truth of the gospel of Christ, then our armor is incomplete and we are exposed to Satan in a most vulnerable way. If we do not know (believe and act on) the truth that we have been crucified with Christ and our sinful nature is dead and gone, the devil can easily deceive, defeat and devour us, making it impossible to bear the spiritual fruit of sanctification. We need to be established in the whole truth of the gospel (Christ died for us and included us in His death so He might sovereignly live in us). This is why the belt of God's truth is the first piece of our protective spiritual armor that enables us to overcome the sin of the world.

Paul lists only one item of offensive armor - the sword of the Spirit, the Word of God. Once again, we need to know the whole truth of God's Word concerning Christ's triumph on the cross (Christ disarmed Satan by completely replacing our sinful nature with His holy nature; therefore sin no longer has any power over us and the devil no longer has any foothold in us). If we do not know (believe and act on) this Biblical fact of the gospel, we will not be empowered to overcome the enemy. As we can see from Paul's teaching on the armor of God, it is not enough to experience "momentary" fillings of the Spirit. These fleeting experiences are not enough to spiritually arm us to steadfastly resist the devil and live the overcoming Spirit-filled life, with its attendant hardship, persecution and suffering. "Therefore, since Christ has suffered in the flesh, arm yourselves also with this purpose, because he who has suffered in the flesh has ceased from sin (1 Peter 4:1)." We must know *how* to put on the full armor of God so that we can walk in the fullness of the Spirit. Only when we stand firm by faith in Christ's triumphant work on the cross will we be continually filled with the power of the Holy Spirit. "And the disciples were continually filled with joy and with the Holy Spirit (Acts 13:52)."

To sum up, the "Spirit-filled life" is a life of sanctification. The Bible says, "Pursue... sanctification without which no one will see the Lord (Hebrews 12:14)." Bearing fruit by living the sanctified, Spirit-filled life is not an option. Any so-called "believer" who does not learn to walk by faith in sanctification (being continuously filled with the Holy Spirit) will not "see the Lord." Jesus said, "Every branch *in Me* that does not bear fruit, He takes away...if anyone does not abide *in Me*, he is thrown away as a branch and dries up, and they gather them, and cast them into the fire and they are burned (John 15:2&6). Jesus also said we prove we are His disciples by bearing fruit (John 15:8). It is clear from these Scriptures and many others that practicing lawlessness (Matthew 7:21-23) instead of being continuously filled with the Spirit and practicing "the obedience of the faith (Romans 1:5; 16:26)" eventually results in eternal spiritual death and separation from the Lord, even if someone has at one time been "born again."

It is absolutely essential, therefore, to understand what it means to be Spirit-filled, and even more importantly, how Jesus' death on the cross has enabled us to live a life of sanctification. This is the true key to living the overcoming, victorious, Spirit-filled Christian life.

Q30.   How can the church fulfill God's eternal purpose?

A30.   There is only one answer to this question: the church must abide in (remain connected to) her head, Jesus Christ (Colossians 2:19). But what does this mean? Some have thought that returning to New Testament church principles and practices would enable the church to express the purity and power of Christ's life in the same way as the first century church. While there is some merit to this, it is not the whole truth and God's complete design or remedy. With this thought in mind, the New Testament records that the first century church was characterized by several recognizable features:

1. The first century church normally met in believers' homes and whenever the church grew too large to meet in one member's home, they simply multiplied from house to house throughout their geographic locality (Romans 16:5; 1 Corinthians 16:19; Colossians 4:15; Acts 2:46; 5:42; 20:20);

2. The first century church experienced spiritual fellowship and shared close community life among its members. They met on the Lord's Day (Sunday) to share the Lord's Supper together as a full fellowship meal. The primary purpose of this covenant meal was to remember and proclaim the Lord's death together through the sharing of the "bread and the cup." In doing so, the church celebrated their communion with the Lord and with one another (Luke 22:19-20; Acts 2:42-47; 4:32-33; 20:7; 1 Corinthians 10:16-17; 11:20-26; 12:12-27; Ephesians 4:15-16; Philippians 2:1-5);

3. The first century church did not practice Old Testament tithing; they practiced giving and periodically took a collection to help those members of the body who were suffering and in need (Acts 4:34-35; 1 Corinthians 16:1-2; 2 Corinthians 8:1-15);

4. The first century church had a vibrant, functioning priesthood of all believers who were gifted and equipped by the Holy Spirit to do the work of the ministry to-gether and build up the body of Christ (1 Corinthians 14:26; Ephesians 4:12; 1 Peter 2:5);

5. The first century church was led by mature brethren, called elders, who as servant-leaders were accountable to the church and the chief shepherd Jesus Christ to provide over-sight and pastoral care for God's local flock (Acts 14:23; 20:17, 28; 2 Timothy 3:1-7; Titus 1:5-9; 1 Peter 5:1-4).

These are the basic features that formed the first century church. However, the church cannot fulfill her divine des-tiny and God's eternal purpose by simply adhering to a "New Testament form" and hope to have Christ's life. No, there is far more required: the church must, both as individuals and as a body, abide in Christ. But how do we individually abide in Christ and how can the church corporately abide in Christ?

First, let us look at what it means for us to abide in Christ as individual members of the body of Christ. Jesus Christ said, "Abide in Me and I in you." This is both a command and a promise. If you abide in Christ, He will abide in you. The Greek word for abide is *meno*, which means "to actively dwell in." This can also be expressed as "stay rooted in" or "remain united or connected to." As with all of God's promises, this one is also conditional upon the obedience of our faith. If you stay united to Christ by faith, He will remain united to you and you will bear spiritual fruit. However, if you do not stay rooted in Christ by faith, you will not bear spiritual fruit. It is vital that we stay rooted in Christ because we have no spiritual life in ourselves apart from Christ and without His life we cannot bear His fruit. Jesus said, "Truly, truly, I say to you, unless you eat the flesh of the Son of Man and drink His blood, *you have no life in yourselves* (John 6:53).

In order to abide in Christ, we must abide by faith in the truth of His word. If our faith is not rooted in Biblical truth, it will not bear true, life-giving fruit. Jesus said, "If you abide in My word, then you are truly disciples of Mine, and you will know the truth and the truth will set you free (John 8:31-32)." The apostle Paul said the cornerstone of truth for the church is Jesus Christ and Him crucified (1 Corinthians 1:23; 2:2). Therefore, in order to be able to abide in Christ, it is essential that we understand the full provision of Christ's death on the cross. All Christians know that Christ died for their sins (Romans 5:8); however, many believers do not know that their sinful nature died with Christ and was completely removed from them when they were born again (Romans 6:6-8; Colossians 2:11). Knowing this truth is vital if you want to abide (stay rooted) in Christ.

Why is this? Because God knew we not only needed forgiveness from the penalty of our sins; we also needed

deliverance from the power of sin in order to stop practicing lawlessness. We cannot hope to abide in Christ if we
continue to practice sin (1 John 3:6). To abide in Christ
requires our repentance (turning away) from lawless thinking and behavior. Christ died to make this possible for
everyone who believes the truth of the gospel. Therefore,
when Christ died, He not only bore our sins on the cross,
He also bore our sinful nature on the cross with Him
(1 Corinthians 5:21). Consequently, when Christ was crucified, our sinful nature was crucified with Him and buried
with Him (Romans 6:6). And since our sinful nature is dead
and gone, we have been freed from the power of sin (Romans
6:7). Once again, hearing, believing and acting on this divine
fact of Christ's crucifixion is the essential, foundational truth
that enables us to abide in Christ. This is also the spiritual
lesson that God wants every new believer to learn when they
are baptized (buried) into the watery "grave" and emerge as a
new person in Christ (Romans 6:4; 2 Corinthians 5:17).

In the Scriptures, Jesus Christ inseparably links abiding in
Him with carrying our own cross (Matthew 16:24: Mark
10:34). Christ bore our sins on His cross, but He also said we
must carry our own cross. "Whoever does not carry his own
cross and follow Me, cannot be My disciple (Luke 14:27)."
What does it mean to carry our own cross? The cross of
Christ, which was the implement of His death, must now
become the implement of our *own* death (the death of our
self-willed, self-governed soul-life). Therefore the cross is
not just His; it must by faith become ours. Jesus said that we
carry our own cross when we lose our soul-life for His sake.

"Anyone who does not take his cross and follow Me is not worthy of Me. Whoever finds his soul-life will lose it, and whoever loses his soul-life for My sake will find it (Matthew 10:38-39)." Our soul-life (the Greek word is *psyche,* from which we get the English word *psychology*) is our individual personality and comprises our will, intellect and emotions.

Does this mean that God wants to destroy our soul? Of course not! Then what does it mean to lose our soul-life? It means God wants our soul to be governed by the Holy Spirit as we lay down (turn away from) all attitudes and thoughts that originate from our unrenewed mind (the unconverted and unsubmitted soul-life). The apostle Paul taught, "If you are living according to the flesh *(the unsubmitted soul-life),* you will die; but if by the Spirit you are putting to death the misdeeds of the body, you will live. For all who are being led by the Spirit of God, these are sons of God... now those who belong to Christ Jesus have put to death on the cross the flesh *(the unsubmitted soul-life)* with its passions and desires (Romans 8:13-14; Galatians 5:24)." If we belong to the body of Christ and we are led by the Spirit, we will put to death by the Spirit our unsubmitted and unconverted soul-life for Christ's sake and our brethren's sake (John 15:13; 1 John 3:16).

How do we "put to death" our unconverted soul-life? First and foremost, we *believe* the divine truth that God has exchanged our sinful nature with Christ's nature *to the point* that we act on this truth each day. We then present ourselves daily as a living and holy sacrifice to God and immerse ourselves in the truth of His Word. The Holy Spirit then renews and transforms our mind so that we are able (by faith) to "put off" our soulish attitudes and thoughts and "put on" the mind of Christ and His attitudes and thoughts (Romans 12:1-2; 2 Corinthians 2:16; Ephesians 4:22-24). In this way, "we take captive every thought to make it obedient to Christ (2 Corinthians 10:5)." The apostle Paul taught, "Do not be conformed to this world, but be transformed by the renewing of your mind, so that you may prove what the will of God is (Romans 12:2)." The Bible calls this ministry of the Holy Spirit (to transform our soul into Christ's image) the work of "sanctification" (Romans 8:29; Philippians 3:10; 1 Thessalonians 4:7-8; 2 Thessalonians 2:13).

Now let us see how we can apply this truth of the cross of Christ to our life together as the church, Christ's body. Since the body consists of many members, as each member individually abides (stays rooted by faith) in Christ, the church will then corporately abide in Christ as one body (1 Corinthians 12:12). As the members of the body lay down their soul-life out of love for Christ and one another, God will cause His spiritual growth in the church and together as one body we will bear much fruit (Mark 14:26-29; 1 Corinthians 3:6-7). When we are planted, both individually and corporately, in the whole truth of the cross of Christ and abide in Him, we will be like a branch that bears much fruit as it abides in the vine (John 15:1-8). We will experience community *(koinonia)* resurrection life together as the living body of Christ instead of organizational or institutional life, which is really no life at all. "For if we have been planted together in the likeness of His death, we shall be also in the likeness of His resurrection... now if we have died with Christ, we believe that we will also live with Him (Romans 6:5 & 8)." Jesus said, "My Father is glorified by this, that you bear much fruit, and so prove to be My disciples… you did not choose Me but I choose you, and appointed you that you would go and bear fruit, and that your fruit would remain (John 15:8 & 16).

However, if we have not been individually and corporately planted in the truth of the cross, we have no other alternative than to try to live and function together as the body of Christ by the best of our natural ability and soulish *(psychikos)* understanding and strength. We will then mistake our soulish enthusiasm for faith and our soulish energy for Christ's life (Galatians 3:3). If this persists, it is tragic and of grave concern. Jesus said, "Every plant that My heavenly Father did not plant will be uprooted (Matthew 15:13)." Consequently, the church will only corporately fulfill God's eternal purpose and bear the fruit of Christ's life *if* she abides (stays rooted by faith) in the truth of Christ's death and submits to His headship and authority. "Therefore, as you received Christ Jesus as Lord, continue to live in Him, firmly rooted and built up in Him (Colossians 2:6-7)."

Paul instructed everyone who desires to build the house of God, His church, to be careful to build *only* on the foundation of Jesus Christ and His crucifixion; or else whatever they build will not stand the test of fire (1 Corinthians 1:23; 2:2; 3:9-15). It has been insightfully said, "In God's service, what matters most is the man; not the methods. Unless the man is right, right methods will be of no use to him or his work; for carnal men to use spiritual methods will only result in failure… the real danger to the work of God is our soul-life and natural energy, untamed and uncontrolled by the Holy Spirit." Building the church according to a New Testament pattern only works if we spiritually understand and practically apply the cross of Christ in our lives. Ultimately, it is not New Testament principles and methods that matter; it is whether the work of the cross has accomplished its divine purpose in us. Otherwise, we will only produce soulish converts and soulish churches. "Unless the Lord builds the house, its builders labor in vain (Psalm 127:1)."

Therefore, everyone who aspires to build the Lord's house, His church, should ask themselves: "By faith in the cross of Christ, am I putting to death my unsubmitted soul-life so that I might serve Christ and His church by the spirit and not by the flesh?" This was Paul's own personal example and testimony: "I have been crucified with Christ and I no longer live but Christ lives in me; and the life that I now live in the body, I live by faith in the Son of God who loved me and gave Himself up for me (Galatians 2:20)." We can do no less. Indeed, this is the *only* way the church can be planted to bear the fruit of God's eternal purpose. Therefore, let all those who truly love our Lord Jesus Christ "kiss" His cross, the implement of death for our own soul-life, and carry our cross every day, knowing that when we are conformed to His death, His life will manifest through us, both individually and corporately, as the church of the living God (2 Corinthians 4:10; Philippians 3:10).

Afterword

This book was forty years in the making. This is the story behind the book. When my wife and I became Christians over forty years ago, we dedicated our lives to doing our "Utmost for His Highest." We tried to live the Christian life and do Christ's work by the very best of our ability. We were actively involved in both institutional churches and house churches and I served in a variety of ministries including shepherding, teaching, evangelism and editor of a Christian magazine.

But God wanted to reveal much more of Himself to us and led us into a difficult, decades-long "desert wilderness" experience designed to purify our faith. During this prolonged period of testing, we encountered a baptism of fiery ordeals and major crises adversely affecting our health, family, finances, work, and church life. After twenty years, our lives came to a critical crossroads when I was asked to serve as dean of students for a Bible school. It was then that we honestly admitted to ourselves that our spiritual lives were still lacking something essential, but we did not know what it was. We did not feel we were inwardly experiencing God's true transforming power, which we knew was possible and had expected when we were saved. We knew something vital was missing in our Christian experience and asked God to do whatever was necessary to bring us into a closer and more dynamic walk with Him. We declined the invitation from the Bible school and decided to give up all ministry from that day on until the Lord brought us into His life and power. During this time (since we were married), I also had a secular career job (and sometimes worked a second job) to provide for our family and enable us to preach the gospel without charge.

God lovingly answered our prayer to really know Him by intensifying our furnace of affliction. Another series of severe trials then pressed us far beyond our natural ability to endure, until we reached a crisis of faith that only He could possibly bring us through. It took twelve more years for this fiery crucible to accomplish His divine purpose and bring us to the absolute end of ourselves. During this time, however, we became so distressed and disheartened from three decades of suffering (with no end in sight) that we fell away ("ran away" might be a better term) from the Lord in despair and confusion. Like the apostle Peter, we were sifted like wheat and wept bitterly at our unfaithfulness. Our precious Lord Jesus then mercifully and miraculously called us back to Himself in brokenness, repentance and faith.

God's appointed time in His school of the wilderness had finally broken us of our self-confidence, false sense of moral virtue, and reliance on our natural ability. It was at this point that Jesus Christ revealed to us that, not only had He died for us, *He had included us in His death* so that He might sovereignly live through us. The Lord had shown us how to cross the Jordan into the Promised Land of our full spiritual inheritance in Him. It was out of this difficult travail and divine revelation that, seven years later, we published this book. Our hope and prayer is that the cross of Christ will also become your door to eternal union and intimate friendship with God.

Peter Newman
December 2012

Made in the USA
Las Vegas, NV
23 March 2024

87650420R00184